5/05/00

Anna Held

and the Birth of Ziegfeld's Broadway

Otto Sarony Co.

Anna Held

and the birth of
ZIEGFELD'S BROADWAY

Eve Golden

THE UNIVERSITY PRESS OF KENTUCKY

Publication of this volume was made possible in part by a grant
from the National Endowment for the Humanities.

Editorial and Sales Offices: The University Press of Kentucky
663 South Limestone Street, Lexington, Kentucky 40508–4008

04 03 02 01 00   1 2 3 4 5

Frontispiece: Anna Held in her biggest hit, *Miss Innocence* (1908). Culver Pictures.

Library of Congress Cataloging-in-Publication Data

Golden, Eve.
    Anna Held and the birth of Ziegfeld's Broadway / Eve Golden.
      p.cm.
    Includes bibliographical references and index.
    ISBN 0-8131-2153-1 (cloth : alk. paper)
      1. Held, Anna, 1877?-1918. 2. Entertainers—United States—Biography.
  3. Entertainers—France—Biography. 4. Ziegfeld, Flo, 1869-1932. I. Title.

PN2287.H42 G65 2000
791'.092—dc21
[B]   99-047298

To David Blazak

The Brightest of the
Bright Young Things

Contents

Illustrations follow pages 86 and 150

Acknowledgments

The following people and institutions provided invaluable help in the writing and researching of this book: Ruta Abolins (Wisconsin Center for Film and Theater Research); Academy of Motion Picture Arts and Sciences; Jennifer Axt; Sarah Beitling (John K. King Used and Rare Books, Detroit); Ray Cunningham; Norman Currie (Corbis-Bettmann); Sally Dumaux (Frances Howard Goldwyn Hollywood Regional Library); Audrey Edwards; Robert Edwards; Richard Erickson (*Metropole Paris*); James V. Ford (Gate of Heaven Cemetery); Kim Korby Fraser; Eleanore Golden; Jonathan Gray (National Museum of the Performing Arts, London); Grace Houghton; Jorge Jaramillo (AP/Wide World Photos); Bob King (*Classic Images*); Robert Klepper; Miles Kreuger; Arthur Lennig; Jo Lowrey; The Lyndhurst (N.J.) Public Library; Pat Marsh; Stephen O'Brien; Jonathan Pettit; Photofest; Brian A. Porter (University of Michigan); Mary, William, and Michael Powazinik; Kevin Profitt (American Jewish Archives); Joe Rocco; Richard Ziegfeld.

This book certainly would not be possible without the help of Anna Held's descendants, who provided both documentary material and encouragement (without requesting any kind of editorial veto power). My sincere thanks to Anna Held's granddaughter Antoinette Martensen, her grandson-in-law Paul Isola, her great-granddaughter Paule-Antoine Isola, and her great-great-granddaughter Alexandra Nicole Isola.

Prologue
The Hotel Astor
New York, December 31, 1913

It was New Year's Eve and the Sixty Club was throwing its annual costume ball for the theatrical elite. "The ballroom was filled with fashion's throng;/It shone with a thousand lights." Everyone seemed to be there: Ethel Barrymore, Laurette Taylor, Marilyn Miller, playwright Harry B. Smith and his wife, actress Irene Bentley. Theatrical producer Florenz Ziegfeld Jr., already famous for "Glorifying the American Girl" in his yearly *Follies*, attended in a tramp costume, accompanied by his breathtakingly beautiful mistress, Lillian Lorraine, who was decked out in lace and curls as a Dresden shepherdess. But the most eye-catching trio consisted of an overweight businessman and his two dazzling companions. On one arm, Diamond Jim Brady escorted Lillian Russell, an over-the-hill sex kitten who still managed to brighten up the room with her personality and slightly fading charms. On the other, dressed as the Empress Josephine, was Lillian Russell's good pal and reigning successor, Anna Held.

At forty years of age (more or less), Anna Held had been the queen of American musical comedy for more than a decade. Her flippant Parisienne naughtiness had thrilled and titillated turn-of-the-century America, as it had enriched her discoverer, champion, and husband, Florenz Ziegfeld Jr. Anna and Ziegfeld had been divorced for more than a year by late 1913, but she was once again under his management and the two had been spotted dining and riding together. All eyes were on the estranged couple (and on Lillian Lorraine), waiting to see who would approach whom. Despite Ziegfeld's mistresses, his gambling losses, and his lies, Anna had never really gotten over him, and this might be the night for a reconciliation.

Sometime before midnight, fireworks broke out: The hard-drinking and mercurial Lorraine fought with her escort and stormed out of the Astor into the darkness of Times Square. Ziegfeld, upset and embarrassed, went into the men's lounge to change back into street clothes, while Anna's friends apprised her of the situation. To cheer up the crowd and give herself a little confidence, Anna climbed atop a table and entertained with a few of her hit songs. It was around this time that some new guests wandered in. Writer Somerset Maugham had just left another party and had stopped by the Sixty Club with his date, twenty-eight-year-old actress Billie Burke, who was currently starring in Maugham's *The Land of Promise*. A delicate natural redhead with china-blue eyes, she was an arresting sight at the top of the staircase. When Flo Ziegfeld came back into the main ballroom, it was Billie Burke he spotted, not Anna Held. Indeed, there seemed to be no other woman in the room for him, and Burke, as she later recalled in her autobiography, fell "desperately and foolishly" in love with him at first sight. The two danced off into the crowd, while Anna stood helpless and aghast.

At this moment, her life reached a major turning point, just as the world itself would reach a turning point within half a year. La Belle Époque was doomed to end in 1914 as the world plunged into the century's first "Great War." By the time another year had passed, Anna Held, the epitome of carefree glamour and joy, would be transformed into a single-minded heroine, risking her life at the front lines and heading blindly to her own tragic destiny.

When midnight struck on January 1, 1914, Anna Held's old world of Diamond Jim, Lillian Russell, ostrich plumes, and champagne dinners had ended. It was time to reinvent herself.

—1—
Heaven Will Protect
the Working Girl

Anna Held's stardom burst onto the new century like a fireworks display. For that brief prewar period known as La Belle Époque, Anna represented everything that was glamorous about Broadway, everything that was naughty about Paris. Backed by the demented zeal of her husband, producer Florenz Ziegfeld Jr., she sang and danced and flirted from one hit show to another. A later Ziegfeld star, Eddie Cantor, reminisced about the impact of Anna's stardom. "For a generation America succumbed to the Anna Held craze," he wrote in 1934. "There were Anna Held corsets, facial powders, pomades, Anna Held Girls, Anna Held eyes and even Anna Held cigars. She toured the country like a conqueror and no matter where her private car stopped, she had to step out on the observation platform and greet laborers and shop girls who waited since daybreak to catch a glimpse of her before reporting for work. Anna Held was the most buoyant and cheerful spirit that ever swept across our stage. To this day stage-hands throughout America doff their hats at the mention of her name."

This carefree, lighthearted Parisienne lived the life of an empress for more than a decade. But her working life began in the sweatshops of the garment industry and ended in the frontline trenches and field hospitals of wartime France. The Anna Held of the fabled milk baths and champagne giggle died a decorated war heroine. But while she played, she held the world in the palm of her hand.

Anna Held's birthdate and hometown are a dark mystery, thanks to her own mythmaking. Theatrical history books claim she was born in Paris on March 18,

1873. This is certainly not the case. Actresses can be forgiven for lying about their age, and Anna was no exception: No birth certificate exists, but a careful look at Anna's early career suggests that she was born closer to 1870. Her gravestone reads 1872, but gravestones are notoriously inaccurate. Jacob Shatzky of the Institute for Jewish Research wrote a letter to the *New York Times* in 1956 claiming that Anna had been born in 1865. But Shatzky offered no sources for his assertion, and this date seems a little too early when taking into consideration Anna's career and the testimony of her neighbors. Even her birthday is somewhat cloudy, as one newspaper report has her celebrating it in November rather than March.

Equally problematic is Anna's nationality, as she was the very embodiment of France to prewar Americans. Called "the musical comedy Sarah Bernhardt," Anna spoke and sang in a heavy French accent, vacationed in Paris every summer, and virtually gave her life for France in World War I. "I was born in Paris," she stated point-blank in 1907. "Voilà! That is settled. For they have had me born everywhere else, even in Indiana. . . . They have had me from Poland, but that was not I but my mother. And my birth the chroniclers had made to occur in London. But I did not see London until I was twelve years old. It was Paris, Paris, Paris."

It was Warsaw, actually. Her passport and the reminiscences of childhood neighbors and early coworkers all give lie to her almost violent claims of French birth. But Anna's early escape from Poland with her family was so hair-raising, and her experiences in London so hellish, that it's no wonder she claimed Paris for her own. In one very real sense, "Anna Held" *was* born there.

Her father was a modestly successful glovemaker, Shimmle (he later anglicized his first name to Maurice) Held; her mother, Yvonne Pierre, was later described by Anna's daughter as conservative, "rather helpless," and very religious. Anna later said that her father was probably of German origin, accounting for the name Held (which means "hero" in German). If he had emigrated, mid-nineteenth-century Warsaw was not an unfriendly place for Jews. Poland was occupied by Russia, where the liberal Czar Alexander II had been in power since 1855. Alexander II lightened some of the harsher laws against Jews; they were allowed into universities, into more professions and towns. By the late nineteenth century, Warsaw was 40 percent Jewish, and most of its citizens felt secure in their own little world. It never paid for Jews to get too secure, of course. They were still not officially citizens and had few recourses to law. Poland was a heavily Catholic country: If you were not Catholic, you were not Polish, in the opinion of most citizens. Many Jews converted for business and social reasons, but Judaism was still considered a "race," not a religion. Converted or not, a Jew was a Jew.

Helene Anna Held (nicknamed "Hannelah") was the youngest child of Maurice and Yvonne. She was also the only one to survive childhood; her six brothers and sisters all died young. She became, naturally, her mother's spoiled darling and was allowed to accompany her father to work and chat with his wealthy customers. Anna learned to sew at her father's shop, a skill that soon came in handy. The Helds lived a comfortable middle-class life until all hell broke loose in 1881.

On March 1 of that year, an event occurred that affected the lives of all Eastern European Jews: Alexander II was killed by a bomb thrown by a Polish student. The new czar, Alexander III, had long hated Jews and blamed them for this assassination (as well as for most of the other problems in Russia). Incited by police and mobs of street gangs, the worst of the pogroms began in southern Russia shortly after the assassination. Jews were attacked and murdered throughout the spring and summer of 1881. All the advances gained under Alexander II were overturned: Jews were thrown out of most professions, out of universities, and out of their homes. Jewish women were forbidden to wear silk, velvet, or gold. Synagogues were looted and burned.

Alexander III did all he could to punish the Jews of Russia and the countries it controlled, including Poland. Jewish schools were closed, presses outlawed, communities broken up. Impoverished refugee camps sprang up around Eastern Europe. Thousands of Jews took whatever few belongings they had left and fled to America, Palestine, England, or France. The Helds were soon part of the horde. In the spring or summer of 1881, Anna and her parents packed up and moved to Paris.

Paris in the late 1800s was growing and reinventing itself, lurching toward the twentieth century—just as little Anna herself was doing. Electric lights, improved heating, ready-made clothes, better food, water, and transportation were becoming available even to the middle classes (though not yet to poor immigrants like the Helds). Everyday implements like telephones, bicycles, typewriters, and elevators were slowly becoming accessible to the public at large.

The press, freed from government control in 1881, reported on all this to an increasingly literate population. The widely distributed newspapers also brought crime, drugs, and depravity to the attention of the reading public. Oddly enough, the rate of murder, arson, robbery, and assault rose alarmingly during the years Anna lived in Paris, then dropped when she left (one can only hope this was a coincidence). Anna, who was conversant in French, became an avid newspaper reader and for the rest of her life tried to read a paper cover-to-cover each day. The four most popular papers during Anna's lifetime were *Le Petit Parisien*, *Le Petit Journal*, *Le Journal*, and *Le Matin*—as well as the conservative *Le*

Figaro, whose ill-fated editor Gaston Calmette would later play a minor role in Anna's life.

Vagrancy in France had doubled between the 1870s and 1890s, and poor immigrants like the Helds were hardly welcome, especially in the crowded Quartier Montmartre where Anna and her parents lived along a street full of other Polish refugees. The fact that the Helds' French was accented and rusty didn't really set them apart; many people from far-flung French villages spoke regional dialects and were even more unfamiliar with Parisian French. Paris in the early 1880s, like Warsaw under Alexander II, really wasn't a bad place to be Jewish. There were not many Jews in late-nineteenth-century France—they accounted for only .18 percent of the population—so few people bothered about them one way or the other. Organized anti-Semitism really didn't take off until the legislative elections of 1889, by which time Anna already considered herself a born Frenchwoman. When the Helds arrived in Paris, if they were hated at all, it was for being Polish: Poles, Germans, and especially Italians experienced much more prejudice than did Jews. As historian Eugen Weber once noted, "The fact that [the French] may not particularly like the Jews is irrelevant . . . because the French do not particularly like anybody."

Anna, however, loved the French, and especially Paris. She fell for the city at first sight. Perhaps her terrified exit from Warsaw had turned her against her homeland, but for the rest of her life she considered herself a born Parisienne. The wide airy boulevards with their active street life, the ornate Second Empire architecture, the flourishing theater, art, and literary life—Anna adored everything about Paris. Even as a poor newcomer, unsure of her pronunciation, she wandered in her spare moments around the city, gazed at the beautifully dressed women, the shop windows, the expensive hotels and restaurants, and planned her future.

For a few a months, Maurice Held managed to eke out a living making gloves in Paris, but his health was failing and soon his business, as Anna later put it, "went up in smoke." He was reduced to taking a janitorial job at a neighborhood synagogue. Yvonne Held was an expert cook, so the family opened up a small kosher restaurant, and Anna helped in the kitchen. "I am very, very proud of my ability as a cook," she later said, "and I am not ashamed of the way in which I learned it. There is no disgrace in working. . . . There was no silver spoon around at the time I was born and whatever success I may have attained is due to the fact that since I was old enough to work at all my ambition has never deserted me."

It was a good thing for Anna that she possessed such a tough, matter-of-fact attitude, as things got worse and worse for the family. It's a well-worn platitude to call a hard-knock childhood "Dickensian," but the life survived by Anna truly sounds like a chapter from *The Old Curiosity Shop* or *Little Dorrit*. Yvonne Held's restaurant failed, and Maurice soon became too ill to work. So it was up to Anna to pay the rent and buy groceries. Child labor laws were not passed in France until 1892, so it was easy for Anna to find work in the garment district. She got a job curling ostrich feathers; then her tiny fingers and skill at sewing got her a factory job making buttonholes. "Because I was little and the youngest, they gave me the darkest corner," she recalled.

Anna could only take so much of that treatment and left to get a position making fur caps in a friendlier factory. She admitted to mixed emotions when she saw rich children trotting off to school in the fashionable caps she'd just finished sewing. But Anna made friends in her new workplace and entertained them by singing songs she'd heard from her neighbors. She had a light, nasal voice, but one with a lot of verve and personality. At the suggestion of her coworkers (and her boss, who felt she was spending too much time entertaining and too little sewing), she spent her off-hours singing for loose change on the streets.

According to a neighbor in Paris, Anna got a job singing at a little Jewish theater as well. Mrs. Joseph Kutzen spoke to a Detroit newspaper in 1908, by which time Anna had become the queen of musical comedy. "I taught her 'The Cuckoo Song,'" Mrs. Kutzen reminisced, "and, oh, she made a hit." When asked if perhaps the actress she'd recently seen onstage and her little Parisian neighbor were two different girls, Mrs. Kutzen drew herself up and snapped, "Haven't I taken her across my knee often enough to know her, no matter how she has grown up? Spanked her? Cuddled her? I should say I have."

Looking back through rose-colored glasses, Anna referred to this time as "the happiest days of my life," perhaps remembering the early weeks of her love affair with Paris. At night, after her workday had ended, Anna sold flowers for a franc or two per bunch on the boulevards, singing her heart out. "My clothes were ragged and torn, and I slept in a little attic room, which was cold and barren," she said of these "happy" days. She had her regular customers, wealthy men who would slip her an extra franc for a song or perhaps a kiss, though Anna seems to have been lucky enough to escape having to give them more than that.

Sometime around 1884, Maurice Held died at a *hôtel-Dieu*, or charity hospital. He was buried in a pauper's grave, and Anna and her mother were at a loss as to their future. Yvonne recalled having a paternal aunt in London, so the two women packed up and took the train and ferry across the channel, despite being largely unable to speak English. When they arrived at the aunt's home, she had moved, leaving no forwarding address. Once again, the two immigrants were alone in a strange country.

London's small Jewish community had exploded in numbers throughout that decade, the poorer settling in the slums of Whitechapel (it was here that Jack the Ripper conducted his brief reign of terror in 1888 and 1889). The charity organizations were overwhelmed, and in the cold winter of 1883–84, coal strikes resulted in large numbers of starving homeless, Jews and gentiles alike, wandering the East End.

The Whitechapel that Anna and her mother moved into in the mid-1880s could only have reinforced her love of Paris. Whitechapel was a veritable medieval horror of ancient, crumbling buildings overhanging narrow, winding streets. Dubious shops competed with pushcarts selling food and other necessities. Sad, frightened families, many (like Anna and her mother) not able to speak English, were huddled in garrets and cellars, wandering the streets in search of someone from their home country who could help them. The cold, the fog, and the overcrowding all contributed to illness, and Yvonne Held already was not very healthy. There were synagogues and government organizations to help as best they could, but one had to find them and wait in very, very long lines.

Happily, Anna was fluent in Yiddish and that saved her life. A curious blend of Hebrew and German (with dollops of Polish, Russian, French, and other languages thrown in over the centuries), Yiddish was the secular language of many Eastern European Jews. Yiddish theater had been flourishing since the 1870s, due largely to its three most prominent proponents, all of whom would play roles in Anna's life: Jacob Adler, Yisrol Gradner, and Avrom Goldfaden. Goldfaden was a teacher, journalist, and poet who teamed up with folksinger Gradner in 1876 and began writing, adapting, and performing Yiddish plays throughout Romania. Within a few years, the two split up and toured in competing companies. In 1879 Adler, then only twenty-four years old, cofounded a Yiddish theater troupe in Odessa. Competition between these three men was often cutthroat.

In 1883 Yiddish theater was officially outlawed by Alexander III, and the theatrical community fled along with their fellow Jews. Most of them landed in London, where Yiddish theater quickly caught on. Hordes of people hungry for entertainment, for Yiddish, and for the company of fellow refugees flocked to the shows. Even wealthier Jews from London's West End began to show up, and by the mid-1880s there was a flourishing Jewish theatrical community in Whitechapel. Describing his work at this time, Adler said, "our life together had . . . the heart-warming spirit of the commune. . . . We laughed together, ate, drank, jested together." Adler's company specialized in dramatic plays, while Goldfaden leaned more toward lighter musicals.

In late 1885 Jacob Adler moved into Smith's Theater at 3 Prince's Street. This became the headquarters of London's Yiddish theater for the next two years. The company played every night (except Fridays, of course), and Adler's people were paid a fixed salary, an unusually generous practice at the time. Although the plays (and performers) were largely secular, the company was closely monitored by the religious community to make sure they didn't do anything offensive to observant Jews.

Anna later said her entrance to the theatrical world came through a neighbor who managed a local theater. Knowing how ill her mother was, he asked Anna if she'd like a job. "Yes, but I don't know what to do," she answered. By this time, though, she was hardly an amateur, having worked as a street singer for some time (more than a generation later, Edith Piaf would come to fame via that same route). For five shillings a night, Anna joined the chorus of Yisrol Gradner's company, eventually working her way up to bit parts. ("I was so young the only way they could use me was to dress me up as an old woman. I must have played all the silent old women in the Jewish repertory.") Anna's coworkers later remembered Yvonne Held accompanying Anna to work several times to make sure it was respectable enough for her daughter. It was more than that: Gradner ran a tight ship, and Anna was much safer in his theater than in the garment factories.

Safe from sexual advances, anyway, but not from jealous chorus girls. Anna had only been with Gradner three weeks, she recalled, when she was attacked backstage by a fellow chorine, jealous of her quick rise. Anna stayed home for a week with two black eyes and various bruises, "but the attack only seemed to make sympathy for me. The manager began giving me parts to play and songs to sing, and my salary increased."

It was around this time that Yvonne Held died, leaving Anna an orphan— she was twelve years old, according to her own chronology, but probably actually in her mid teens. Anna had saved just enough money to give her mother a decent burial but not more than that. Then, shortly after he'd moved into Smith's Theater, Jacob Adler spotted Anna and stole her away for his own company. He was the first to notice something really special, some incipient star quality, in her. "There was so much coquetry in her speech," he later wrote; "she spoke each word with such sweet glances, looking at whomever she addressed with such graciousness and moving her clear white fingers in a manner so adorable, it was impossible to resist her enchantment."

Little "Hannelah" became the pet of Smith's Theater. She was befriended by actress Dinah Feinman, who loaned the poorly dressed girl shoes and dresses to wear onstage. It was a close-knit community. There was Adler, of course, as well as leading men Max Rosenthal and Max Radkinson, and actresses Fanny Epstein, Sophia Goldstein, and the dark, attractive Jennye Kaiser. Anna was soon supplanted as the company's up-and-coming starlet by Kaiser, who became the married Adler's mistress and the mother of his child. Within a few years Anna would have good reason to empathize with Adler's actress-wife Sonya. Tragically, Sonya Adler died in childbirth in 1885, and Jennye vanished from Adler's life (she herself later became a theatrical producer).

Anna's story about being only twelve years old is made even less likely when one considers that her first major role with the company was the lead in the dramatic folk opera *Shulamith*. The work had been written and first performed some years before by Avrom Goldfaden, based on a fable about a girl whose fiancé forgets her and marries another. *Shulamith's* curse causes the death of the couple's children, and the wife gives her husband up; the old lovers are reunited (though one doubts they lived happily ever after). Anna's street-trained voice was put to use in this show: One of the numbers, "Raisins and Almonds," had already become a popular folk song. It was her first major role and Anna was terrified. She was only given the chance because Adler's current leading lady had left without giving notice. Anna hurriedly learned her lines and songs and was practically pushed out onstage to make her debut as a leading actress. The jealous chorus girls in the company may have been plotting her demise, but the more professional members of the company helped Anna out, prompting her in whispers when she went up in her lines, patting her on the back behind the scenes, and bucking her up enough to get through that first night. She was enough of a hit in *Shulamith* that she went on to appear in other shows with Adler's company: *Bar Kochba* (a drama about the Maccabean rebellion), a Yiddish-language version of the popular hit *The Ticket-of-Leave Man*, and others.

Anna's days with Adler's company ended on January 18, 1887, when Smith's Theater burned to the ground during a performance of *Gypsy Girl*. Seventeen people (most of them women and children) died in the ensuing panic, many from suffocation or from being trampled. This tragedy seemed to take the heart out of London's Yiddish theater community. Jacob Adler sailed for New York later that year, where he went on to become the founder of a great theatrical dynasty.

After the fire Anna left London and returned to her beloved Paris, where she acted with former Adler costar Max Rosenthal, who'd formed his own theatrical company. She later joined Avrom Goldfaden (she may have already been familiar with his work, as Goldfaden had run the El Dorado Theater in

Warsaw during Anna's youth). A director told her she would never get very far with the failing Yiddish theater company and suggested she work up some songs and routines and enter the music hall. "I did, and so I succeeded," she succinctly summed up, making it seem like child's play. Actually, the next five years were ones of hard work, travel, competition, and fighting to avoid becoming a kept woman. The late 1880s were a booming time for music halls, which meant both more opportunities and more competition for Anna. Through hard work, clearheaded planning, and the wits to make herself different and noticeable, Anna Held joined the group of colorful performers who made late-nineteenth-century Paris so vibrant.

Cafés chantants were establishments peculiar to France; first popularized in the 1700s, these were coffee houses and cafés featuring live entertainment. By the late 1880s, there were dozens thriving on the main Paris boulevards, patronized by families, tourists, and playboys alike. The Eldorado, the Chatelet, and La Scala (a high-class establishment at 13 Boulevard de Strasbourg) were among the most popular, but the plush, glittering Folies-Bergère, which had opened in 1869 at 32 Rue Richer, was the goal of ambitious young singers. At the same time, grittier cafes were opening in Montmartre and the Latin Quarter (Le Mirliton, La Chat Noir, Le Moulin Rouge). Anna had to compete with established singers, dancers, comics, and various other assorted acts. Anna had beauty, freshness and youth going for her. One writer on the period noted that *café chantant* singers tended to vary between "beefy, middle-aged females" and "libertine little lambs. . . . Most of the favorites had little education, depending for success largely on spontaneity and pungent individuality." Anna had plenty of both, as well as a steely determination to succeed and an astounding amount of energy.

Some of the most successful artistes were ladies better known as *"grandes horizontales."* Ballerina Liane de Pougy and dancers La Belle Otero and Cleo de Merode got acres of press coverage and attracted rowdy audiences more because of their reputations as courtesans than their onstage talents. All these ladies were vituperative in defending their professional credentials, however: De Merode said of Otero, "She was no dancer; she was a cocotte, a woman of the streets; she would sleep with anybody willing to pay her price." For her part, Otero dismissed a rival named Carmencita with, "There are plenty of Carmencitas in Europe. Every tom cat knows a Carmencita there."

There were also the "professional beauties": society girls, minor royalty, and ladies-about town whose postcards were sold in shops and some of whom—notably Lillie Langtry—tried for stage careers. Writer John Brown remembered them as "ladies who, when they went driving in the park, would have people leaping up on chairs and benches, in order that they might catch a better glimpse of them as they passed." Among the more successful performers of the day were the ethereal dancer Jane Avril, the Dutch-born "exotic" dancer Mata Hari, the brilliant and innovative Loïe Fuller (famed for her colorful and abstract "Butterfly Dance"), and the chubby, self-destructive Louise Weber, known as La Gouloue ("the glutton"). Perhaps the most bizarre act during Anna's reign in the Paris music halls was that of Joseph Pujol, known as Le Petomane (loosely translated as "The Fartomaniac"). Through amazing intestinal control, he was able to sing, do imitations, play instruments, and blow out candles with his nether regions. "They fell over themselves to hear him," recalled singer Yvette Guilbert, "and the laughter, shouting, the women's shrieking and the whole hysterical din could be heard a hundred yards away."

Anna's main competition was not Le Petomane but Guilbert herself, described by one writer as "the embodiment of seduction." Thin, vibrating with energy, Guilbert was about Anna's age and came to fame about the same time. Like Anna, she was more of an actress than a singer; her voice was thin and nasal (the same was said of Anna's own voice), and she sang low songs of love, the rough life, and contemporary scandals. Though she traveled the world, her fame was more confined to Paris than Anna's was. Her biographer noted that Guilbert's character numbers "were biting or sardonic rather than gross; a few even glowed with pity or chastised with wit, but always it was a degraded or morbid side of life they were preoccupied with. These were songs with a glitter all their own, though undeniably a darkened glitter."

Anna was a diamond to Guilbert's black pearl. Anna sang naughty, sinful ballads and childish double entendres, but, unlike Guilbert's, her numbers did not deal with subjects like the guillotine, abortion, and betrayal. But as different and fresh as Anna tried to make herself, there were always comparisons drawn. One reviewer rather inaccurately noted that Anna's songs were "much the same order as those of Guilbert, and for the most part deal with things which are not the ordinary subjects of conversation in polite society. She sings about the frayed edges of humanity, the sinful and unfortunate of both sexes." Anna became frantic with rage when she was called a Guilbert imitator and was far from happy when one critic wrote that comparing Anna to Guilbert was like comparing "a trick horse with a Bach fugue." For her part, Anna could be as catty as the next actress. "I am very fond of Yvette," she told a newspaper reporter. "She is a good comrade, but—well, remember. . . . I do not say anything from jealousy—I do not admire her. She is an artist, yes, but she has no voice." Anna sweetly added, "I am very fond of her, though. She is a good fellow."

Anna did not confine her act to Paris but also traveled with music hall troupes and alone back to London, to Holland, Berlin, and smaller towns around France. She had a bad reception while playing Amsterdam, where she was mistaken for a woman who'd recently been paroled from jail after killing a policeman and had taken to the stage. This was compensated for by a wonderful tour of Norway around 1890, where she got to chat with Arctic explorer Fridtjof Nansen in Norwegian ("I was very adept at acquiring languages," Anna noted modestly) and to see the midnight sun. She was so dazzled by the sight that she went out for a late-night frolic behind her hotel and was so intent on sky-gazing that she knocked herself out on a low-hanging branch.

She also returned to London, where she was featured in their popular, rowdy music halls. The London stars were bouncy and often coarse but essentially innocent, and audiences saw Anna's French double entendres as pleasantly shocking. The popular British singers of her day included jolly, bucktoothed Marie Lloyd and her lovely sister Alice, bumptious Cissy Loftus, male impersonators Vesta Tilley and Vesta Victoria, cockney Kate Carney, and such now-forgotten artistes as Billie Barlow, Katie Lawrence, and May Yohe. There was nothing quite like Anna Held in London, and audiences took her to their hearts. There was little outrage over her naughty lyrics or eye-rolling; it was all taken in good fun, and Anna felt more and more secure in her act.

By 1893 Anna was a minor star and had many male admirers; she banked their gifts of money and wore their jewels. She developed a good relationship with Edouard Marchand, director of the Folies-Bergère and manager of La Scala. Marchand was the first director to emphasize pretty girls at the Folies-Bergère, and he often hired Anna to headline at his two glittering theaters (though, unlike Yvette Guilbert, Anna avoided the smaller, darker establishments of Montmartre). She was no innocent flower by this time, though she had certainly avoided (through smart money management and old-fashioned morals) becoming a *grande horizontale* like Otero or de Pougy. Still, no one had really captured Anna's heart.

Then in 1893 she met Maximo Carrera, a rather notorious playboy-about-Paris. He didn't look the part; nearing fifty, he was rather short and balding, with dark, flashing eyes and a walrus mustache. He spotted her first: Every night he would appear in a box seat for Anna's performance and leave after her last curtain call. According to their daughter, Anna openly flirted with him from the stage. She spotted her still anonymous admirer again while performing in Trouville; an actress in a more paranoid time might have labeled him a stalker. But Anna was charmed, and the two got acquainted in the gambling casino at Trouville's Hôtel de Paris.

Carrera was of Spanish descent, but his family had lived in Uruguay for decades. He'd been in that country's army but was now living the life of a stage-door Johnny and hard-gambling playboy in Paris, while his two older sisters managed their large tobacco plantation back in Uruguay. He lived in a huge bachelor apartment on the Champs-Élysées and had a troupe of mistresses flocking in and out. His daughter later reminisced that "he was reputed to have in and around Paris some twenty mistresses, every one kept in great luxury." He was also a confirmed gambler, and for the first time Anna got a close look at the addiction that was to cause such grief in both of her marriages. Carrera's indulgent sisters sent him sufficient funds to cover his debts, but he put little aside for his own future.

It was around this same time that Anna bought her own home, a four-story townhouse at 86 rue de Faubourg Saint-Honoré. It stood just across the grand boulevard from the beautiful, ornate Élysée Palace, the residence of France's presidents. From her front windows, Anna could view crowds of tourists, the comings and goings of the world's politicians, the handsome red-uniformed guards at the gate. (The house was also just up the street from the site of the infamous 1847 scandal at 55 rue de Faubourg Saint-Honoré. It was there that the Duchesse de Praslin was murdered by her husband, a crime which inspired the novel and film *All This and Heaven Too.*) Anna's apartments were a riot of eighteenth-century French furniture—both real and faux—all curlicues shining with gilt. Lace curtains and tablecloths, heavily framed paintings, and shelves holding knickknacks from her travels filled the space. One reporter described it as "an exquisite little home of the bijou type . . . its furnishings in blue and white and gold and as delicate as those of a fairy bower." And, like a fairy bower, its bathing facilities were somewhat primitive. Anna had running water in the downstairs kitchen but just couldn't see her way to spending for a modern bathroom. Her dressing room faced the back courtyard, which contained the block's communal water supply. Her *cabinet de toilette* was a folding screen covered in red cambric with a sunburst design; this was set up to hide her large bathtub. Anna's maids carried water up from the courtyard, and Anna sprinkled the tub with either bran, cornstarch, or salt, depending on her mood. After soaking, she'd sponge herself with perfumed water, and the poor maids had to empty the tub—accidents were not uncommon. After fame and fortune descended on Anna, she finally updated her bathing facilities to the extent of arranging for a large hose to pump water from the courtyard directly to her dressing room, but she never did opt for the hot-and-cold running water that most wealthy people thought essential by the early years of the twentieth century.

It's not likely that Anna was able to buy her new house—in what is still one of Paris's most fashionable districts—on her own. She had quite a respectable bank account, but the savings and salary of an up-and-coming variety artist could not come close to affording such luxury. Since Anna bought the house shortly after meeting Maximo Carrera, it's fairly safe to assume that he at least helped her with the purchase price, if not the whole amount.

Then, suddenly, Anna put her career on hold and unexpectedly married Carrera. It was an odd match on both sides: Why would the career-obsessed Anna, fawned over by men in a half-dozen countries, marry a middle-aged gambler with dozens of mistresses? And why would the notorious playboy (but nominal Catholic) Carrera marry a Jewish variety actress? The explanation seems to be an old one and a simple one: Their daughter, Liane Carrera, was about to be born. Her birth supposedly came in 1895, but the timing seems a bit off. Anna and Carrera married, so they said, in Trouville in the spring of 1894, and Liane was said to be born about a year later. But Anna had returned to the stage with great success by February 1895, and her movements can be followed from then on. Even if Liane had been born in January of that year, February was a bit soon for Anna to be back onstage. So it would appear that Liane got in just under the wire and that Anna had insisted on marriage when she discovered her predicament.

There were immediate problems with Anna's new in-laws. Carrera's sisters in Uruguay looked the other way when their rapscallion brother gambled and kept mistresses, but when he married a music hall girl, it was the last straw. It was probably at this time that Anna converted to Catholicism, for many reasons. One of them may have been, of course, genuine religious belief in her new faith. But the fact that Anna was never seen near a church and never made reference to her religion other than denying her Judaism does not indicate a sincere belief in Catholicism. And Anna's insistence—even in the face of so many facts—that she was born Catholic leads one to believe there were deeper forces at work as well.

For one thing, the Carreras never would have let Maximo marry a Jewess. For another, anti-Semitism was growing by leaps and bounds in Anna's Paris of the early 1890s. A particularly nasty political campaign was fought on anti-Jewish feeling in 1890, and in 1893 the failure of the Panama Canal Company was blamed on influential Jews. The following year the epoch-making Dreyfus Affair began gaining public notice. In 1894 Capt. Alfred Dreyfus of the army general staff was arrested for passing information to Germany. He was convicted and sent to Devil's Island (though many felt that he deserved execution).

Dreyfus's Jewishness became a huge issue in this case, which dominated public discussion when it became clear by 1897 that he had been railroaded.

Emile Zola's incendiary newspaper commentary in early 1898 brought the case back to court (and into the streets, where deadly anti-Jewish riots took place). Dreyfus was finally pardoned in 1899. But from 1894 till well into the twentieth century, anti-Dreyfusards cluttered the newspapers and streets with violent anti-Semitism. Many felt—and said—that Dreyfus's fellow Jews had exerted pressure to get him released. All in all, France was becoming a less friendly place for Jews as the nineteenth century closed.

Anna had already seen her family run out of Poland; they had been secure and patriotic, well liked and "safe." Anna could see it all easily happening again, being forced to leave her beloved adopted homeland because she was a Jew (and events of the 1940s prove she was not just being paranoid). Her parents were dead, she had no relatives, her name didn't sound Jewish; it was very simple for Anna to become an instant "cradle Catholic." Life suddenly became a lot easier for her—until, of course, childhood acquaintances and early coworkers began showing up and shooting their mouths off to the newspapers.

But Anna never backed down. She spun an imaginary childhood for herself and shamelessly reminisced about it. Early in her fame she invented a fanciful tale about her favorite childhood Christmas. She was given permission, she recalled, to leave "the convent," to join her parents on vacation in Germany. The train was delayed outside of Nuremburg and a farmer put them up in "a dear, old-fashioned place, with immense porcelain stoves and furniture." The farmer dressed as St. Nick and the Helds had dinner and spent the night. "I bear few Christmases in mind more clearly than I do this one," she sighed. She never made any kind of anti-Semitic statements, but Anna was firm in her story. When a newspaper offered to reunite her with her old Paris neighbors the Kutzens, she said, "No, I do not know them. Tell them I am not a Jew," and changed the subject.

She had become Anna Carrera in name only; the couple never lived together. Anna wanted to return to her burgeoning stage career, and Carrera wanted a quiet little housewife who would stay at home, bear children, and look the other way at the goings-on in the Champs-Élysées apartment. Almost immediately, the two began to amicably drift apart. Both had played their role in the social game, had given Liane a name, and had no hard feelings for each other. But they hardly considered themselves man and wife.

The Carreras back in Uruguay may also have had something to do with the breakup of the marriage. Maximo Carrera's sisters severely reduced his allowance, making it quite clear that his new wife was not welcome in their family. But it was too late for that: The very-Catholic family did not believe in divorce, and there Carrera agreed with his sisters. Anna and Maximo never divorced, but they never lived together either. It was a marriage in name only, and accomplished its purpose of saving their daughter from being illegitimate. Divorce had been legalized in France in 1884, but it was still highly irregular and unpopular. The only causes for divorce were adultery, cruelty, slander, or criminal conviction, and Anna and Carrera were on such good terms that neither wanted accuse the other of those crimes.

Anna and her husband remained cordial, but by the end of 1894 he was back to his mistresses and whatever gambling he could still afford, and Anna was back at her old stand, competing with Yvette Guilbert for audiences' affections. It's a good thing the Carreras remained on friendly terms: As a married woman, Anna had no say over her own money. Not until 1895 could a woman even withdraw money from a bank without her husband's permission, and until the early 1900s married women did not "own" anything they themselves had earned. Happily, though, there were few financial quarrels between Anna and her husband, and those were several years in the future.

There were also few quarrels on what to do with their baby daughter: She was promptly sent off to a wet nurse in Rueil, then a good two hours' ride from central Paris. Aside from a visit or two when convenient, both of her parents pretty much forgot about her for the next few years. When she was old enough, Liane and her pet puppy were sent to the Pension Gelot, a boarding school in Neuilly run by two elderly women. Liane herself later claimed that her two aunts in Uruguay wanted to adopt her but that her father fought them "tooth and nail." Liane idolized her father, though, and her claims must be viewed with some suspicion. She was clearly hurt by her mother's abandonment: "It was practically the life of a princess in a fairy tale that my beautiful mother was living," she later wrote with some bitterness. "Everywhere the whole world was at her feet. Why should an old man or an insignificant child intrude?"

Anna's career had lost some momentum with her year-and-a-half break. Finally, in February 1895, she introduced a newly tooled act. No longer did she sing of the sadness of love and the futility of life. The new Anna Held was all gaiety, champagne, naughtiness, and high kicks. She discovered a talent for suggestively using her arms, and especially her large, expressive eyes. No more ragged, plain clothes and simply tied-back hair. She spent as much as possible on flouncy, low-cut dresses and jewels, and she accentuated her full, unruly hair with huge feathered hats and side-combs.

Her songs were still of love, but of the kind of love tourists in France want to hear about: naughty boulevard girls, loose actresses, bits of fluff on the side. Her biggest hit was "Die Kleine Schrecke," which she'd learned at the Berlin Wintergarten; German audiences enjoyed hearing something in their own language, and Anna's stumbling linguistic mistakes were considered cute. Back in England, she had the childishly naughty song translated, and it became her biggest hit:

> I wish you'd come and play with me,
> For I have such a way with me,
> A way with me, a way with me,
> I have such a nice little way with me,
> Do not think it wrong.
> I should like you to play with me,
> To play with me, to play with me,
> I should like you to play with me,
> Play with me all the day long.

It was a cute, lilting tune, and Anna's eye-rolling, shoulder-wiggling rendition brought down the house. She would choose a susceptible-looking man from the "bald-head row" and direct the song to him, much to his delighted embarrassment. "Won't You Come and Play with Me?" soon became her theme, and audiences demanded it at every show—she eventually had to have special encores written for her curtain calls. Another hit song was "Le Colignon," for which Anna dressed as a tough Parisian cab driver, complete with whip and tight pants. She also sang a postage-stamp number; in a frothy white ballet dress covered with stamps, she suggested her audience come up and "lick" her. Not only did her fans throw bouquets to her, but many a man, carried away in his enthusiasm, threw his pocket watch. Anna kept these in her French bank vault back at the Credit Lyonaisse and after a few years had quite a collection.

Audiences may have been charmed by Anna's new persona, but moralists were not. One noted that Yvette Guilbert "was not risqué for the mere purpose of purveying impropriety that would attract audiences, a plan which comprises Anna Held's sole conception of art." Anna's new act, unlike Guilbert's (and her own former) songs of the slums and life in the raw, shocked this particular reviewer: "Such winks, shrugs, wriggles, kicks and grimaces accompanied by words freighted by insolently impure meaning, convey impressions that cannot be described without impropriety." Readers did not wait to have them described; they lined up at the theater to be pleasantly shocked for themselves.

She was becoming something of a public figure and was interviewed and photographed more often for the popular press. Anna's habit of riding horses astride, wearing a split skirt, caused much comment, and in 1896 when the bicycling craze hit, Anna became one of Paris's most enthusiastic cyclers—again in her scandalous split skirt. Enough modern, devil-may-care women had begun wearing these "culottes" that the minister of the interior released a statement that "the wearing of masculine clothes by women is only tolerated for the purposes of velocipedic sport."

New York theater critic Alan Dale saw Anna perform in 1895 and brought Americans their first mention of her. After noting that her name was on posters all over town, Dale said that "she came on late—like all star attractions," and when he later briefly met her, he reported that "Miss Held is young and comely, and as far as I could discover she has no very exalted views to profess. . . . I like that." Anna's presence was also requested at benefits. She wasn't paid for these performances, but it was quite an honor to be asked to help out fellow artists, war widows, the unemployed. Only top stars were on these bills, and Anna began developing a social conscience. For the rest of her life, she would take time off from touring to appear at bazaars and benefits.

By the summer of 1896 Anna was headlining at London's Palace Theater of Varieties. Newspapers that season noted that she had been "the rage of Paris and London" for more than a year, billing to her as a "café-concert singer." The article also noted that she combined "the talent and originality of Yvette Guilbert with beauty of a remarkably high order." Her voice, it was said, "has melody," and she herself possessed "an ability to use it intelligently." Anna was used to receiving flowers from her fans, so when bouquets from someone named Florenz Ziegfeld Jr. began arriving, she took little notice. Even the diamond bracelet attached to the bouquet made little impression. It took a good bribe to the stage doorman to get Ziegfeld into Anna's dressing room. One night after her performance, he simply burst in unannounced and—with an enthusiasm unusual even for an American—proceeded to sweep her off her feet.

While Anna Held and her parents had been struggling for a living in the slums of Europe, Florenz Ziegfeld Jr. was being raised in the lap of upper-middle-class luxury in Chicago, Illinois. He was born on March 21, 1867, making him perhaps a year or two older than Anna. He was the eldest child of the German-born Florenz Ziegfeld Sr. and his French-born wife, Rosalie de Hez. By 1875 the family also included younger siblings Carl, William, and Louise. Ziegfeld Sr. spent much of the late 1860s trying to establish himself in the music business: He had a rickety music school above the Crosby Opera House, published music and sold instruments with Ziegfeld, Gerard, and Co., and finally opened the Chicago Musical Academy in 1867. The school started small but—like Chicago itself—grew by leaps and bounds and by 1871 was a respectable concern.

That was the year of the disastrous Chicago fire, the blame for which myth lays upon Mrs. O'Leary's cow. Myth also says that Florenz Ziegfeld Jr.

developed his love of colorful spectacle by watching his hometown burn from his family's perch under a bridge in Lake Park. Chicago was rebuilt, and so was the Chicago Musical College, as it was renamed in 1872. Ziegfeld scored a coup that year by enticing famed composer Johann Strauss to participate in the Boston Peace Jubilee. While Flo Jr. grew up, his father became one of Chicago's leading citizens, his Musical College the most successful and elite of its kind in the area.

Ziegfeld Jr. was basically a spoiled rich kid with a lot of charm. He did his lessons sporadically and with no good grace, working for his father while attending Ogden High School in the early 1880s. After graduating, he was sent out west to "become a man," probably because his boundless energy and lack of respect for his father's business was driving his parents to distraction. From the older generation's point of view, this trip was a mistake: Flo Jr. fell in with Buffalo Bill's Wild West Show, and the Chicago Musical College seemed even duller by comparison.

Back home, he buckled down to work as assistant treasurer for his father's college (he couldn't have been a very good one, as his later life shows he had no more financial sense than a goose). As a wealthy young playboy, Ziegfeld divided his free time between dancing and dating, and trying out his own show-business schemes. These included the infamous (and possibly apocryphal) Dancing Ducks of Denmark, an appalling act in which the ducks "danced" in a gas-heated cage. There was also the bowl of water billed as "The Invisible Brazilian Fish" (not even the dumbest rubes fell for that one).

Ziegfeld's big break came with the Columbian Exposition of 1893, which was held in Chicago and which his father saw as a great opportunity to introduce hordes of tourists to his college. Ziegfeld Sr. and Theodore Thomas were put in charge of the fair's many and varied musical programs, and Ziegfeld entrusted his son with rounding up some of the talent. In late 1892 Ziegfeld Jr. sailed for Europe and began booking acts: There wasn't enough money for the classical orchestras and famed pianists and violinists his father would have preferred, so young Ziegfeld improvised.

The acts that he brought back to Chicago included the Von Bulow Military Band, the Muhlemann Swiss Mountaineer Trio, Iwanoff's Russian Singers and Dancers, and myriad European music hall performers: jugglers, magicians, acrobats. Ziegfeld Sr. was not pleased, and for good reason. His personal exhibition, peopled by these acts, flopped. Tourists were more interested in seeing Little Egypt do the hoochie-coochie, wasting money at the gambling halls, or visiting the breathtaking architectural and mechanical wonders of the fair.

So in the summer of 1893, Ziegfeld Sr. sent his son to New York to scout

out some more promising and audience-drawing acts. In a move calculated to annoy his father, young Ziegfeld zeroed in on Eugen Sandow, a German-born strongman performing at the Casino Theater, under the management of one Rudolph Aronson. Sandow is generally dismissed as an empty-headed pretty boy, but he was actually a brilliant businessman who invented and popularized the modern concepts of the gym and bodybuilding. That he was also breathtakingly handsome was the icing on the cake.

Ziegfeld's genius for promotion and for guessing just what the audience wanted kicked in. He bought Sandow's contract and, in August of 1893, he presented the new act at the Chicago World's Fair. Rather than the run-of-the-mill weight lifting and posing, Ziegfeld "glorified" his new acquisition, with a combination of sex and spectacular nonsense: Both of these elements would later play a role in Anna's success as well. Sandow performed eye-catching stunts, such as lifting a man with the palm of his hand, wrestling three takers at once, and hefting a barbell containing a man in each "bell."

The sex part of the act was even more effective: For one thing, Sandow posed dressed in little more than a thong (in many of his postcards he wore nothing at all). And Ziegfeld invited prominent ladies backstage to politely grope the agreeable muscle-man. It was all a huge success, and at the end of his Chicago run Ziegfeld packed up his new star and took him on the road. Ziegfeld, Sandow, and their little troupe of second-string performers toured successfully through the end of 1895 (the only disaster being a lion-fighting act wherein the tired old lion collapsed upon entering the ring). In 1894 Ziegfeld took Sandow to Thomas Edison's laboratory in New Jersey, where a brief film immortalized him.

But the independent-minded Sandow moved on, and by early in 1896 Ziegfeld found himself in New York with no act. There he met Charles Evans, coauthor and costar of the long-running comedy *A Parlor Match*. The show had opened in 1884, featuring Evans and his brother-in-law, William Hoey, as a couple of ne'er-do-wells trying to bilk a rich mark out of his fortune. The show was very loosely constructed, which is why it was able to tour the United States for nearly ten years: New material and new performers were added from town to town, without disturbing the plot. The popular songs "The Man Who Broke the Bank at Monte Carlo" and "Daisy Bell" (better known as "A Bicycle Built for Two") were first introduced to the public via *A Parlor Match*.

Ziegfeld had the idea of reviving *A Parlor Match*, with its original stars and some flashy new talent. It seems Ziegfeld could talk anyone into anything, as he would prove time and again. His enthusiasm infected Evans and Hoey, and the two wealthy stars agreed to his plans. Ziegfeld and Evans sailed for Europe to scout new talent for the revival (and to cut a swath through Paris: Both men were young, handsome, and full of mischief). While in London, the two met up with T.D. "Teddy" Marks, well known as a snappy dresser, boulevardier, and incidentally a theatrical manager. When Marks heard what Ziegfeld and Evans's mission was, he directed them to the Palace Theater, where Anna Held was performing. It was a tip that would change both Anna's and Ziegfeld's lives in ways no one could imagine. It was like nitro meeting glycerine.

—2—
It Pays to Advertise

W hen Anna Held and Florenz Ziegfeld Jr. met for the first time in her dressing room that summer of 1896, they had a lot in common. Both were young, attractive, and ambitious. Both were risk-takers and rule-breakers. And both loved show business with every ounce of their beings. We are more familiar with Flo Ziegfeld from his later photos, when he had taken on the appearance of a disgruntled tortoise. But when he first met Anna, he was a bright-eyed, dark-haired young man, thin as a whippet and vibrating with enthusiasm and harebrained schemes for conquering the theatrical world.

Anna had never heard of Florenz Ziegfeld, either Sr. or Jr. Few had. Flo had never produced a Broadway show. But he did have the well-known Teddy Marks and Charles Evans to back him up, which kept Anna from showing him the door. And a trip to America was tempting: All big stars went there sooner or later and usually came back with great gobs of cash and some funny insulting stories about the backward savages of the United States.

Anna was already booked for the winter of 1896–97 at the Folies-Bergère, but that didn't slow Ziegfeld down; he offered to pay off director Edouard Marchand. Such a show of self-confidence impressed Anna. Then Ziegfeld got down to business: He would offer her fifteen hundred dollars a week for a three-month engagement in *A Parlor Match.* That was a higher salary than Anna could earn in Europe, and she was caught up in the excitement of seeing America and spending several months with this interesting young Mr. Ziegfeld.

Besides, she needed the money badly: Maximo Carrera had not slowed down his gambling, even with his allowance cut back. He was badly in debt, and bailiffs had taken everything they could from him. Now they came knocking at Anna's door: As his wife, she was legally responsible for his debts. She ended up using her savings and marriage settlement to pay off Carrera's gambling losses and was again staring poverty in the face. Ziegfeld's fifteen hundred dollars a week was too good to turn down. Edouard Marchand agreed to accept four thousand dollars to let Anna out of her Folies-Bergère contract, and Ziegfeld deposited an additional four thousand dollars in Anna's bank to cover some of what she had given to her husband's creditors (it was later rumored that the money came from Ziegfeld's friend, railroad tycoon Diamond Jim Brady). As quickly as he'd arrived, Ziegfeld vanished in a cloud of flowers, promises, and bank checks. Anna half-wondered if the whole thing hadn't been a dream, it was so sudden.

Ziegfeld arrived back in New York on August 6, and began laying the groundwork for Anna's debut. He hired newspapermen (always anxious for a little extra spending money) to plant stories in the press about her. Startling red-and-white posters reading "GO TO HELD!" appeared on ash cans and the walls of construction sites around the city. Anna's picture appeared in the pink pages of the racy *Police Gazette*; this was the 1890s equivalent of being a *Playboy* centerfold. By early September the *New York Dispatch* noted that "Miss Held's photographs are already becoming conspicuous in the Broadway shop windows."

There was no shortage of actresses ready to compete with Anna Held. In those premovie days, stage performers were idolized; their postcards sold briskly, fan clubs multiplied, crowds waited for them at the stage door, and newspapers covered their every move. The unknown foreigner had to meet New York's stars head-on, and there were some impressive acts in the 1890s. In addition to popular dramatic stars like Mrs. Fiske, Mrs. Leslie Carter, Julia Marlowe, Maxine Elliott, and Viola Allen, plenty of light comedy and musical actresses competed for the same section of the public that Anna targeted.

Breathtaking Maude Adams was about to burst into stardom in James Barrie's *The Little Minister*. Roly-poly blondes May Irwin and Marie Cahill were already well established by the mid-1890s, as was ugly-duckling British import Marie Tempest. Raucous redhead Fay Templeton had been a favorite since her debut as a child star in the 1870s. The imposing Canadian-born comic Marie Dressler had her first hit in 1896, starring as *The Lady Slavey*. And waiting in the wings were promising, hardworking youngsters like Blanche Ring, Trixie Friganza, and Della Fox. Anna and Ziegfeld had their work cut out for them, making an impression against that competition. There was also Anna's bête noire from Paris, Yvette Guilbert. She'd come to the United States for the first time early in

1896 for a brief tour, her East Coast engagements managed by the same Teddy Marks who had tipped off Ziegfeld about Anna. Guilbert was to return again later that same year and make further U.S. tours, but she was a little too dark and scary for American audiences to take fully to heart.

After bidding farewell to Ziegfeld, Anna had traveled to Lucerne, where she was booked to perform for a few weeks. While there, she got word that Eduoard Marchand had changed his mind about letting Anna out of her Folies-Bergère contract; he demanded she perform for the rest of the season. He had indeed received Ziegfeld's check for four thousand dollars, but never deposited it. As far as he was concerned, the deal was off. And Carrera, for his part, was panicking at the thought of his meal ticket leaving for the United States. Rather than set foot back in Paris, Anna sneaked from Lucerne to Southampton, where she sailed for New York on September 8.

Like New York, America itself was undergoing a tumultuous and exciting period in the late 1890s. One hundred years later, it's easy to look back on turn-of-the-century America as quaint and picturesque: Gibson Girls playing lawn tennis while their strawhatted beaus sipped lemonade; couples strolling through the town square listening to the band play "In the Good Old Summertime." It was all that and more for some people. But it was also a time of upheaval and change, as the old folks, with one foot still in preindustrial America, gave way to the new generation that would lead the country into two world wars.

Anna's first ocean voyage, on the *New York*, was both exciting and terrifying, if some of the newspaper tales are to be believed. Press reports (probably planted by Ziegfeld and his minions) later claimed that the trip was full of trauma and adventure: A crazed jewel robber was found in the baggage room, "eyes blazing and a cut-throat razor in each hand," and Anna of course happened to be present when he was overpowered and put in irons. A deck steward was washed overboard (or in some versions committed suicide) and Anna nobly arranged for a ship's concert to aid his widow and children. All this may or may not have happened, but when Anna's ship docked in its namesake city on September 15, she merely called the trip "delightful," adding the only real excitement was seasickness. "I cry all the time, and feel so sorry I left my home," she said in broken English. "Then I got better and began to enjoy myself. My little dog, he did not get ill. . . . It is so funny that people get ill on a boat and dogs do not."

Anna's welcoming party—including Ziegfeld and Teddy Marks—whisked her uptown to a suite at the Hotel Netherland, on the corner of Fifth Avenue and Fifty-ninth Street. The New York that Anna saw for the first time on her carriage ride uptown seemed to be a small provincial city compared with Paris. The streets were narrower, the buildings smaller and darker. Most buildings in New York were still three or four stories and made of brick or brownstone, with a few light-colored limestone facades thrown in. Traffic was ill controlled, and the streets were hectic with carriages, people, and animals rushing to and fro with frequent collisions. The skies were darkened on some streets by loud, clattering elevated trains. New York at the time was home to some 150,000 horses, who produced large amounts of odiferous waste and who lived in equally smelly stables throughout the city. During dry spells the manure turned into dust, which blew into everything, including noses and mouths.

As her carriage jostled its way uptown, Anna would have spotted a few private mansions, built in heavy Romanesque or light, fantastic French revival styles. There were even a few of the famed New York skyscrapers for her to gape at: The first had been the 1889 Tower Building on lower Broadway, a steel skeleton supporting its thirteen stories. The twenty-two-story American Surety Building was only two years old when Anna arrived in New York, but other early landmarks, like the Flatiron and Woolworth Buildings, were still only in the planning stages. As she rode up Fifth Avenue toward the Hotel Netherland, she would have seen the ominous tomblike Croton Reservoir on Forty-first Street (which would be demolished in 1899 to make way for the New York Public Library); some impressive old churches; and, as she neared Central Park, the breathtaking mansions of Mary Goelet, Henry Clay Frick, and various Vanderbilts; and finally a cluster of hotels around the Grand Army Plaza at Fifty-ninth Street.

The Hotel Netherland was an imposing Romanesque building made of rough stone blocks, with a huge arched entrance and corresponding arches at the windows. The very afternoon she arrived, Anna was interviewed by the press, and quite a performance it was. As she spoke little English, Teddy Marks stood in as translator and Ziegfeld hovered nervously in the background (his name misspellings in these early days ranged from Ziegfried to Leigfeld to the one he hated most—Ziegfield). The experience of Alan Dale was typical: Shown into the large suite, he was told that Anna was just emerging from her bath and would have to receive him in her negligee. Dale was wise enough to be amused at such a cunning stunt.

Shown into her dressing room, Dale encountered his subject lazing in an armchair, hair disarrayed, wearing only "a nightie, filmy with laces and gew-gaws." The effect was marred only by a bandage-covered mosquito bite over one eye. "Do not write that Mlle. is hideous and mosquito-bitten," she pleaded in vain, adding perceptively, "I am afraid of your journalists. They tell everything." She promptly won Dale over, and he was a very powerful man in the theater world. "She laughs at her own candor, and I like it immensely," he said. "She is frank, and naive with it all." With Marks's help, Anna tried to describe her act and particular allure. "I sing softly, cattily, and languorously," she explained. "All my gestures are carefully studied, and they mean much." Her act, she emphasized, "is not coarse; it is not rude; it is not shocking." And she downplayed any thought of great art: "Those who go to hear ditties don't want to imagine themselves at the grand mass."

More reporters crowded into Anna's Netherland suite over the next week or two, and there were few subjects not covered in these earliest interviews. Anna mentioned that in Paris she wore bloomers to ride her bicycle ("they are much more comfortable") but that in the United States she would bow to convention and wear a short skirt over them. She also admitted to riding a horse astride in jodhpurs, at a time when ladies rode sidesaddle. She denied that this was at all "coarse or vulgar" and insisted that riding astride "is the most healthful and the most comfortable fashion. . . . I have more purchase, more command. It is not good to ride twisted. Any doctor will say the same thing."

She also spoke of her dislike for low-heeled shoes. In the day of the open-air, athletic Gibson Girl, Anna sniffed, "It is all very well for so-called sensible people to recommend flat heels and short skirts, but—well, most of us prefer not to be sensible." And her horror of any form of violence came to the fore when a reporter asked her about the popularity of boxing in America. "Fighting, pugilism, killing one another!" she gasped. "My! but it is horrid. I cannot see why they allow it here, this sport of punishment." She chatted politely of America, Central Park, how she longed for her bicycle, and how no, she was entirely different from Yvette Guilbert. Keeping a relatively straight face, she described her hobbies as visiting the poor and paying their rent.

Anna had won over at least some of the New York press, but she still had other worries before her show even opened. One worry was Lillian Russell, the darling of Broadway and the reigning queen of musical comedy. "Airy Fairy Lillian" was thirty-five years old in 1896 and was generally acknowledged to be the greatest beauty of her era. Blonde-haired and blue-eyed, Russell had perfect features that put her in an entirely different league than Anna; Russell's clear soprano voice also outclassed the singing skills of the foreign newcomer.

The Iowa-born Russell had first achieved fame as a Gilbert and Sullivan soubrette in the early 1880s and over the next decade starred in more than twenty shows, becoming the premiere musical comedy diva of her day. That day, some felt, was passing by 1896; Russell's problems with debt, husbands, and her weight were well publicized. But just before Anna landed in New York, Russell had her biggest hit yet with *An American Beauty*, in which she played an amnesiac heiress who winds up performing in the circus (at the final curtain, of course, she recovers her memory and marries an English earl).

With that show, Russell was back on top. The press and the theatrical crowd hoped and prayed for a feud between Russell and the younger upstart Anna Held—nothing was more fun than a public catfight between actresses. Russell's patron and (probably platonic) friend Diamond Jim Brady was a pal and business associate of Ziegfeld, and he arranged for the foursome to get together. To everyone's vast disappointment, Anna and Lillian Russell became instant and lifelong friends. The two could be seen strolling along Ladies' Mile together, as Russell introduced Anna to New York's fashionable shopping district. Russell—also a bicycling fanatic—loaned Anna a machine and the two rode together through Central Park. Both gourmands, the ladies were often seen dining at Rector's, the "Lobster Palace" and tourist trap that moved to midtown in 1899. Through the ebb and flow of both of their careers, Anna and Lillian Russell never let professional jealousy get in the way of their close friendship. They were each other's greatest cheerleaders and consoled each other through romantic traumas as well.

A Parlor Match opened for a month of out-of-town tryouts in Boston, but Anna did not join the company until it moved to the Herald Square Theater in New York on November 21. At that time, the Herald Square was smack in the heart of New York's theater district. Fourteenth Street had been the theatrical hub until such palaces as the Herald Square, Koster and Bial's, the Manhattan, and the Metropolitan Opera House drew audiences uptown in the 1880s and early 1890s. There were already a few scattered theaters farther up Broadway, near Forty-second Street, but that was still considered a declassé neighborhood of stables, butchers, and bordellos.

The humor in *A Parlor Match* was broad and none too demanding: Character names included Abel Leever, I. McCorker, and Vesta Bule. There were nearly twenty songs crammed into the evening, aside from Anna's contributions. None of these other songs were very memorable, consisting of such ephemeral tunes as "Dear Golden Days" and "Your Baby Is Comin' to Town." At the high point of the action, Evans and Hoey try to convince Capt. William Kidd (played by James Galloway) that his house is haunted. They bring out a "mysterious cabinet," which was the centerpiece of the show: A seance ensues, and a handful of performers emerge from the cabinet to do musical or comedy turns as "spirits." This was where Anna came in: She popped out of the cabinet, sang several numbers, and vanished again. Most performers pretended to be great characters of history, but Anna was simply billed in the program as "Mlle. Anna Held, Etoile de Paris, Exclusively engaged for America by Mr. F. Ziegfeld, Jr." Three other new girl acts also popped out of the cabinet. Ziegfeld was hedging his bets: If Anna was not a success, perhaps Beatrice and Millie Tate, or Gracie Scott, would be.

What did audiences see when Anna materialized from the mysterious cabinet? Well, for one thing, she was tiny—only about five feet one inch tall. She was also shaped like a miniature hourglass, due less to her cinched-in waist than to the padded roundness of her hips and bust. Her head was disproportionately large and looked larger because of the thick auburn hair piled loosely atop it. "She wore tiny dresses and tiny shoes," wrote Alan Dale. "She sang in a tiny voice and she spoke in a tiny voice. . . . In fact, she talks like one of those French dolls which, when you pull a string, say 'Ma-Ma,' 'Pa-Pa.'"

Anna's face was her fortune: It wasn't classically pretty, but cute and pert. She had good "stage bones," which caught the light well, and strong features that could be seen from the back row. She had a large, expressive mouth and good white teeth (which were rare in the nineteenth century). Her nose was long and prominent, but it was her eyes that dominated her face. Large, brown, and turned-up at the outer corners, they protruded just slightly. By this time Anna had learned to use them expressively: She rolled her eyes like a pair of dice, but they paid off much better than any honest dice ever did.

Anna received an unexpectedly hearty reception on opening night. After her rendition of "Won't You Come and Play with Me?," William Hoey came out onstage to continue with the action. But the audience wouldn't let up, applauding so loudly that Anna would obviously have to do an encore or two. Flustered, she looked at Hoey, who was stranded onstage. Ever the professional, he grabbed a chair from the set, sat down with his back to the audience, and joined in the applause. Anna gratefully sang a few extra choruses directly to him, as he reacted in a broadly comic style, to the audience's delight. When she finished her song, Hoey cried, "You won't have to wait long—I'm comin'!" and waltzed her offstage. That night, a theatrical myth was acted out as fans unhooked Anna's carriage from her horses and pulled her up Broadway to her hotel. Of course the fans were probably paid off by Ziegfeld, and a terrified Anna was jostled to the wrong hotel, but it made for a good story in the papers.

The revival of *A Parlor Match* and its stars were enthusiastically received by the large audience and the stage was "literally loaded with barrel of flowers" (arranged for ahead of time by the management). One paper noted that the show's centerpiece, the spirit cabinet, "produces a neat little variety show, which is applauded as before." Anna's big hit, "Won't You Come and Play with Me?," invariably elicited several encores and a speech of thanks in French and prettily broken English. One critic concluded that the show "is good for another profitable tour in the provinces."

But Anna's critical reviews were mixed. "She is always vivacious and daring," read one, "and last night she outdid herself." The *New York Mercury* was delighted with her, claiming that "Never was the like of the Anna Held 'shoulder wriggle' seen on the New York variety stage. Its caressing fascination was simply enthralling." That same paper noted the variety of Anna's onstage giggles and laughs: "In one of the most notable of these she would lay her left hand against her heart, press the other to her brow, and shake all over with merriment." The *New York Times*, then as now a powerful vehicle, gave Anna a backhanded notice. "Her abilities are of the most ordinary kind," wrote Edward Dithmar, "Yet the impression Mlle. Held makes is not quite disagreeable." A reporter from *Vogue* went completely 'round the bend in October 1896 and described "such a perfect little figure, as if really born in fairy land, and sprung from the heart of a rose."

But America was still a very moralistic country, and many newspapers inveighed against this fast, foreign woman. "In a short time," hoped one outraged journalist, "she will pack up her little stock of tricks and manners and go away, leaving us to forget all about her." This same man had just spent four columns of newsprint chastising Anna as "brazen," "sensual," "bawdy" and "wanton," surely the kind of publicity on which Ziegfeld would have spent huge sums. Happily, Anna's grasp of English at the time probably prevented her from reading that particular notice. Even a fellow performer, Edward Harrigan of the popular comedy team Harrigan and Hart, lashed out at her and other foreign influences in print. "The nasty songs of Anna Held and Yvette Guilbert and others of their ilk are raved over by people who couldn't order dinner in a Parisian cafe," he said in a press release.

Anna's pedigree as a Parisienne was already in question: As early as September 30, 1896, one paper referred to her as "a Polish Jewess." Years later it was said that when she got to New York, Anna took a carriage to the Second Avenue Jewish theater district and paid a call on her former Adler coworkers. But given Anna's terror of her true background being found out, it's unlikely that this trip was ever made. As long as Anna's name was spelled right, Ziegfeld was happy (Anna mentioned in one interview that both she and Ziegfeld got antsy if a day went by without "Anna Held" appearing in at least one paper). He had her pose for seemingly endless sets of publicity photos, looking as naughty and French as possible: In a shockingly knee-length and low-cut dress, she applied stage makeup ("a dash of rouge to the cheeks applied by means of a hare's foot"), played with her jewelry, adjusted her hat and corset stays, and rolled her eyes engagingly.

Ziegfeld hired struggling playwright and *New York World* journalist Max Marcin as a freelance press agent. This relationship led to what was acknowledged as the most successful publicity stunt of its era, perhaps of all time. Marcin claimed to have been inspired by reading of Cleopatra's milk baths. He knew that if he tried to plant a story simply saying, "Anna Held bathes in milk," few newspapers would run it. So he snuck in the back way: Marcin convinced milkman R.H. Wallace of 25 Patchin Avenue, Brooklyn, to lend his name and released a story that Wallace had sued Ziegfeld for an unpaid bill for sixty-four quarts of milk. Marcin's friend Herbert Lome leaked the story to the press (Marcin, as a *World* man, wanted to keep his name out of it).

When pressed about the bill, Ziegfeld admitted sheepishly that Miss Held bathed in milk every day—then said that he'd not paid Wallace's bill because the milk was sour. Every New York paper ran the story on October 10 except the *Sun*, whose reporter tracked down farmer Wallace. Infuriated, Wallace was anxious to set the record straight: "I didn't see what harm it would do to let him use my name," he fumed. "But when he says I sell sour milk, that's another matter. I never heard of Anna Helid or Held or whatever her name is, and I never sold her or anybody that represents her a drop of milk in my life."

Few Broadwayites took the milk bath story seriously. "The habitués of the Rialto put a finger to the nose and said: 'Aha! The press agent,'" noted one reporter. Through some stroke of serendipity, a cow in Port Chester managed to kill itself that same week by wedging its neck in the crook of a tree. The press leaped gleefully on this, and a cartoon appeared of a cow hanging itself, leaving the note, "As Anna has soured on me there is nothing left but suicide." Even though the milk bath story had been disproved almost immediately, it developed a life of its own: For years after Anna Held's death, the tale of her milk baths stayed fresh in the public mind. Other press agents tried again and again to equal this legendary stunt, but none ever could. As late as 1930 artist John Held Jr. (no relation) published a scratchboard cartoon of Anna in the *New Yorker*, subtitled, "When the Theatre Was Fraught with Romance: Anna Held's Milk Bath." Max Marcin, incidentally, had netted a grand total of $250 for his idea; milkman Wallace was calmed down with a bribe of $10 and some show tickets.

Ziegfeld's role as a promoter was already well established, and his future as the Glorifier of American Girls seemed assured: "He has not sang her songs," a paper reported of Anna and Ziegfeld, "he has not worn her clothes; he has not posed openly. But Anna Held is the pretty feminine reflection of this gentleman's seething brain. One of these days Ziegfeld will write a book called 'How to Make a Star Twinkle,' and future generations will read it in amazement." For all her gratitude, Anna must have been somewhat nonplussed. Her ten years of very hard work in the theater were brushed aside and she was already treated as nothing more than a brainless Trilby to Ziegfeld's Svengali.

Alan Dale professed himself somewhat less than bowled over by Anna's press. "I have no objection at all to the press agent, when he is at one end of Manhattan Island and I am at the other," wrote Dale. "I love reading his stories, when they are particularly obvious, and warranted not to deceive a babe in long clothes. I am very partial to infantine literature, and the press agent is more ingenious than Grimm or Hans Christian Andersen." But the constant barrage of newspaper stories, photos, ads papered all over New York for a yet-little-known actress were beginning to backfire.

Ziegfeld could turn anything into a publicity scheme, as press agent Will A. Page later stressed. While backstage at a rehearsal, Ziegfeld tripped over a piece of wood and slightly bumped his knee. "Send out a story at once that Ziegfeld was seriously injured by an accident during the rehearsal due to falling scenery!" he ordered. It's easy to think Page was exaggerating, except for an incident in late 1896 when Anna suffered a similar spill. Riding her bicycle in Brooklyn, she tumbled off and bruised herself; a paper or two thought this worthy of a small story. But Ziegfeld had bigger fish to fry and released a statement that Anna had actually leaped off her bike to stop a team of runaway horses, thereby saving the life of former judge E.C. Murphy.

Very few papers fell for this one, and it seemed Ziegfeld had finally gone too far in crediting their gullibility (it must be noted that one of the few papers that did run the story straight had on the same page articles about the world's largest barrel—three thousand three hundred feet—and 104–year-old Barney Morris, a "queer old man" who collected stray scraps of paper). The *Evening Journal* stood back in awe of Ziegfeld's gall and published a poetic tribute:

> Where do you buy your hasheesh? What is your brand of dope?
> Will you ever reach the end of your imaginative rope? . . .
> Now tell us, Mr. Ziegfeld, when the date and hour are set
> For Miss Held to jump off Brooklyn Bridge and get no more than wet?

But Ziegfeld was just getting warmed up, and not a day passed in late 1896 without a mention of Anna in New York's many newspapers. She gave out beauty tips, and at one point a palmist was called in to read Anna's hand, telling the *New York World* with notable accuracy that "the head line is a little stronger than the heart line, indicating that she is not entirely governed by her feelings" and that "she will have one slight break that will cause considerable trouble." Of course the palmist also saw her having two children and living into old age. Ziegfeld began selling Anna's image to advertisers: Soon she was seen plugging Pozzoni's Medicated Complexion Powder, a hair tonic, and a corset, as well as gazing into a new American Mutoscope machine.

Theatrical publicity was nothing new in the 1890s; even zanier stunts had been tried before. Sarah Bernhardt was already famed for being photographed sleeping in her coffin, horse-whipping enemies (both male and female), and trying her talents as sculptress and fencing-mistress. In the 1880s, American actress Mary Anderson was the first to hire a press agent to specifically invent stories about her to be placed in newspapers. But never had the public been subjected to so constant, so unrelenting, and so shameless a barrage of publicity as Ziegfeld now unleashed on Anna's behalf.

Will Page wrote that "in the old days a press-agent was a man who cooked up ingenious, but not very credible, lies and by hook or crook, got them printed." By the time of the 1920s, he ingenuously averred, "We make, not fake, news. It may be synthetic in the sense of being carefully planned, but it is real." In his biography of Walter Winchell, Neal Gabler described exactly the kind of hack Ziegfeld relied upon to promote his new discovery: "On the face of it, press agents were a strange, colorful breed, who prided themselves on being characters in the Damon Runyon mold," Gabler wrote. "But just beneath the surface of the image, one found an unsavory and largely forlorn group of men. Some were lapsed journalists in mid-career who were frantically searching for a way to make money. Some were fresh high school kids who liked to wisecrack and hoped they might become humorists or even columnists. Others were orphans and vagabonds who had drifted into publicity because they didn't know how to do anything else." But these men—and a few women—put their life's blood into making sure everyone in the United States knew exactly who Anna Held was.

A Parlor Match ended its New York run on October 31, 1896, and Anna took off on her first American tour with the show: Confined mostly to the eastern states, the tour encompassed Philadelphia, Pittsburgh, Boston, Chicago, and Baltimore. Anna's first Christmas in America was spent in Pittsburgh, where she sang at a benefit for that city's Humane Society (she was also paid five hundred dollars to perform at a private party that same month). While in Boston, Ziegfeld tried to plant a story about Anna facing down a mugger with her tiny derringer, but the Boston papers proved harder to fool than their New York counterparts. In Philadelphia on March 8, Anna appeared in the three thousandth performance of A Parlor Match, where "the audience went wild over her."

As 1897 dawned, the majority of newspaper critics remained largely unimpressed by Anna's skills, but her audience appeal was growing. To a certain segment of the theatergoing population, Anna was the high point of *A Parlor Match*. One paper noted that the theater lobbies were packed with "listless club men, tired professional men, fashionable folks from Newport and other seaports and the well-dressed riffraff from the hotels and apartment houses" until it was time for Anna's appearance, at which point they rushed into the theater to find their seats. After Anna's last encore, they rudely grabbed their coats and strolled out again. "Better five minutes of Anna Held than a whole evening of *A Parlor Match*," wrote a Boston critic during this tour. "Why we should have to suffer two hours of the most conventional farce-comedy acts in order to reach the one interesting feature is a problem which we leave to the solution of theatrical managers."

Repeat audiences required that Anna add new songs to her repertoire, though "Won't You Come and Play with Me?" was always kept in as her finale. In the late 1890s, newspapers and playgoers alike complained about women wearing huge hats to shows, blocking the vision of anyone behind them. Ziegfeld played on this and developed a "hat dance" for Anna: She performed one song from behind a huge six-foot hat, peeking out occasionally. The audience got the joke and a few women unpinned their hats.

The show finally ended its East Coast tour in March 1897, and Anna returned to New York, where she and Ziegfeld shared an apartment at the Netherland. Friends and business associates knew by now that the two were more than just business partners. Ziegfeld was a quiet, taciturn man who never discussed his private affairs. His nicknames amongst his theater associates included "Ice Water" and "Gloomy Gus" (Anna mangled the latter into "Gussie Gloom," to everyone's amusement). In January 1897 Ziegfeld had hotly denied a newspaper story that he and Anna were engaged. "A false rumor like this does not improve an actress's professional reputation," he managed to say with a perfectly straight face, "and both she and I are annoyed by its publicity."

But the fact was Ziegfeld and Anna were very much in love. They couldn't marry, because she'd been unable to divorce Carrera—but they had a solution of their own. On March 26 they invited some friends, including Lillian Russell and Diamond Jim Brady, to a dinner party at their hotel. Without any fanfare, they stood up, toasted each other with champagne, and announced that—as far as they were concerned—from that moment on they were man and wife. No wedding was ever announced in the press; within a year or two, the couple was simply referred to as a married couple. (By New York state common law, they became legally wed after living together for seven years, so time would accomplish what the Catholic church and the Carreras had tried to prevent.)

In May 1897 the more-or-less newlywed Anna sailed for Southampton, and New Yorkers thought that they had perhaps seen the last of the *chanteuse excentrique*. Anna spent the summer resting, clothes-shopping, and trying to duck Edouard Marchand of the Folies-Bergère, who was still infuriated at her supposedly running out on her contract. She visited little Liane—now about three years old—and bicycled around Paris taking in the sights. Reporters—both American and European—interviewed her on her home turf, one finding her "no hairbrained trifler, but a very level-headed, kind-hearted and womanly little woman." There was never any mention of Anna's ex-husband or her daughter. When Anna visited Liane, no reporters went along. She realized that the middle-aged Carrera and her all but abandoned daughter were not good for her public image.

When Anna sailed back to New York in August 1897, she found that Ziegfeld had teamed up with another producer to showcase her in her next production. Oscar Hammerstein had opened a huge multitheater complex in 1895, at the "uptown" location of Broadway and Forty-fourth Street. He had to fill those theaters, and he and Ziegfeld agreed to team up with an English-language version of the French farce *La Poupée* (The Puppet). Anna was already familiar with *La Poupée*, having performed in a French-language version of it at the Théâtre des Variétés. Portraying Alesia Hilarius, daughter of a toymaker, Anna posed as a living doll purchased by a novice monk who is forced by his uncle to marry. Of course, the "doll" and the unwitting husband (played by handsome blond leading man Frank Rushwood) fall in love and all ends happily. "Where there is Ziegfeld, there is hope," noted one reporter, looking forward to more of Anna's antics.

As soon as she returned to the United States, before she even went back onstage with *La Poupée*, Ziegfeld arranged another stunt, which he vainly hoped might surpass the already fabled milk bath: In October, he staged a kissing marathon at the Hotel Martin. With Ziegfeld and one Dr. Frank Muller looking on, Anna was kissed 156 times by Broadway leading man Julius Steger until at last she "lay back in her chair—panting, exhausted—white as the flower that had fallen from her hair—limp as the roses that were dying in the gaslight."

While the man who was essentially her husband looked on, Anna panted prettily for a *New York Journal* scribe, "Up to the fifteenth kiss I felt calm, comfortable, with no marked sensation of any sort. . . . At the 150th kiss I was muscularly exhausted, overwhelmed with such inertia that I could not stir." As Anna's English was rudimentary at this time, someone (probably Teddy Marks) must have been serving as her interpreter and elaborator. Dr. Muller noted sagely that Anna's collapse occurred because "woman's psychological condition is more delicate than man's."

Another concocted tale, carefully tied in to the plot of *La Poupée*, had Anna going to the popular Eden Musée on Twenty-third Street. Standing in front of the wax figures, lost in admiration, Anna was suddenly kissed by a young man who'd mistaken her for a statue. Mayhem resulted, according to the press releases. Even Anna's "private" outings were turned into press holidays. She and Ziegfeld went to see Ringling's circus, and Ziegfeld insisted that the dubious Anna be hoisted atop an elephant for the amusement of the newspapermen. She convincingly shrieked in terror as the animal swayed from side to side and was much happier while admiring the monkeys from the safety of the floor.

La Poupée also involved a bit of product placement. Popular French dolls called Bébé Jumeau were plugged in the show, much to the delight (and remuneration) of their manufacturer, M. Jumeau himself. Alan Dale dryly suggested that it might be a good scheme for M. Jumeau to break into Anna's apartments and tattoo her with the Jumeau trademark. He also suggested she bathe in champagne and sell it afterward as souvenirs, rather a coarse notion for the time. "Miss Held can fill in vacant time," Dale added, "by careering through the Park on a bicycle built for six, with five trained dogs on the saddles not occupied by herself." Ziegfeld must have been torn between suing Dale or hiring him.

La Poupée opened on October 21, 1897, at Hammerstein's Lyric Theater. This was Anna's first encounter with what would later be known as Times Square. This Lyric, demolished in 1935, is not to be confused with the 1904 Lyric Theater on Forty-third Street, the facade of which still exists. The theater that housed *La Poupée* had been built by Oscar Hammerstein in 1895, as part of a concerted effort to upgrade what was still called Long Acre Square, around the intersection of Broadway and Forty-second Street.

The small but jewel-like Lyric was part of Hammerstein's huge, multitheater complex on Broadway between Forty-forth and Forty-fifth Streets. His Music Hall, Lyric, and Roof Garden all operated under the umbrella name of the Olympia (in 1899, he would open the famous Hammerstein's Victoria on Broadway and Forty-second). There were a few other theaters on Long Acre Square—the Casino, the Broadway, the Empire, the Knickerbocker—but they still shared the neighborhood with leather and saddle shops, stonemasons, and sad little boarding houses. It was Hammerstein's ambitious plan to transform the area into the new theater and restaurant hub. That actual crossroad—the small triangle formed by the intersection of Broadway and Forty-second Street—was still occupied in 1897 by billboard-covered brownstones. The following year, the nine-story Hotel Pabst went up on the site, and it wasn't until 1903 that the famous *New York Times* Building began to rise on what would be finally dubbed Times Square.

For all the press attention, *La Poupée* did not go over with audiences. It would be difficult to think of a vehicle less well suited for Anna. Her whole act was based on infectious charm and bubbling vivacity; in *La Poupée*, she spent most of the show impersonating a wooden dummy. It was hardly a choice calculated to succeed, and succeed it didn't. When Anna left the show two weeks after the opening, claiming illness, Oscar Hammerstein instituted a lawsuit for $17,500 against her for breach of contract and damages. Ziegfeld countersued for $12,500 for humiliation, claiming that Hammerstein had bumped Anna from the show so his mistress, Alice Rose, could replace her. The various suits and countersuits faded away as both producers realized they could ill afford the legal fees. It wasn't the last time that Ziegfeld would regret teaming up with another powerful producer.

Ziegfeld quickly signed Anna to play a vaudeville act at Koster and Bial's Music Hall on Thirty-fourth Street, on the current-day site of Macy's. Earlier that same year, Koster and Bial's had introduced the American public to projected moving pictures at the end of another vaudeville bill. Anna appeared just before the closing act—a good spot on the bill—sharing the program with such acts as British comic Marie Lloyd, "Novelty Sand-Modeler" Mlle Rombello, and the unfortunately named De Kock Troupe of acrobats.

When Anna first entered vaudeville, it had already taken hold of the American public and was not to let go for some time. Most aficionados place its heyday between 1881 (when impresario Tony Pastor opened his 14th Street Opera House in New York) and 1932 (when the Palace Theater folded as a two-a-day house and began showing movies). It was a world unto itself: Thousands of acts were born, became rich and world famous, and died within the world of vaudeville. Frequently, "legit" acts such as Anna, Sarah Bernhardt, Ethel Barrymore, and others would invade vaudeville to spread their fame to the masses and earn extra cash. But the heart and soul of vaudeville were the troupers: singers like Eva Tanguay, Blanche Ring, Nora Bayes; comics like Gallagher and Shean, Bert Williams, Burns and Allen; frighteningly adult children like Baby Rose Marie, Baby June (Havoc). And then there were the acrobats, jugglers, animal acts, dancers, female (and male) impersonators, monologists, magicians, glass eaters—anything you could imagine.

Anna was back in her element, and those who had been disappointed with her in *A Parlor Match* and *La Poupée* saw for the first time what Ziegfeld had seen in London: a charming song-and-dance artist who could use her voice and body with professional verve. "She accomplished one of the triumphs of the amusement season," said *The Player* magazine. She sang, of course, "Won't You Come and Play with Me?" and another song in French, while expertly twirling a parasol. Her other big number put her into the unfamiliar world of blackface. Mercifully Anna herself did not don burnt cork, but she sang "I Want Dem Presents Back" in a bizarre Polish-French-Southern dialect, while cakewalking in front of a huge sheet-music backdrop. Poking through the cutout notes were the heads of thirty-three chorus boys in blackface, who sang lustily along with the star.

A reporter attending a rehearsal for this number noted that Anna was still struggling with her English but that the chorus boys "wrestle manfully with the difficulties and the bad breaks are excused." Anna had finally found her forte, and her two-week engagement at Koster and Bial's was extended through Christmas 1897. She was still playing to standing-room-only crowds, which also benefited the other acts on the bill (which by now included contortionist Pablo Diaz and Jessie, the Equestrian Baboon).

Anna spoke to a reporter from the *Evening World* about vaudeville, and he managed to translate her opinions into a "journalistic English" that sounded very little like Anna's own speech: "The vaudeville stage, as I first knew it in Europe, is a splendid school," she supposedly said. "You learn self-confidence, assurance, and, above all, you instinctively discover how to entertain an audience." She went on to note that, when choosing her songs, the words and music were equally important, and she learned them together. Once she had the songs down pat, she would rehearse her movements—down to the last wink—in front of a full-length mirror. "My feet, my arms, my face—all must do their part." She also explained the secret of her rapport with audiences. "Charm them with your presence as soon as they look at you," she advised, "then acquire the trick of apparently singing to each individual your song. This is done with the eyes and a general attitude of confidential interest you assume toward the orchestra chairs."

If there were any doubts that these were actually the opinions of Anna, they are laid to rest by the hardheaded financial advice. "Above all," she was quoted, "measure the applause of your audience from a commercial standpoint: The more they applaud the bigger your salary will be, and the stage in all its branches is a money-making institution." Anyone who knew Anna knew that this was a sentiment she might as well have had embroidered on a pillow. Already she was showing a clear-eyed concern for money. The once impoverished Anna told a reporter that a woman "must make her fortune before she is 30; or work after she is 30; or get married. Now, I don't want to get married and I don't want to work after I'm 30, so I must manage to make my fortune somehow in the next seven years." The fact that Anna was probably twenty-eight at the time and not the twenty-three she claimed, and that she was already possessed of not one but two husbands did not slow her down. She also continued to keep up the old milk bath story, telling another reporter that "there is nothing to compare with it for the complexion. . . . At home in Paris I take a milk bath two times a week, regularly; but here on the road it is more difficult and I miss them."

In late February 1898 Anna started on a tour of the West and South. She finally had her bicycle but sighed that "I am not able to [ride] in America, on account of being in a different city nearly every two weeks." When in New York, she tried to be in Central Park by nine, either on bicycle or horseback but always in scanty attire. "People look at me and look," she said, "but I do not care." Ziegfeld, of course, cared very much and was no doubt delighted that her riding caused a sensation.

One of the sights she saw on this tour was San Francisco's pre-earthquake Chinatown. This was not the picturesque village of today, with its respectable families and business people. Anna emerged from her tour sputtering with horror. "I think it is the worst thing I ever heard [sic] in my life," she gasped. "That Chinatown should be burned to ashes. It ought not to be tolerated. It is bad for the nation. The vice, the filth, the disease, oh, it is all too horrid!" Her reaction seems a bit extreme, but even theatrical producer Oliver Morosco—no babe in the woods—was shaken recalling a trip to Chinatown at about the same time. "My guide showed me a pen in which Charley Hung had some 80 or100 Chinese slave girls, all under 14, whom he offered for sale or rent," Morosco wrote in his memoirs. "I saw other things that night—things which are not mentioned in polite society, things we don't like to admit human beings will do, that left me incredulous."

By the spring of 1898, Anna was doing so much touring it was decided that she must ride in style, like the star she was. Touring by train was no fun: "She did not enjoy living in a car and inhaling gaseous odors of railway yards," said one of her business managers. So she and Ziegfeld invested twenty-two thousand dollars in a luxurious private railway car, one that had been previously owned by actress and noted royal mistress Lillie Langtry. The car was so huge and well appointed that Anna was able to bypass local hotels and sleep in it on her stops. It contained a stateroom, dining room, a parlor, and a plate-glass-enclosed observation deck, as well as servant's quarters and a well-equipped kitchen (Anna was not impressed with American hotel cookery). She hired a chef who had previously worked on the Vanderbilt yacht; as part of his contract, he was permitted to use the white-and-gold piano and the observation car when not engaged in his duties.

Anna's train was not only good for transportation but also for impressing reporters, and *Metropolitan* magazine did a photo feature on the Anna Held Special. Her parlor was fitted out with music boxes and (for very smooth rides) a phonograph. Her large, soft bed was enclosed by heavy satin curtains, and the whole car was done up in cluttered knickknack-heavy Victorian style. Riding along with Anna were three of her dogs, Chico, Nellie, and Tiger. Chico, a tiny Mexican hairless who ran away later that year, was described rather unkindly in one paper as "a globular, bow-legged creature with pop eyes and an imbecile expression."

But for all the publicity and money, Anna's career was not progressing as quickly as she'd hoped. She was put into a troupe performing the one-act play *The Cat and the Cherub*, a Chinese-themed drama. After an intermission, the audience was treated to a variety of acts: Dixon, Brown and Dixon ("The Three Rubes"), the flying De Kocks, and finally Anna herself, doing the "animated sheet music" act that had been such a hit in New York. One critic sounded positively forced into liking her despite his better instincts: "It is useless to deny that she is interesting," he huffed, "it is useless to attempt to moralize over the blatant lubricity of her style; it is equally useless to forbid her recognition for the remarkable color which she is able to infuse into her voice." Another paper dismissed her thus: "Her way of doing her Parisian things is well known; it is occasionally shrewd, often funny, always vulgar. If it were not vulgar, it would be flat, empty, meaningless." This was not what Anna had come to America for, and her patience was running out. By the end of her tour, she sighed to a reporter, "I do not like vaudeville, but what can I do? It likes me."

While Anna was touring the country, Ziegfeld and coproducer William A. Brady were readying their mistaken identity comedy *A Gay Deceiver* for its February 1898 opening. Anna wound up her vaudeville tour at the end of May, and on June 7 she sailed for Europe on the *Kaiser Wilhelm der Grosse*, accompanied by an equally exhausted Ziegfeld. But Anna's summer vacation was not all fun and games. That ongoing legal battle with her old employer Edouard Marchand of the Folies-Bergère and La Scala had been percolating since she had cut and run in the summer of 1896. Anna and Ziegfeld insisted that Marchand had agreed to a pay-off of four thousand dollars for Anna's contract. Marchand—who had never deposited the check—said in turn that he'd never finalized the agreement and had only considered (and rejected) it. There was "much animated and courtly discussion" between Marchand and Ziegfeld, reported the *New York Telegraph*, "embellished with polite shrugs, grimaces and gesticulations." After some two years of fighting, the courts found in Marchand's favor: Anna owed him five thousand dollars for breach of contract. All parties agreed to shake hands and make up if Anna would play the Folies-Bergère for free during the month of June 1898.

That finally done with, Anna journeyed to St. Petersburg in July and earned a healthy forty thousand francs performing there while Ziegfeld remained in Paris working out the logistics of their next show together, *The French Maid*, another coproduction with Charles Evans. The show had been running at the Vaudeville Theatre in London for four hundred performances, and an American version had opened in late 1897 with Marguerite Sylva in the title role; Ziegfeld hoped to buy the show and replace her with Anna—America's idea of the perfect French maid personified.

She and Ziegfeld return to the United States in August. His show *The Turtle*, a comedy about midlife divorce, opened September 3, while Anna toured in yet another revival of *A Parlor Match* (this time without its original stars, Evans and Hoey) in September. During a typically muggy Baltimore heat wave, one paper noted, "Mlle. Held is in fine spirits and excellent voice, and . . . bursting with anxiety to disclose the splendors of her new stage gowns, one of which is encrusted with diamonds thicker than barnacles on a blockade service battle ship." Her swan song in *A Parlor Match* brought in ten thousand dollars in Baltimore alone.

The couple began setting down tentative roots in the United States, where Anna would now be spending at least half of her time. In the fall of 1898, Anna and Ziegfeld bought a small farm on the outskirts of Belgrade Lakes, Maine. Neither of them got to spend much time there, which was fine with Anna: While Ziegfeld enjoyed roughing it in the woods, Anna was more of a city girl. Between shows they would drive north to their farm and spend a week or so with friends, until the mosquitos drove Anna back to New York. A local Maine paper printed news of Anna's arrivals and departures and noted with tongue in cheek that "guests are invited to visit the place at any time, where the hired man, if requested, will show them her calves."

While rehearsing for *The French Maid*, Anna continued doing a vaudeville turn at the Herald Square Theater at night. When *The French Maid* finally opened on September 26, 1898, it played for one week at the Herald Square, then moved to Boston for eight weeks. But Anna was not playing the French maid in *The French Maid*—she simply wasn't ready to take on such a difficult English-speaking role, and Idalene Cotton starred while Anna studied her—and the audience reaction to her—closely. Anna (billed as "The Peerless Little Parisienne") performed "specialties" during the second act.

It wasn't until early 1899 that Ziegfeld and Evans thought Anna herself was ready to take over the title role in *The French Maid*, on a whirlwind tour that included stops in Detroit, Montreal, and, by April, New York. As Suzette, the flirtatious domestic at a seaside resort, she romanced the entire British fleet, a headwaiter, and a policeman. *The French Maid* had a stellar cast, which included zaftig comedienne Eva Davenport as society matron Lady Hercules Hawser. Anna's leading man, in the comic role of an English waiter, was Charles Bigelow. This was the first of five shows that were to costar Anna and Bigelow, and theirs was to be a stormy pairing. Charles Bigelow was one of those stars who enjoyed a huge popularity for a few years but after his death was completely forgotten. For all his fame and success in the early years of the twentieth century, his name cannot even be found in theater reference books today.

Bigelow was born in Cleveland and had been an actor since his teens. He was only thirty-six when he and Anna first worked together in *The French Maid*, but because of his cadaverous, bald appearance, he was already playing old men. Playwright Harry B. Smith later explained both Bigelow's appeal and his major professional drawback: "Nature had been kind in giving him a perfect physical equipment for his vocation," Smith wrote in his memoirs. "He had a comic bald head and a spectacular nose, and he had developed the latter feature by the alcoholic treatment."

Ziegfeld and Evans's revival of *The French Maid* did not get very good reviews, and neither did Anna. Indeed, only Charles Bigelow and Eva Davenport received unanimous raves. Capt. Basil Hood's script had a few funny jokes, but they were too few and far between; and the music of Walter Slaughter (misprinted in the program as "Walters Laughter") borrowed too heavily from other popular show tunes. Anna's personal notices were far from encouraging. "One might have fancied that the part of a French maid would be exactly in her line," reasoned one critic, but "the little lady showed no skill worthy of mention in her performance and her playing fell flat." Another paper agreed that Anna seemed "considerably out of her element—a square peg in a round hole." The only kind word came from a critic who felt that "she can shrug her shapely shoulders and wink her eyes and make suggestive grimaces as well as she ever could." One Detroit critic seemed especially offended by Anna: "She is not pretty," he wrote. "She cannot sing. She cannot dance. To come down to brass tacks, Anna Held has not even a good figure." He closed the review by suggesting the theater be "fumigated by the health officer" after *The French Maid* closed. Hardly the kind of review that leads to a long and remunerative career.

Ziegfeld latched onto those few lonely critics who called Anna "sweet," "engaging" and "personable." He also noted that she was an audience favorite, no matter what the newspapers might have to say. "Our audiences here don't understand scarcely a word of French," he said, "and yet applaud her wildly.

Why? I can only attribute it to her individuality. I know that if I get a proper vehicle for her she will show herself to be a great actress."

For all the carping about Anna's skills, interviewers found her to be charming and unaffected offstage, and she was well liked by her coworkers. Legit acts coming into vaudeville were known for acting "upstage," but Anna, it was written in late 1898, "has none of the freakish caprices of a prima donna or a star, and is as ambitious and willing to work as a child. She does not demand the star dressing room, nor does she insist upon special billing."

By the spring of 1899, Ziegfeld was in New York preparing two shows, *Mlle. Fifi* (another divorce comedy), which opened for a three-month run on February 1, and *The Manicure* (about, not surprisingly, a flirtatious manicurist), which opened and closed like a camera shutter on April 24. *The French Maid* also closed in late April, but Anna scarcely had time to take a breath before Ziegfeld propelled her into the cast of an odd little comedy called *By the Sad Sea Waves*, which had been running at the Herald Square since February. A broad farce, its plot strongly resembled a Three Stooges short: Two wastrels (the comedy team of Harry Bulger and J. Sherrie Mathews) are mistaken for the new music master and gym teacher at the Finishville Habit Cure Sanitarium; the expected mayhem results.

The show had, in the words of one reviewer, "the merest suspicion of a plot," and no author was credited in the program. The music ranged from Gilbert and Sullivan parodies to ragtime and minstrel tunes. Anna, apparently playing one of the rehab guests, did a few numbers, including "My Honolulu Queen," aided—according to the reviews—by "seven pickaninnies" (just what "pickaninnies" would have been doing in Honolulu is anyone's guess). While Bulger and Mathews vanished from theatrical history, a few other cast members went on to fame: Rose Melville took her comic rube character Sis Hopkins for a long run, and ragtime pianist Ned Wayburn later went on to popularize modern tap dancing and became choreographer and stage director for many Ziegfeld shows, including six editions of the *Follies*.

After *By the Sad Sea Waves* died its unlamented death in early May, Anna and Ziegfeld hopped on the first ship they could book and sailed back for France, where Anna spent her summer vacation reacquainting herself with her favorite town and buying clothes for her next New York venture. Anna made this a lifelong habit: Her shows closed in late spring and she sailed back to Paris just when all the fashionable people were leaving it. The social elite spent the year journeying from one resort to the next: The popular "seasons" were spring and early summer in London, late summer in the German health resorts, late fall and winter at one's country home, and late winter and spring in the south of France.

No one spent summer in Paris, but a working woman like Anna had no choice. Besides, she enjoyed having the city to herself: The rue Faubourg Saint-Honoré had fewer carriages crowding it up in the summer, and her dressmaking establishments were less busy at that time of year. Anna had never been "fashionable" in the social sense, so she didn't mind being in the "wrong place at the wrong time."

One lovely day in June 1899 reminded Anna why she loved Paris so much: She won first prize at the Fête des Fleurs, an annual festival in which all the loveliest ladies of Paris decked themselves and their carriages out in floral displays—kind of a late-Victorian Rose Bowl Parade. All day and into the night, ladies in flower-laden carriages, boats made of flowers and flowered dresses rode up and down the Bois de Bologne to cheering crowds. The all-day celebration converted the streets into "a gigantic pathway of crushed roses and tulips, daisies and carnations." Anna dressed all in pink and white, her hat made of lavender orchids and her dress embroidered with white orchids; her carriage and driver were done up in green and lavender orchids. As she drove by, a cheering Ziegfeld threw her a five-pound bouquet of roses from the sidelines, which only succeeded in knocking her hat off. Anna carried the day, winning first prize (over such competitors as Liane de Pougy and Cleo de Merode).

With money still to be earned (those orchids didn't come cheap), in August Anna took off for Ostend, the popular Belgian bathing resort, where she was booked to do her act for the king of Belgium and his guest, the shah of Persia. Anna drove to Ostend in her first automobile, a nickel-plated Dion-Bouton. She first practiced on the bumpy but less crowded country roads before trying out her city driving skills. She once drove herself in the rickety, uncovered and unreliable car all the way from Paris to Bordeaux, and on another occasion proudly noted that she made it from her home on the rue de Faubourg Saint-Honoré to Versailles ("mostly uphill") in only twenty-two minutes.

But much of that summer was devoted to intensive study: of her new role in the show *Papa's Wife* and of the English language. Her lack of English had gotten her into trouble, and not just with the critics. In Boston she had attended a political lecture with Ziegfeld, and when one speaker referred to the Dreyfus case as having made France "a foul blot on the fair face of modern civilization," Anna—having only caught the word "France"—burst into pretty applause. Ziegfeld hurriedly explained and she sat down abashed as onlookers whispered and giggled. To learn English, Anna tried the submersion method, hiring only English-speaking servants, including a cockney chauffeur who gave her a very odd idea of pronunciation. But she was a naturally brilliant linguist and by the end of the summer had English more or less where she wanted it, along with her half a dozen or so other languages.

Still, Anna had second thoughts about coming back to the United States. She enjoyed great success in Europe, but all she had to show for her two American trips was—besides huge wads of cash—appearances in indifferent shows and limited success in vaudeville. The late 1890s had its share of skyrocketing musical comedy stars: Edna May shot to fame in *The Belle of New York* in 1897, May Irwin enjoyed a huge hit with *The Swell Miss Fitzwell* that same year, and Marie Dressler was still glowing with her success in *The Lady Slavey*. But Anna felt she was going nowhere fast.

She kept her agreement and returned to the United States on the *La Touraine* on August 26, 1899, ready to tackle her new assignment. She'd made a new friend on the voyage, the wife of publisher Frank Leslie. "She has no wrinkles, and she combs her hair so nicely!" Anna stated enthusiastically to reporters about Mrs. Leslie in her newly perfected English. Anna had shipped her Dion-Bouton to the United States with her, and her second vehicle, a Panhard racing car, was being sent on later.

That year, New York saw its first speeding ticket (motorist Jacob German was arrested for going twelve miles per hour on Lexington Avenue) and its first fatality (real estate broker Henry Bliss was struck and killed by a car on Central Park West). Even Anna hesitated to drive in Manhattan, where the streets were narrow and crowded with horses, carriages, and pedestrians. The city imposed a nine miles per hour speed limit, and drivers had to sound a gong until horns were invented. But cars were banned from Central Park, so if she wanted to drive, she had to head up to Westchester. Reporter Ray Stannard Baker rhapsodized about how blissful New York would be when the automobile took over: "In the first place, it will be almost as quiet as a country lane," he predicted, "all the crash of horses' hoofs and the rumble of steel tires will be gone. And since vehicles will be fewer and shorter than the present truck and span, streets will appear less crowded."

The earlier cars that Anna drove cannot be compared with those of even ten years later: They were more akin to being perched atop a washing machine with a rock in it during the spin cycle. Steering wheels had not yet been invented; instead, a vertical bar was connected to the wheels. There were no seat belts or even side doors, and the vehicles frequently tipped over, sending the occupants out onto the road. "Suspension" was a joke, and one's spine and neck underwent a terrible jolting on the unpaved, often rock-strewn, roads. There were no "parking spaces" as such, and garages did not yet exist in the city; Anna had to board her new vehicles in accommodating stables.

Cars were difficult to start, and, as memoirist Mark Sullivan reminisced, even more difficult to run. "Switches had to be pressed, and a complexity of pedals and levers had to be operated simultaneously by drivers woefully inexperienced. Frequently when the driver wished to go one way, the car went another. Not infrequently brakes or pedals refused to function, and terror-stricken drivers were carried helplessly along by iron steeds indifferent alike to prayers or curses from behind or obstacles in front." Nonetheless, the adventurous Anna found all this to be a lot of fun. Despite driving through some of the most crowded cities and desolate country villages in America and Europe, she never lost her love for the automobile.

Ziegfeld saw gold in Anna's new hobby and arranged for another publicity stunt. In September 1899, while her new show, *Papa's Wife*, was still in rehearsal, Anna issued a challenge for any woman to race her by automobile from New York to Philadelphia ("a morning's ride"). There was to be no money involved, just "glory," but "we must go fast, because the race is against time. We must run our own machines. Yes, with the lever and the steering gear we must remain until the race is over." The notice ended with the extremely polite postscript, "Pardon me for detaining your attention to ask you the favor of accepting my challenge." Anna's love of cars never abated, but with the excitement of *Papa's Wife*, no more was heard of this auto race.

She and Ziegfeld realized that this show was her last chance to win over the American public. After her mixed reception in *A Parlor Match*, *La Poupée*, *The French Maid*, *By the Sad Sea Waves*, and vaudeville, Anna was no longer a novelty. She needed more than a cute accent and some naughty songs: If *Papa's Wife* was not a hit, she would have to return to France an artistic failure, and her future would be confined to Parisian and British music halls. But this time Ziegfeld had planned more carefully, and *Papa's Wife* was carefully tailored to fit Anna's talents and charms perfectly. The show was written specifically to highlight her sparkling, innocent naughtiness—but it was no free ride. There were some scenes (especially a tipsy scene at a party) that required delicacy and professional self-control.

Papa's Wife was written by Harry B. Smith, a prolific playwright whose work has all but been forgotten today. He wrote an impressive 123 Broadway shows, as well as many others that played in the provinces. For *Papa's Wife*, Smith reteamed with Reginald De Koven, who had provided the music for the pair's biggest hit, *Robin Hood* (1891). Smith had grown up in Chicago, and Ziegfeld probably knew him from his father's Musical College. Ziegfeld and Anna became great friends with Smith and his wife, actress Irene Bentley, and the couples often traveled together through Europe on their summer breaks. The idea for *Papa's Wife*, Smith said, came not from Ziegfeld but from Anna. She had seen the French play *La Femme à Papa* and thought it might be translated for her. "The plot of *La Femme à Papa* being rather thin," Smith recalled, "I combined it with parts of another French comedy, *Mam'selle Nitouche.*"

In September and October 1899, Anna faced her biggest challenge: learning her first English-language role, one which kept her onstage for nearly the entire play and which would have tested even an experienced star. As the October tryouts in Boston, Philadelphia, and Rochester approached, Anna became manic with worry and Ziegfeld grew characteristically silent.

—3—

The Belle of New York

Papa's Wife was the first show in which Anna received star billing, so everyone knew the success or failure of it rested on her shoulders. But there was more on the line than Anna's career. She knew if she wasn't a success in *Papa's Wife*, her marriage might be doomed as well. For Anna, Florenz Ziegfeld was that once-in-a-lifetime love. She happily followed his advice, rearranged her schedule and career plans, spent less time in her beloved Paris, and jollied him out of his dark moods. She knew he was in love with her, too, but she also knew that Ziegfeld's life was consumed by the theater. His every waking hour was spent arranging or producing shows. "He would get up at six in the morning," recalled Eddie Cantor, "take the telephone into his bed and start calling up his press agent, managers, actors, and authors—who had probably gone to sleep an hour before." Not that Anna thought Ziegfeld just saw her as a meal ticket (which was exactly what some newspapers implied). But how would his love for her fare if she were no longer a popular draw at the theater, no longer part of "his" world? Anna had a lot riding on *Papa's Wife*.

In *Papa's Wife*, Anna played a sweet convent girl (also named Anna) who is wed to a dissipated French nobleman (played by character actor Henry Bergman), much to the horror of his upright son (leading man Henry Woodruff). Despite the efforts of Papa's riffraff friends to corrupt her, Anna remains pure and innocent—and through very circuitous plot twists, she turns out to be married not to Papa but to his handsome young son. In comic supporting roles were Charles Bigelow, as Anna's dancing master, and Eva Davenport, as his long-lost mistress. "Anna" was a difficult role to pull off. She had to be sweet but not cloying and to be able to put over a lot of double entendres and naughty songs. The danger was in going all kittenish and winking knowingly at the audience, which would be the kiss of death. In addition, Anna had a lot of songs to deliver—in character—and she had to compete with a very talented and stage-hardened supporting cast.

Fortunately Anna had as a director George Marion, who also played a supporting role in the show. Marion, only thirty-nine, was already well known for his character roles (he would later come to fame playing the father in Eugene O'Neill's *Anna Christie,* both onstage and onscreen). As both actor and director, he was sympathetic to the plight of actors and was able to calm Anna and coax from her an honest, charming performance. Ziegfeld kept his distance, overseeing sets, costumes, and besieging poor Anton Heindle, the musical director, with suggestions for the production numbers. Anna was not comforted when famed theatrical producer David Belasco attended a dress rehearsal and declared that he could not understand one word she was saying.

The show had its out-of-town tryouts in Boston, Philadelphia, and Rochester, New York, in October 1899. Old theatrical lore had it that a bad tryout meant success in New York, and vice versa; it was a good way to make the cast and crew feel better if the show looked to be a flop and kept them from getting too smug and secure with a "sure-fire hit." Thus Anna and Ziegfeld didn't know whether to be pleased or nervous when out-of-town audiences and critics acclaimed both *Papa's Wife* and its star the best things they'd seen in years.

In Philadelphia Anna was called out to take ten curtain calls, according to the *Inquirer* (the more conservative *Bulletin* said eight). The Boston critics in particular fell all over themselves to praise Anna's performance, and she basked in the first real feeling of adulation since she'd arrived in the United States. "It will no longer do to treat Miss Held as a fad," wrote the *Boston Herald.* "She is worthy of serious critical consideration." The *Globe* added that Anna "shows great talent and . . . thorough appreciation of the opportunities her part affords." The *Boston Post* wrote of her "remarkable skill as an actress. It was a very realistic piece of work, and no one could accuse her of exaggeration or coarseness." The most often heard complaint was that, at nearly three hours, the show badly needed some trimming.

Anna's second-act tipsy scene, which could have been badly overplayed, was one of the hits of the show, and it was noted with undisguised amazement by the *Boston Transcript* that it was "an exceedingly fine piece of art. You felt the poor little drinker to be a lady, and pitied her. Neither was this scene the only place where Anna Held showed her newly acquired powers as an actress." There exists a brief film clip of that scene, the first motion picture ever taken of Anna

Held. Filmed in semi-closeup by F.S. Armitage of the American Mutoscope and Biograph Company, Anna is seen lifting a champagne glass, dizzyingly whirling her head back and forth, singing, rolling her eyes, and touching her hand to her forehead. She's utterly delightful in what amounts to a twenty-second glimpse of her technique. She's beautifully lit (especially for such an early film) and her features stand out—it's easy to see how her gestures could be appreciated from the back row—yet still not a gesture or expression seems overdone. She also posed for an advertisement for the film company, which was headquartered in a still extant building on New York's Union Square.

Another high spot of *Papa's Wife* was an automobile number Ziegfeld had added after the success of his New York-to-Philadelphia auto race scheme. Toward the end of act I, Anna made her entrance seated gingerly on the front of her tiny Dion-Bouton car, piloted from the back seat by a driver. Her chorus girls were already singing and dancing and, as one Rochester paper noted, the effect onstage was as great as the effect on the audience. Most of the girls at this point had never even seen a car, much less been caught in the path of one. "There is always something closely approaching a panic when [the chorus girls] hear the preliminary puffing and snorting of what they are pleased to call 'the infernal machine,'" wrote the reviewer. "The latter has the right of way, and for 20 [*sic*] young and beautiful comediennes to dance and sing and maintain expressions of joyous abandon while at the same time being compelled to skip out of the way of this petroleum fed monster is no trifling matter."

At the Philadelphia tryout, the car refused to work, and the somewhat relieved chorus girls expected Anna to simply dance out on her own. But Ziegfeld—by now somewhat of a good driver—leaped into the seat and managed to pilot the car onstage after all. Once in New York, the auto behaved itself. *Papa's Wife* opened on November 13, 1899, at the Manhattan Theater on Sixth Avenue between Thirty-second and Thirty-third Streets. Among the celebrities in attendance were Spanish-American war hero Admiral Dewey and his family (the audience held up the curtain till he agreed to take a bow). The theater was packed to standing-room-only, but this could be misleading. Often opening nights were "papered" with celebrities and friends of the star, to make sure the attendees would look enthusiastic and applaud convincingly, impressing both reviewers and passersby. Frequently no profit was made on opening night, even if the house were packed. Some managers also gave free tickets to office workers and shopgirls, who spread good word of mouth. At musicals, "gallery boys" (messengers and such) were paid to whistle along with the second chorus of a song, to convince the rest of the audience that a popular hit was in the making. About eighty orchestra seats were reserved for critics; after the show, press agents would swoop down on them and try to jolly them up, taking the more susceptible ones out for drinks or dinner. Bribery was rampant.

The New York critics came to *Papa's Wife* with chips on their shoulders. For three years now they had been savaging Anna Held, laughing at her pretensions and her silly publicity stunts. For out-of-town critics to suddenly praise her to the skies was like a slap in the face. Although Anna had friends out front that night, she had just as many enemies who were waiting for her to fall on her face. But—to everyone's surprise—*Papa's Wife* was a smash hit in New York as well. True, the papers were divided on Smith's script: Some felt the plot and lines were paper-thin, while a few called it "smart, pretty, picturesque, and up to date." But the cast came in for unmitigated praise. All of the New York critics were big enough to admit they'd quite underestimated Anna's potential. The editions of November 14 read like extended love letters to her.

"She acted capitally the role of Papa's innocent wife thrust into the company of soubrettes that had been Papa's old-time companions, and did the part in a manner that won well-deserved applause," read a typical review. One critic who had reservations about the show itself admitted that Anna "reads suggestive lines in a way that is not suggestive, and always appears to be what the part intends—an innocent and unsuspecting seminary girl who knows nothing that she has not learned in books." As in *The French Maid*, Charles Bigelow and Eva Davenport received raves for their broad comic turns. Anna's still heavy accent was noted, but her newfound command of English applauded. "It would be an agreeable thing indeed if Miss Held were to bring her English education to a close right where it stands at this moment," suggested one writer. "She will never speak more charmingly than now." Anna agreed: "I am rewarded for having studied so hard to learn English," she said, adding, "I am quick at imitation. If I live here too long I should lose my accent!"

There were some, of course, who felt the show too suggestive (oddly, there were more complaints about this in New York than in supposedly staid Boston). Ziegfeld and Harry B. Smith had tried to make this show less racy than Anna's previous outings had been, hoping to attract a family crowd. But some still were offended. One paper felt that *Papa's Wife* might be all well and good for Paris but was "too unsavory" for New York. The fact that women and children were being admitted to such shows as this—as well as to other current hits like *Make Way for the Ladies* and *The Girl from Maxim's*—shocked the writer. "Some episodes in the piece would be decidedly out of place in a Christian Endeavor Hall," another critic amusedly remarked.

After nearly fifteen years onstage, Anna Held was an "overnight success." Perhaps the sweetest acclaim came from the powerful Alan Dale, a hard man to fool and one who up till now had not been impressed with Anna's doings (though he was always fair to her and gave her an even shake). But Dale was big enough to admit that he'd underestimated her potential. "Here I had been taking her little 'will you come and play with me' girl as a pretty little fool without brains," he wrote on November 14, "a charming picture for susceptible ninnies and vacillating schoolboys. . . . Not a bit of it. While we were laughing at her she was laughing at us—in her sleeves. She was working like a Trojan—or whoever it is that works. . . . Throughout the evening she made a good many of us feel like 30 cents. We had never believed her capable of sustained dramatic effort. Last night we got one that was dainty and consistent throughout—one that will probably cause Anna Held to play with us for a long time."

Papa's Wife had more than just Anna going for it. This was the first Ziegfeld show that showcased beautiful chorus girls: sixteen of them, many playing characters with such ooh-la-la names as Zizi, Ninette, and Fifine. It was noted that Ziegfeld already had no peer when it came to choosing breathtaking chorines. "There is not a homely girl in the bevy," one paper stated enthusiastically, complimenting Anna for not being afraid of the competition. "She can mingle with a score of beautiful women without having her luster dimmed for an instant," she was assured. Vivian Blackburn, Olive Wallace, Emma Levy, and Frances Wilson were mentioned as being among the prettiest of these first "Ziegfeld Girls," though none of these Zizis or Ninettes seem to have gone on to stardom.

Along with beautiful girls, *Papa's Wife* featured what was to become another theatrical trademark of Ziegfeld's: breathtaking, trendsetting, and expensive costumes. Everything Flo Ziegfeld knew about women's clothing, he'd learned from Anna. In the previous seven shows he'd produced or coproduced, costumes played only a minor role. Some of the outfits Anna had appeared in provoked comment, but credit was given to her French dressmakers, not to Ziegfeld. In *Papa's Wife*, however, a stage legend began: the incredible fashion show of a Ziegfeld first night. Anna's clothes were made to her own specifications by Mme Landoff in Paris (the rest of the company contented themselves with W.R. Barnes's designs, which were little noted by the press). In all her years on the variety stage, Anna had learned the importance of eye-catching gowns. The men came to the theater to see her legs and shoulders and to hear her sing insinuating songs. But the women came to ogle her scandalously expensive gowns and to get ideas to suggest to their own dressmakers. Female audience members were frequently spotted peering intently through their opera glasses and making swift sketches on their programs for future reference. Fashion magazines and ready-to-wear were not common at the time, so Anna was serving as a Paris runway for eager American women. Anna impressed this upon Ziegfeld, and he was a quick learner. The legendary costumes of the *Ziegfeld Follies* really started here, with Anna and *Papa's Wife*. From *Papa's Wife* on, every show with which he was associated concentrated just as much (sometimes more) on gowns as on sets and script.

In December, Anna received an elaborate "flower gown" from Mme Landoff. When it had its debut in *Papa's Wife* that month, it received an astounding amount of newsprint. The dress itself looks dreadful to modern eyes, like an overdecorated wedding cake. "It is made of crepe de chine of a delicate rose petal pink over soft silk of a slightly deeper hue," wrote one paper. Scattered over the gown were large bulging roses of silk and velvet, with a train of orchids. The flowers' centers were made of rhinestones, and the sleeves of pearl ropes fastened with diamonds. Even for Anna Held, it was a bit much, making her look short and bulky.

The high fashions of 1899 were as beautiful as they were impractical: Women were essentially works of art, Anna more so than most. Collars were chokingly high (except on evening gowns, when shoulders were bared to the bustline). Skirts were sweeping morning glories bedecked with acres of lace, ribbons, silk roses, and chiffon. The waistline was the oddest part of turn-of-the-century gowns. An "S-curve" was created by having the front of blouse overhang the waistline, making women look, as one fashion historian noted, "as if the female body had been cut in two at the waist, and the pieces put together again after the upper portion had been pushed several inches forward, so that the whole looked like a ship's figurehead, carved to fit the prow of the vessel."

Even the daytime clothing of turn-of-the-century women was annoyingly restrictive, though admittedly beautiful. Novelist Kathleen Norris recalled that the average woman of the period went out every day wearing

> a wide-brimmed hat that caught the breezes, a high choking collar
> of satin or linen, and a flaring gored skirt that swept the street on
> all sides. Her full-sleeved shirt-waist had cuffs that were eternally
> getting dirty, her stock was always crushed and rumpled at the end
> of the day, and her skirt was a bitter trial. Its heavy 'brush binding'
> had to be replaced every few weeks, for constant contact with the
> pavement reduced it to dirty fringe in no time at all. In wet weather
> the full skirt got soaked and icy. Even in fair weather its wearer had
> to bunch it up in great folds and devote one hand to nothing else
> but the carrying of it.

Indeed, picturesque and ladylike skirt-lifting was an art, much like the handling of a fan or a muff.

One aspect of nineteenth- and early-twentieth-century clothing that has gotten an especially bad reputation is the corset—and Anna loved her corsets. Her reputed eighteen-inch waist became as much a trademark as her rolling eyes. "I have never known the time when I did not wear stays," she said in late 1899. When asked if she wouldn't be more comfortable without them, she replied, "I believe not. My stays are part of me." Corsets are mainly associated with the nineteenth century, but women (and men) had been cinching in their waistlines long before Anna was born. Paintings from Crete nearly four thousand years ago show people in beautifully decorated, wasp-waisted corsets. But the zenith of the corsetmaker's art began in the 1820s and lasted for nearly one hundred years. By the time Anna was a girl in the 1870s, no respectable woman would have thought of going uncorseted.

There were corsets for day, evening, sport; as dress shapes changed through the 1880s and 1890s, so did corset shapes. And one did not simply go out to a store, buy a "size 8" corset, and slip it on. "To put on a corset properly is as much of an art as to make a corset properly," Anna lectured. Too many women would buy a ready-made corset in the wrong size or shape and, Anna sighed, "shoves them in here, shoves them out there, stretches them to meet over her abdomen or her bust, crosses the strings at the back, ties them in a bow at the front of the stomach, and she considers herself ready for her corsage."

Anna had special corsets made for her stage appearances. These were thirteen inches long in the front and only eight inches in the back, for low-backed gowns. She and Lillian Russell often went to their corsetmakers together, for intensive, all-day fittings (they were sometimes accompanied by Russell's friend, female impersonator Julian Eltinge, who later marketed his own brand of corset). Anna admitted that being corseted was not always easy. "I have made certain concessions to them," she said. "For instance, I do not allow myself too excessive comfort without them. . . . I do not lounge without stays during the day. It is a temptation to come in after a fatiguing day and discard one's stays, resuming them perhaps not at all that evening. It is a temptation which I resist. To eat without stays is frequently a temptation to the appetite."

That having been said, it is important to note that corseting itself was not harmful. *Tight* corseting was. Even Anna said it was important to "allow yourself ample room to breathe. To crowd the lungs would be criminal, and not pretty." Today we look at fashion drawings and photos of nineteenth century women with impossible hourglass figures, read about Scarlett O'Hara types proud of their eighteen-inch (or even sixteen-inch) waists, and shake our heads in horror. But those women were few and far between, and they were looked upon as bizarre and ridiculous creatures in their time, much as eighty-five-pound fashion models are today. It's easy to see that fashion drawings (with hips sometimes actually narrower than waists) were unrealistic, but what is not obvious a hundred years later is that many photos were also misleading. A close look at Anna Held's professional studio portraits reveals that her waistline was usually airbrushed (and not too skillfully, either—there's often a visible aura around it). Anna herself admitted freely that "with my corsets I am an inch smaller than without it," hardly an example of overly tight lacing. "That inch!" she elaborated. "Ah! It is everything. It is the modeling, the chiseling. But do I sacrifice my health to it? No, I am sure not. I am in a perfect state of health, so I fancy that one inch more or less makes little or no difference." Anna, a very tiny, slim woman, actually padded out her slight bustline and hips more than she cinched in her waist.

One benefit of corsets that is not generally remembered is that they helped the posture: Women in the nineteenth century did not slouch (and slouching is certainly as bad for the internal organs and spine as is tight lacing). In short, corsets were like dieting, high heels, and drinking wine: perfectly harmless in moderation but given a bad name by those who misused them. Anna's ill health and death were later blamed on "tight lacing," but she was never guilty of this fashion error. For years after her death, it was even rumored that Anna had had her lower ribs surgically removed to make her waistline smaller and that this had led to her death. This was, of course, sheer nonsense. Any such operation—especially in the days of uncertain surgical techniques and no antibiotics—would have led to death within a week or two. Still, even today one can read in otherwise authoritative works that Anna's lower ribs—and life—were sacrificed to her shapely stage persona.

As *Papa's Wife* continued its successful run through the end of 1899, the praise continued to pour in. It certainly helped that there were no other big hits that season, except for the Weber and Fields burlesque *Whirl-I-Gig*. To Anna's delight, that show costarred her friend Lillian Russell. The two ladies often got together to toast each other as that season's reigning queens of Broadway. The tributes to Anna continued to accumulate. One critic gushed, "America has been anxiously awaiting the advent of a true comedienne for several seasons. She has recently arrived in the piquant person of Anna Held"—as if this were her U.S. debut. Another paper agreed. "The season before last it was Maude Adams; last season it was Mrs. Carter; and now it is Anna Held. . . . Hitherto she has been regarded as a petted and spoiled child of the music hall—a piquant feather brain with no deep emotional substrata. But presto change! All at once she reveals herself as an artist of wide range and admirable skill!" The *New York News* found both the show and Anna herself "as clean and sweet as a rose and sparkling like diamonds. Anna Held in *Papa's Wife* proves that degeneracy and salaciousness are not essential to a long run. For months it has jammed the Manhattan." By the autumn of 1899, tickets to *Papa's Wife* had become all but impossible to come by; sidewalk scalpers made a fortune selling even bad seats. Everyone seemed amazed at Anna's sudden improvement from the cute but unremarkable song-and-dance act of only a year before to the accomplished actress of late 1899. "Perhaps you have forgotten how hopeless Anna Held was in *The French Maid*," began one typical review. There were several reasons for this turnabout. For one thing, *Papa's Wife* was a perfect vehicle for Anna; her previous shows had not displayed her to good effect. For another, in George Marion she finally had a director both sympathetic and capable. But chiefly it was her new command of the English language.

Previously Anna had been acting all but phonetically. She spoke enough English to know the meaning of her lines, but she could not have known which word to put emphasis on; she didn't know enough to play with the meanings, to shade her speeches as a good actress must. Now, with her amazingly quick mastery of English, she was able to implement the same skills that she'd been able to in French and Yiddish. The talent that had propelled her to the forefront of Jacob Adler's company was no fluke. She was able finally to strut her stuff to Americans, and the effect was like a sneak attack, an unexpected bombshell in their midst.

On a cold and snowy Sunday, December 31, Anna and Ziegfeld toasted the advent of the new century (some pedants insisted it wouldn't begin until 1901, but few paid attention to them). Ziegfeld was thirty-two; Anna maybe a year or two younger. Both were on top of the world: At that moment success was within reach and Broadway had finally opened up to them. Both France and America were optimistic and financially sound. Paris was planning a huge fair for that summer, and the Dreyfus scandal was finally simmering down. America was still preening over its recent victory in the Spanish-American War and its controversial expansionism into the Philippines, and both President McKinley (a Civil War veteran) and New York Governor (and soon to be Vice President) Theodore Roosevelt were reaping the rewards.

Of course, no era is truly "calm." In 1900 unemployment was high, prohibition and women's rights were being fought over state by state, union and antiunion violence broke out, and many U.S. citizens still lived in the same primitive conditions their ancestors had suffered through a hundred years earlier. In Germany, Kaiser Wilhelm II proclaimed on January 1 that he planned to rebuild his nation's navy so that "the German Empire may . . . be in a position to win the place that it has not yet attained." It was the first dark portent of events that would bring Anna's world crashing down in another fourteen years. But in the big city, with Paris just a week away by ship, things couldn't have looked better as the twentieth century began. Anna saw a bright future for herself, and—for a few years—her every expectation was fulfilled.

Papa's Wife had a healthy New York run, taking off on tour in the beginning of April 1900. By this time, Anna was getting accustomed to the ups and downs of the touring life. As the twentieth century dawned, so too dawned the heyday of the touring theatrical company. Shows played in New York for as long as they could (until receipts dwindled or the next show had to occupy the theater), but it was on the road that shows really made their money. Most took off from New York in the spring and toured through early summer, when the weather got too much for them (not even the biggest theaters were air conditioned until the 1920s, and most not until after the Depression).

By the time *Papa's Wife* took to the road, the expansion of the railways had completely reinvented touring. Previously theatrical companies had to rely on the main train routes or on riverboats or horse-drawn stages. This left all but the largest towns out of the loop, and for entertainment they had to rely on local companies and traveling circus caravans. But with the new century came more railway lines, and smaller towns began building their own theaters and "opera houses," though some of them were not much more than glorified tents or shacks. As late as 1905 many local theaters were still lit by gasoline or even kerosene. Ziegfeld shows, of course, were only booked into theaters large enough to hold troupes of chorus girls and unwieldy scenery flats. Out of the three thousand-odd theaters in the United States at the time, maybe one thousand could handle a show like *Papa's Wife*. Even so, this offered Anna and her company a three-or-four month tour of the United States, playing a week in larger cities like Chicago, New Orleans, San Francisco, and Kansas City, and only one or two nights in whistle-stops like Chattanooga, Lincoln, Topeka, Peoria, and East Saginaw.

The arrival of a show troupe was quite an event for small towns before the age of television and radio. The performers themselves—Anna Held! Sarah Bernhardt! Richard Mansfield!—would not only be appearing in person at the local theater but would be staying at their hotel, eating at their restaurants, maybe (time and weather permitting) strolling Main Street to see the sights. Stage-door Johnnies got out their clean collars and set out to charm the show's chorus girls (maybe even the star!) and stagestruck locals showed up every night, befriending the stagehands in case a job opening might come up. Members of the company were sternly lectured to be on their best behavior. It hadn't been that long since actors had been looked upon as little more than tramps, and Anna ran a strict little family.

There were many tribulations on the road. Even with a private railway car, Anna and her troupe were at the mercy of railroad schedules, such as they were. Connections were haphazard, tracks were ill maintained, and often the entire company had to bunk down in their cars, which were stuck overnight in some out-of-the-way junction. "Train schedules of the period might as well have been calibrated by sundial or calendar," wrote photo archivist Otto Bettmann, "especially on small trunk lines in winter. Connections were more miss than hit, partly because of competing railroads." By the time the company arrived at their destination, their advance man was long gone to the next town, and they had to find their way to the hotel (if they had time to check in) or to the theater (if they were running late).

Hotels were another problem. Even the big cities sometimes refused to let Anna bring her lapdogs with her, and she would indignantly cancel her reservation and sleep in her railway car, cuddled up with her current pet. Smaller towns might let dogs stay over, but they were also lax when it came to bugs and rats. To save money and time, the company stayed at hotels convenient to the theater or the train station, and these were often cold in the winter, hot in the summer, and outfitted with lumpy furniture and highly suspicious mattresses (Anna, of course, carried her own bed linens with her).

Ziegfeld only toured his shows in theaters that could accommodate them, but that didn't mean that the dressing rooms were luxurious. It took Anna well over an hour to dress and to do her hair and makeup, and this was often accomplished in freezing or sweltering dressing rooms, always crowded and badly lit. Reporters and local big shots often burst into her dressing room and Anna would have to hastily cover herself with a wrap. The show's entrances and exits had to be hurriedly reblocked according to the layout of each house (some of them had no "backstage" behind the last drop curtain). And some of the more bluenosed towns insisted on having their mayor, sheriff, or religious leader see a run-through of the show before approving it for community standards.

Touring was a mental and emotional workout as well. Anna was careful to remember the names, birthdates, and personal quirks of everyone she would encounter: local newspaper columnists and reviewers, politicians, religious leaders, and the social elite. Like a political candidate on the stump, Anna charmed and flirted with these regional fans both out of career considerations and from her own desire to be liked and remembered. She also acted as a mother hen to her troupe of actors and crew members. All the maternal feelings she had withheld from her daughter were lavished on her chorus girls, costars, carpenters, scene-

painters, and dressers. Anna was famous for the family atmosphere she culti-
vated and the fact that she treated even the lowliest chorine like a person, not a
prop.

The summer of 1900 was the most leisurely and pleasant one Anna could
recall. For once, she had no "homework." Her English skills were growing by
leaps and bounds, and Ziegfeld had decided to take *Papa's Wife* on a grand tour
of the United States in late 1900, so there was no new play to learn. Her
newfound stardom made her glow with self-satisfaction, and her bank account
reflected her new success. Ziegfeld himself was not planning any new shows, so
the two had lots of time and money and the world was at their feet. Their
relationship was as easy and passionate and devoted as it had ever been. With
few worries, Ziegfeld did not fall prey to his dreaded dark moods. He and Anna
sailed to Europe, where they paid a flying visit to Liane in her school. The girl
was hugged and petted and showered with toys, then her mother and stepfather
took off back to Paris.

Paris was the place to be in the summer of 1900. The Universal Exhibition, which helped popularize the swirls and swoops of the art nouveau style,
had opened in the spring and would run through that November. A far cry
from even the impressive "White City" atmosphere of the Chicago World's
Fair of 1893, this event seemed to showcase the apex of La Belle Époque. A
huge statue, *La Parisienne*, greeted visitors, who marveled at the colored, lighted
dome at the place de la Concorde, the recreated "old Paris" along the Seine's
right bank, the many foreign exhibits, and—what interested Anna the most—
the auto show.

Of course there was always time to fool the press into a couple of non-
sensical tales, just to keep Anna's name in the newspapers. The most successful
of these included that huge gold *Parisienne*. Anna herself was reported to be
posing for a solid gold (not just plated, mind you) statue to be exhibited at the
Exposition. W.H. Mullins, who had sculpted the notorious nude Diana atop
Madison Square Garden, was reported to be vying with the firm of Tiffany's
for the honor of portraying Anna. The statue was first to be cast in plaster, then
125 pounds of gold would be poured into the mold (Anna's weight in gold was
worth $31,500, readers were informed). Her pose (a photo shows her holding
some cloth under one arm and another arm atop her head, in a modified "I'm
a Little Teapot" stance) was exhausting for the poor girl, the papers reported.
For all Anna's exertions, the statue—if it was ever really planned—vanished
from the world's press as soon as its usefulness was over.

Relaxed and eager to get back to work, Anna and Ziegfeld arrived back in

New York in August. *Papa's Wife* reopened for its second season in Boston in September 1900, with a few cast changes. Charles Bigelow and Eva Davenport had departed for greener pastures, and the roles of both Papa and his son were taken by the enterprising Max Figman (this required some scene-shifting and rewriting, as well as some very hasty costume changes for Mr. Figman). Another new cast member was Frankie Bailey, then somewhat past the height of her fame as the quintessential chorus girl. She was known as "The Girl with the Million Dollar Legs," and indeed "Frankie Baileys" had become a contemporary slang expression for great legs. Bailey never became a star but remained a well-known Broadway character right up till her death in 1953 at the age of ninety-four.

The opening was packed with society figures and boisterous Harvard students (Anna was already popular with college boys). She wore a whole shopful of new gowns bought that summer in Paris, and the show proved as big a hit in its second season as it had in its first. The autumn of 1900 was spent taking *Papa's Wife* on tour, arriving back in Manhattan by the start of 1901. Then back on the road through spring—by May 7, Anna reached a milestone with the five hundredth performance of the show, quite an impressive run in those days. Small silver boxes with Anna's autograph etched into them were given out to ladies attending that performance.

But Anna's show had some real competition. On November 12, 1900, the British import *Florodora* opened at the Casino Theater and became the hit of the year, almost an emblem of the era. The plot of *Florodora* was circuitous in the extreme: something about a perfume heiress, a tropical island, some soldiers— the plot shifted as new cast members, specialties and numbers were added or dropped. The real draw of *Florodora* was the number "Tell Me, Pretty Maiden," sung by six chorus girls and their top-hatted beaus. The tune became perhaps the first Broadway hit to transcend its own show; it remained popular for well over fifty years and even today it remains recognizable. The *Florodora* Girls became instant celebrities: Daisy Greene, Marjorie Relyea, Vaughn Texsmith, Margaret Walker, Agnes Wayburn, and Marie Wilson went down in theatrical history as the first superstar chorus girls, seven years before Ziegfeld began "glorifying" the genre. But *Florodora* wasn't the only hit to start out the new century. George M. Cohan had his first Broadway show produced, *The Governor's Son*. Weber and Fields showcased Lillian Russell in *Fiddle-Dee-Dee*, May Irwin appeared in *Madge Smith, Attorney*, and Edna May in *The Girl from Up There*. It's a testimony to Anna that *Papa's Wife* continued to be a big draw in its second year, even with those other shows pulling in crowds.

As the last season of *Papa's Wife* finally drew to a close in the spring of

1901, Anna basked in the continued praise. It was noted that she was no longer just attracting "tired businessmen" and college boys but that she now had a firm claque of female admirers. "If she is not the most delightful, the most fascinating, the most bewitching of women, she appears to be," one Boston paper stated enthusiastically, "and it is worthy of note that it is not the men alone who rave over Miss Held, but the women, even the plain ones, go into ecstasies about her." "Anna Held was a woman's favorite from the start," opined another paper. "She was soft and winsome, with . . . the exuberant spirits and harmlessness of a playful white kitten. The harshness, audacity and strident assertiveness of the typical chantant singer did not enter into her method." Asked around this time to define her own peculiar appeal, Anna told the *New York Telegraph*, "I don't want to depend upon beauty. Indeed, I do not think I am beautiful myself, but I think I have what you call charm; personality. I don't know what it is, but it is not beauty." She summed up: "I attract by my art, not my beauty. I am very much ambitious. I think about my work."

The summer of 1901 was a busy one. Again, Anna didn't have any English to learn (indeed, she had to lose her newly acquired "American" accent). But there was a new show—*The Little Duchess*—to prepare for and new gowns to be purchased. Anna visited her daughter and went on short day trips in her automobile, but most of that summer was spent in Mme Landoff's, being fitted and pinned into some of the most elaborate and showstopping gowns ever to be seen onstage. Even if this new show didn't turn out to be as big a hit as *Papa's Wife*, Anna realized, the gowns alone should carry it respectably through one season. After three months of being a dressmaker's dummy, Anna sailed back to New York early in September 1901.

By this time Ziegfeld and Anna had left the Netherland and had taken up residence at the Savoy, which had also been built in 1892 and stood right next door, on the northeast corner of Fifth Avenue and Fifty-ninth Street. Here Alan Dale visited them, remarking upon the still sparse furnishings—the most notable decorations were large framed photos of Anna on the mantel, bureau, shelf, and writing table. "There are no pictures of Anna Held on the ceiling," Dale noted acidly, "and the floor is not carpeted with them." By this time, Anna was comfortable with Dale. He was a very important journalist and could have hurt her career had he wished to, but Anna knew he was fair and would only slam her when she deserved it. She entered the room all in white. "She waggles slightly as she enters on tip-toe," Dale told his readers, "and her hips move rhythmically, as though swayed by coquettish zephyrs. Her mouse-colored hair is tousled."

Anna opened up to Dale, revealing perhaps more than Ziegfeld would have thought wise. She admitted that both she and her husband were quite publicity-mad. "I love to see 'Anna Held' in the papers," she laughed. "I read them every day just to discover if one mentions Anna Held. And if I do not find it I am no longer interested. The papers seem very dull if I do not see my name in them." Ziegfeld was even worse, she confided. "If he sees that a man is 'held up,' even that pleases him, because he seems to read my name," she joked, proud to coin a pun in English. "I speak English so well I am no longer cute," she sighed prettily. Most Frenchwomen—even Sarah Bernhardt, she noted— refused to learn English. "They are so proud, they think there is nothing but French. . . . I speak English all day, and my tongue itches for French." Ziegfeld, she added, knew just enough French to worry bilingually.

Anna also admitted, though, that playing the naughty French "Anna Held" in interviews could become dull and tiring. "That is when people come to find merely a pretty woman, and I have to sit and make grimaces and pose and look charming. Of course, I know I am very beautiful," she modestly blushed, "but I like to talk. I like to be natural, and myself." As for all those photos, she later admitted to another reporter that she found them rather intimidating. "Don't you get tired of them?" she asked. "I do. . . . They flatter me. No one could possibly look all the time like my photographs. . . It is dreadfully hard to live up to them. They stare at me everywhere, stare at me reproachfully as if they thought I was not doing my duty by them."

Out-of-town tryouts of *The Little Duchess* were promising; critics and audiences were already warmed up to Anna, and they seemed to accept both her and her new show, in which she had to create an entirely different—and harder— character than "Anna" of *Papa's Wife*. She played in Boston, Philadelphia, and Rochester, though the tryouts were held up by national tragedy in early September, when President William McKinley died a week after being shot. *The Little Duchess* opened in New York on October 14, 1901, at the Casino Theater. The Casino was the Grand Old Lady of Long Acre Square. Built in 1882, it was a huge Arabian Nights fantasy of turrets and cupolas on the corner of Broadway and Thirty-ninth Street. It had been the home of many hit musicals, and had just been vacated by the record-breaking *Florodora* when Anna's company moved in.

In *The Little Duchess*, Anna played Claire de Brion, a bankrupt actress who disguises herself as a duchess to escape from bill collectors. The script and music were written by the team who had helped put *Papa's Wife* on top, Harry B. Smith and Reginald De Koven. A note on the program told the audience right away what they were in for. The show was billed as "An entertainment devised simply to amuse. Owing to the length of the performance the plot has been eliminated." This line must have been the work of Smith; Ziegfeld, while he loved elaborate practical jokes, was verbally humorless. The show consisted of Ziegfeld's new recipe for a hit: one-third glamour, one-third merit, and one-third advertising.

The amiable George Marion again was called in to direct, but this time Herman Perlet was hired to stage the musical numbers. Joining Anna were director Marion as Claire's uncle, Count Casabinca, and her reliable old comic costars Charles Bigelow (as Gustave, "a bathing master and hero") and Eva Davenport (as Baroness Juliette Koffupsky). Another sixteen beautiful chorus girls were featured in the show, with promisingly naughty character names like Pierette, Susette, Nanon, and Fifine. One unintended laugh came on opening night when Anna laid her head lovingly against the coat of her leading man, and noticed that she'd left some face powder on his costume. She walked back to him and brushed it off, to the audience's delight.

Alan Dale, reviewing *The Little Duchess*, said that "Anna, who began to be a real actress last season, is keeping it up. Joking, clothes, and hair apart, she shows a sincerity and an aptitude that are continual surprises." Noting the new wardrobe, Dale continued that her talent was "combined with a chic you can't buy, because it is not for sale." This season's crop of chorus girls was also commended. "There isn't a girl in the Anna Held company who, as far as beauty and clothes went, couldn't head a company of her own and go triumphantly through the country," Dale wrote. "Meek, unselfish, noble, altruistic little Anna! What a heart must beat beneath that gorgeous raiment (if it has any room to beat)."

More than any of her previous shows, *The Little Duchess* was a fashion extravaganza. Anna's gowns were again designed by Mme Landoff of Paris, the company's, by the New York firm of Simpson, Crawford, and Simpson. The program noted proudly that the chorus girls' embroidered evening gowns in the "Sadie" number were made "from special plates secured by Mr. Ziegfeld in Paris, from the leading fashionable modists [sic] of the day, representing their latest creations." Indeed, the dresses in *The Little Duchess* got as much press as the performances. The most famous gown—worn by Anna in some of her best-remembered portraits—was a breathtaking high-necked number made of pink-and-lavender panné velvet, finished at the hemline with green ruffles. The dress made her look like "some delicate new orchid," according to those who saw it (we only have black and white photos to judge it by). The bodice was decorated with scrolled appliqués of electric blue spangles that ran down the front of the gown, and the three-quarter-length sleeves had an underlining of embroidered gauze. Topping it off, Anna wore a huge pink hat decorated with pink, white, and lavender ostrich plumes. This dress was an astonishing example of Belle Époque dressmaking as an art, the kind of gown that simply could not be manufactured today—but it was only one of the creations enjoyed by *The Little Duchess* audiences.

In act 2, Anna wore a negligee of lavender crêpe de chine, decorated with spangled brilliants, silk rosebuds, and a border of pearls. Later in the same act, she appeared in a white chiffon dress with silver spangles, black-and-green tulips down the front, and a panel of black chiffon and black spangles running down the back. In the finale, Anna appeared in a gown of "custard yellow velvet. An appliquéd design of white velvet narcissus is embroidered on the gown," a newspaper breathlessly reported. "A huge black hat and a wondrous boa with six ends leaves her feminine audience gasping as the curtain falls." They had gasped as it rose on act I, too, as Anna and her chorus girls danced onto the bathing resort set in abbreviated swimsuits. One shocked critic called Anna "a vivified dummy for the display of boldly scanty costumes. She is often an exhibit of which, if she were not physically dainty and delicate, would strike most of us as indecent."

Most male reviewers did not know what to make of—or write about—Anna's costumes. They couldn't be simply ignored, any more than an elephant in the parlor. "Whereas some actresses very much underdress, Miss Held very much overdresses," wrote one stunned newspaperman. "Her laces and bows and gimcracks and things . . . are astounding in their multiplicity and bewildering in their effect on a poor, lone bachelor who doesn't know the difference between a cambric basque and an alpaca bodice."

"In *The Little Duchess* it seems to me I am dressing and undressing all the time," Anna complained to a reporter. "I even have to take off hair and put on hair [in one scene Anna appeared as a blonde]. For the privilege of that blonde wig that nobody likes I paid $150." Anna herself saw all this display as a necessary, audience-pleasing evil, one that kept her in dressmaking establishments all through her summer break. "I live at the dressmaker's," she sighed. "I am being moulded into clothes, all day long. I get no rest. For three months last summer I have been fitted, and draped, and assassinated by clothes. And then you marvel that they fit!"

In 1901 Ziegfeld hired a clever publicity woman, Nellie Revell, who came up with a fashion-related scheme that might have cost Anna her friendship with Lillian Russell. Russell was currently costarring in the Weber and Fields show *Hoity-Toity,* in which she wore a much-commented-upon scarlet-and-yellow gown. At Revell's suggestion, Ziegfeld had sixteen copies made of that dress (at $175 apiece) for his chorus. The audience held up the show with applause when they made their appearance, and the duel of the dresses was the talk of Broadway. Weber and Fields, of course, had to buy a new gown for Russell. Happily, that lady took the whole affair as a grand joke, and her relationship with Anna emerged unharmed.

The chorus girls' other costumes also invited remarks from reviewers. "Cloth and leather are perforated to look like lace," wrote one reporter, "and lace and gauze are used for the foundation upon which are built fascinating creations of passementerie and gold and silver embroidery." Again, we are left with only black-and-white photos of these gowns, so the full dazzling stage effect must be imagined. "There were not enough colors in silk and chiffon," the same writer continued, "so shaded fabrics have been employed, and material of the finest texture is covered with handiwork, embroidered and jewel-studded, chic and startling." No wonder that, already, chorus girls from near and far clamored to be in Anna Held shows.

Before the first week was out, it was obvious that *The Little Duchess* was a hit. On the night of October 19, it took in a record-breaking $2303 (with ticket prices ranging from fifteen dollars for box seats to one dollar for the rear balcony). It trounced the previous records held by the Casino shows *The Princess Nicotine* (an 1893 Lillian Russell musical) and the smash hit *Florodora*. There were no showstoppers like "Tell Me, Pretty Maiden" in *The Little Duchess*, but Anna did have two songs written to highlight her already famous eyes: "The Maiden with the Dreamy Eyes" and "Those Great Big Eyes." She also sang a minstrel tune, "What'd Yo Do Wid de Letter, Mister Johnson?" On November 4, a new number was added to the show, "Pretty Mollie Shannon." This marked the first time Anna appeared on Broadway in trousers. In those days of long skirts, producers found any excuse to get actresses into revealing trousers, and actresses found as many excuses to avoid them. The term "actresses in tights!" was hurled at even the most respectable amateur performers. Lillian Russell had balked at putting on tights early in her career, but Adah Isaacs Mencken became notorious for playing Mazeppa in what amounted to long underwear.

Anna was nervous about this new number, which she performed as a "Paris Street Gamin" with Mabel Barrison playing the titular Mollie Shannon. Wearing checked pants and shirt, a ragged jacket, and a newsboy's cap covering her hair, Anna "assumed a bold swagger and rude manners," said one critic, adding the ungentlemanly observation that without skirts and heels, "she seemed to have lost six inches of height and gained twice that amount of beam." Anna hated the number, thought it put her back into her vulgar old music-hall days, and felt her female audience would much rather see her in beautiful gowns. "I make a very absurd boy and I do not look like one," she groused. "I have too much hip. But what can I do? They clamor to see me in this costume and that is that, so I try to oblige them." The number stayed in the show.

For Christmas in 1901, Anna bought Ziegfeld a new car, which she had seen at the Madison Square Garden Auto Show. The steam-driven Toledo Stanhope set her back fourteen hundred dollars. "A swell thing, with a monogram," she exulted. "He will be furious with my extravagance. I cannot help it." She then added, "I have also bought him a note-book. In America everybody uses note-books. It is extraordinary. It is droll. You tell a man a funny story. He says, ha! ha! Then he takes out his note-book and says, 'excuse me while I jot it down.' So I have bought one for Flo." It's not known what Anna herself received that Christmas, but Ziegfeld was a renowned gift-giver, handing ludicrously expensive jewelry to female friends and coworkers without blinking. Oddly, he never wrapped his gifts, just took them out of his pockets and dropped them into the surprised recipient's hands.

On January 17, 1902, *The Little Duchess* marked its all-important one hundredth New York performance (at that time, if a show passed the one hundred mark, it was considered a hit). The standing-room-only audience that night received silver-topped cut glass powder jars, with Anna's name inscribed on them. At the end of the month, the show had to leave the Casino to make room for the next play, *On the Quiet*, and to fulfill its touring obligations. After a stop in Harlem, *The Little Duchess* moved west to San Francisco, where record-breaking advance sales awaited. Through March, April, and May, Anna and her troupe played a week or two each at Philadelphia, Boston, Chicago, Texas, Kansas, St. Louis, and a good many small one-night stops in between. The rave reviews continued. The show was "as delightful as a journey to Paris," said a Boston paper. "Miss Held is a treat as a comedienne, and everything that she does is thoroughly artistic."

Anna tried to socialize in each town, and there were plenty of invitations. Just as she loved to investigate small towns and villages on her European trips, in the United States Anna wanted to see how "real" people lived. "On Sundays I go to visit very perfect American families," she said, "most gentle and interesting. It is very satisfying, and I enjoy myself so much." Ziegfeld traveled with her for much of this tour and accompanied her on her side-trips and visits. On Sundays when "perfect American families" were not available, the couple rose late and tried to spend the day completely by themselves. Together for six years now, they were hardly honeymooners anymore. Still "Annie" and "Flo," as they called each other, enjoyed these quiet country days, with no business managers or reporters to disturb them. They went for drives, had quiet meals, and retired early to bed.

Anna and Ziegfeld were in many ways opposites, but they'd learned to live together and accomodate each other's differences. Anna was chatty and humorous; Ziegfeld quiet and moody. His humor was pointed. "Flo was a person of triple or quadruple personality," wrote his second wife, Billie Burke, "a bewitching person when he wanted to be, troublesome, fascinating lover, but he possessed a world of his own to which he could and often did retire. There were times, many times, in my presence or in any company, in which he would utterly withdraw. Suddenly, he would not be there."

Eddie Cantor also remembered how infuriating Ziegfeld could be—he "had no notion of time, space, or money. He never kept an appointment, and could never pass a phone booth without going in to call up the world." Cantor recounted a time when Ziegfeld was supposed to see Anna off to Europe, stopped at a phone booth to make a call, and completely missed her sailing. Anna was not a yeller; when Ziegfeld annoyed her, she took off on shopping trips, or called on her girlfriends to complain. Neither Ziegfeld nor Anna ever held a grudge, so their occasional fights faded away quickly.

The Little Duchess finished its 1901–02 season in early spring, and Anna returned to New York. Ziegfeld decided the show had been such a hit that it, like *Papa's Wife*, would continue in the fall for one more season on the road. By this time, Ziegfeld felt he no longer had to rely on wacky publicity stunts, so there were no more milk baths, no more runaway carriage rescues, or kissing contests. Anna's career was beyond the need for that kind of thing. There were, however, an endless series of silly "human interest" interviews, the kind that all actresses had to giggle and primp through and that remained popular through the days of the movie magazines of the 1930s and 1940s. During her so-called free time, Anna played hostess to reporters from all over the world. Serving tea, sitting at her dressing table, or dining in a restaurant, she answered every question they could throw at her.

Anna talked about flirting. "For a married woman to flirt is a sin," she declared. That would be humiliating to her husband, she explained, and thus a wife should never even look another man in the eyes. Admitting that she'd flirted in her single days, Anna maintained, "I think every woman feels proud to have many gentlemen admire her. That shows her her own value. Every woman wants to have more admirers than some other women. It makes her popular!" Asked for a Frenchwoman's flirting tips, Anna pretended to think carefully and answered, "Well, I think the eyes flirt most, don't you? There are so many ways to use them. . . . The society girl will use her eyes discreetly. . . . The wicked woman will wink and look sly, so! Some women flirt more with what they say and some with what they do."

Anna talked about the difference between American girls and French girls. American girls, she said disapprovingly, flirt when they are quite young. "Girls

14, 15. In France we never see young men [to be able] to flirt until we are grown up. [Girls] all go out with chaperons there. They say Paris is so wicked. I think New York is just as bad as Paris and in some things this country is worse." Anna talked about her yearly vacations in Paris. "It is not that I do not love America," she diplomatically explained to reporter Emma Kaufman in late 1901, "it is only that I fear to lose what it is you call my individuality, my charm, the thing that makes me Anna Held. . . . So I go to my home on the Faubourg St.-Honoré every summer to recover from the fatigue and the accent of dear America that I love so much. For three months I talk only the French, I breathe only French air, I hear only the French tongue. Without my accent, oh, it is pitiful to think how my star would fall!" As of yet there was no public hint that she might be returning to France to see a daughter or ex-husband.

Anna talked about her beauty regime, which in America (land of modern indoor plumbing) included a cold bath every morning. "How many women have the courage to start properly with a cold, cold bath early in the morning?" she asked. "I jump in, throw the water, cold as ice, on the back of my neck, catch my breath strong, and after the first plunge I am happy. Most women are indulgent of themselves. This is a mistake. It should be only the reward of old age. They permit themselves hot baths, for instance," Anna scoffed. She cleansed her face, she added, not with soap but with white (not yellow!) perfumed Vaseline. She ate little, never let out her corset stays after a meal, and made her own perfume of white heliotrope, "chypre," violet, and *peau d'espagne.* Seeing reporter Kaufman write her private perfume recipe, she snapped, "I warn you that . . . I shall invent something else."

Anna talked about American women's clothing. "Americans wear too much, too many colors. If I may criticize them. A woman should be like a single flower, not like a whole bouquet. For example, it is a temptation for me to wear all my rings at once. . . . But even though she over-dresses, I love America." Perhaps the height of silliness was reached when a reporter brought up the popular song "Jus' Because She Made Dem Goo-Goo Eyes." Anna's own eyes were goo-goo, were they not? She objected. "I will say 'dreamy' and not 'goo-goo,' she insisted. "Dreamy eyes are long and almond shaped." Without defining what goo-goo-ness consisted of, Anna added flirtatiously that she did know one or two men with eyes as goo-goo as those of any women.

The goo-goo-ness of Anna's eyes having been dispensed with, she and Ziegfeld took off for their summer vacation in France. Their peace was somewhat disturbed in July when Maximo Carrera sued Anna for some bonds and for custody of their daughter. Nothing more was heard of the bonds, but Anna won custody of Liane—perhaps because, even though she lived most of the time in America, she worked and saved her money. Carrera still lived on the kindness of his sisters and gambled away what little they sent him. He was also suffering from diabetes (much less treatable then than now). Why Anna wanted custody of Liane is somewhat of a mystery. Her existence was still unknown to the American press, and Anna saw her daughter less often than she saw her in-laws, the Ziefelds. According to Liane herself, Maximo visited her rather frequently and spent most of his time sighing over his loss of Anna. Liane found her mother distant and glamorous, her father likable but slightly pathetic.

Anna had a lot of ideas on her own as to what she wanted to do next professionally, but Ziegfeld managed to put the brakes to them. She hoped to perform in Paris that fall, but her husband saw more money in a second season of *The Little Duchess*. She even made noises about doing some dramatic work—*La Dame aux Camellias*, *Du Barry*, or *Marie Antoinette*, maybe. Anna sounded out Clyde Fitch about writing a new play for her; he had just catapulted Ethel Barrymore to stardom with his *Captain Jinks of the Horse Marines*. But this too came to nothing. "I do not care for the money, but just for the glory," the already-wealthy Anna said that summer. A new comedy by Fitch, she thought, "may give me the chance." The music would not be by Reginald De Koven, whose work she felt was "too pretty-boy to work." But while Anna wanted to stretch her wings, her husband told her to let well enough alone. "That is so like Flo," she sighed.

As for himself, Ziegfeld was thinking of building his own theater and bid against Sam and Lee Shubert for a spot opening on Broadway and Thirty-ninth Street that June. But the Shuberts prevailed. A more personal loss was the death of their friends Mr. and Mrs. Fair. Anna and Ziegfeld had gone motoring with them in France, and the next day the Fairs were killed in an auto accident. Somewhat shaken, Anna and Ziegfeld arrived back in the United States on the *Kaiser Wilhelm* on September 2, and went right to their Maine farmhouse to regroup for the fall season.

Anna, of course, had brought back a new contingent of gowns to show off in *The Little Duchess* (one newspaper even reported that—at the suggestion of La Belle Otero—Anna had had the gowns molded onto her with wet honey so that they clung "like serpents skin"). Among Anna's haul for 1902 was a new lace-covered corset lined with rose-colored silk and a ruby over each front clasp, a pair of driving gloves in white kid with scarlet cuffs and gold clasps, and silver-heeled shoes with stars made of rubies and diamonds. Even her bedroom slippers rated notice: They were black satin and their modern aluminum heels were decorated in sapphires and diamonds. Before starting her tour, Anna attended a women's exhibition at Madison Square Garden (a march from *The Little*

Duchess was played as she entered the hall, to her delight). Though not a feminist, she enjoyed reading the exhibition newspaper published entirely by women and agreed to sell silver spoons for charity, at two dollars apiece. She even got fifty dollars for one spoon on which she scratched her autograph with a pin. One vendor wanted her to endorse his Anna Held dolls, but their namesake found them rather creepy and declined.

The Little Duchess reopened on October 13 in Washington, D.C., and went on a nationwide tour that lasted until May 1903. Ziegfeld accompanied Anna on most of this tour, as he had no other shows running. As usual it was an adventurous and exhausting time. In St. Louis Anna was pressured by a salesman into taking out the biggest life insurance policy ever issued to a woman, for one hundred thousand dollars (this cost Anna five thousand dollars a year). Anna tried to take out a policy on her poodle, M'sieu, but was turned down.

While in San Antonio, Texas, Ziegfeld managed to coerce Anna into a trip to a gambling hall, where the company had gone to spend some of their free time (and their salary). Much to her surprise, Anna and cast member Marie Courtney won thirteen hundred dollars and celebrated till daybreak. But if Ziegfeld hoped that this would change Anna's mind about his own gambling habit, he was quite wrong. The tour went on, breaking box-office records wherever they landed: the deep South, Denver, Salt Lake City, Fort Worth, Dallas, San Francisco, Seattle, Chicago (for a total of six weeks), St. Paul, and, by March 1903, Minneapolis. In Fort Worth the show took in twenty-one thousand dollars for nine performances, with top seats going for ten dollars (and offers of twenty dollars being made by desperate fans). A band of pickpockets followed the troupe through the Southwest, preying on customers in the lobbies; the thieves were finally captured in Dallas. The exhausted *Little Duchess* troupe finally blew back into New York in April 1903 with a net profit of $142,000 to their credit. Additionally, Anna received a personal salary of one thousand dollars a week, which she promptly deposited in her Paris bank. The railroad car had cost Ziegfeld one hundred dollars a day, for 130 days (Anna's own railroad car apparently had been sold, as it vanished from her press), and there had also been Anna's five servants to pay.

Anna spent a week fighting off mosquitos in Maine while Ziegfeld made flying trips to New York to arrange their summer vacation. In May they sailed on the *Kaiser Wilhelm*; this vacation began with something of a dustup when Ziegfeld discovered that he'd left his tickets at home and had to pay again. They didn't go alone to Europe this year; Ziegfeld and Anna had a regular troupe with them: Grace Van Studdiford, who was to appear in Ziegfeld's upcoming show (*The Red Feather*), to be produced in tandem with his next Anna Held spectacular; director George Marion; and, most colorfully, twelve chorus girls hired as fitting models for the gowns for next season's shows. The "Anna Held Girls," as they were dubbed, took off in a flurry of high spirits and wonderful chorus girl slang. One of them, Mabelle Courtney (perhaps the "Marie" of Anna's Texas gambling trip?), told a reporter that "we shall butt into Paris to acquire the savoir faire of the French capitol." Already reeking with savoir faire, Mabelle continued, "It's like some French 'shine' coming here to keep tabs on [comedian] Dan Daly and his push."

Among the giggling, excited girls—all packing tour books and French dictionaries—were Anna St. Tel, Louise Royce (who memorably declared, "I guess I will be able to take care of myself with the swells!"), and Luella Drew. Play adapter Joseph Herbert lectured the girls on deportment and overspending, sighing, "I expect to give my consent to the marriage of several of you, ere we return. Who knows, many may never come back, which, heaven forfend, after all the expenses Madame will be put to!" *The Red Feather* and a dozen gold-digging chorines aside, Anna and Ziegfeld had big—very big—plans for the 1903–04 season.

—4—

Poor Little Rich Girl

I t's a truism among actors: Comedians want to try tragedy, dramatic actors want to make people laugh, and everyone "really wants to direct." Anna was no exception. She'd scored a huge success over the past few years in comedy roles but couldn't quite forget that her earliest successes with Jacob Adler had been in heavily tragic operettas. Something within her wanted to "show them" that she, like Bernhardt and Duse, could wring hearts. "Not always do I want to be 'Anna Held,'" she said in 1903. "I wish to please the people, of course, but I have the ambition to make them cry, perhaps. There, I have said it. I sometimes want to experience what so many have told me—to work hard and see the people turn and writhe; make them feel things they cannot see and sometimes do not know." Ziegfeld disagreed. Not that he didn't think Anna could be a fine dramatic actress, but why tamper with success? For once he was trying to be financially sensible. People would pay good money to see Anna Held roll her eyes, show her legs, and sing humorously naughty songs. But would they pay to see Anna suffer nobly, die piteously, or sacrifice herself for love and honor?

Finally Anna and Ziegfeld came to what they thought was a happy compromise. French playwright Jean Richepin had just enjoyed a great success in Paris with a play about Mlle Mars, a favorite actress of Napoleon Bonaparte. It was a huge Anna Held-like production, with elaborate costumes, beautiful sets, and spaces for varied songs to be inserted. But it also gave Anna the chance to play heavily dramatic scenes as well as to reemphasize her affinity for all things French. When the Ziegfelds landed in France, they handed Grace Van Studdiford and the gaggle of chorus girls off to George Marion and went to work. They holed themselves up with M. and Mme Richepin and Joseph Herbert, whose job it was to translate *Mlle Mars* (retitled *Mam'selle Napoleon*) into English—not just regular English, but "Broadway English." While continuing to work, the fivesome also piled into Ziegfeld's new steam-car and took an eight-hundred-mile road trip through France, Switzerland, and the Alps.

Back in Paris Anna and her little troupe of models spent weeks being fitted for the *Mam'selle Napoleon* costumes, which were their first essay into period clothing. The high-waisted Empire gowns weren't flattering to Anna, so—historical accuracy be damned—the dresses were retrofitted to her famous hourglass figure. That summer also provided Anna with a lifelong companion and helper, an Italian woman named Beatrice Brianchi. Anna hired her as a maid, but within a short time Beatrice proved herself to be an able social secretary, dresser, travel agent, press liaison, and just about anything else Anna needed. Beatrice became the sister Anna never had and the daughter she never really got to know; she stayed with Anna till the very end.

The company arrived back in New York in mid-August, and Ziegfeld set about casting and rehearsing his two shows (*The Red Feather* opened in November 1903, running through early 1904). *Mam'selle Napoleon* was a huge, unwieldy, and expensive experiment: three acts (with four decorative "tableaux"), forty-four speaking parts, and one hundred chorus members. Act 1 took place at the Comédie-Française in 1803, which Ziegfeld was determined to recreate exactly. Act 2 took place on a moonlit island on a lake in front of Napoleon's residence, and act 3 contained not one but two costume balls, at the Café de la Paix and the Opéra. The whole production was reported to have cost Ziegfeld one hundred thousand dollars to stage by opening night.

Anna's usual comedy cohorts, Charles Bigelow and Eva Davenport, weren't cast in this show. Frank Rushworth portrayed Mlle Mars's fiancé, Noel Gilot, a ne'er-do-well Imperial Guard, and Arthur Laurence was Napoleon, who condemns Gilot to the firing squad. Anna, as the Comédie-Française star, manages to save her fiancé's life by telling Napoleon a heartwarming fable (the one about the injured lion and the helpful mouse) and singing a few Anna Held tunes by Gustav Luders ("The à la Mode Girl," "The Art of Simulation," "The Language of Love," and a few others). There were a total of twenty musical numbers in the show, including several huge choral displays ("On to Paris," and the hopefully titled "Hit Enormous"). Theatrical historian Gerald Bordman describes Luders's music as "small, clear, and enchantingly sweet." He'd had a huge hit that same year with the show *The Prince of Pilsen*, but his *Mam'selle Napoleon* songs were, unfortunately, not quite up to those standards. The show was directed by Joseph Herbert, who also portrayed a secret policeman and had a few songs of his own. He had the difficult task of wrenching Anna's first English-language dramatic performance out of her—from a script he himself had translated. It was really too much for one man.

Mam'selle Napoleon had its first out-of-town tryout in Philadelphia on October 27, and things looked very shaky. Everyone commented on the breathtaking costumes and scenery, but audiences were underwhelmed by the plot, music, and performances. Even the costumes had their downside; few women wanted to copy Napoleonic gowns to wear to their next dinner party or opera opening. Critic Acton Davies, for one, was enthusiastic, calling *Mam'selle Napoleon* "something new in musical comedy" and "a distinct triumph for Anna Held . . . to say that it was the best performance she has ever given conveys no idea of the artistic charm of her work." But Anna knew something just wasn't working, and the old adage of "good tryout, bad opening" kept ringing in her ears. After playing New Haven, the huge company packed up and moved to New York. A nervous Anna told a reporter, "I am so afraid for Tuesday. One may play in all the little places and some of the big ones and they will like one very much, but—brrr. One is to face the big city of New York, and cosmopolitan people who have seen so many things."

In a touchingly human and unusually candid interview, she continued to babble on nervously. "I hope they will like us so much. . . . Sometimes they are so terrible, the critiques! Perhaps they will not like me and, oh, I hope they do. After all, you know, one does not really achieve the grand success until the people here in New York have seen one and said it was good. Out of the city— the provinces? Poof! It is nothing! until New York." *Mam'selle Napoleon* opened in New York on December 3, at the Knickerbocker Theater, on the corner of Broadway and Thirty-eighth Street. That house had seen the hits *Quality Street* and *Sherlock Holmes,* and the Eddie Foy comedy *Mr. Bluebeard* had just vacated to go on tour.

Perhaps Anna was not wise to "poof" the small towns, but she at least knew enough to fear those New York "critiques" and their opinion of *Mam'selle Napoleon.* Her earlier ambition to make the audience "turn and writhe" came only too true. Her old friend Alan Dale turned his guns on her full blast: He found the show "about as dreary and tiresome a proposition as one could well attempt to endure." Of the Gustav Luders score, Dale admitted that "musical comedy leads itself readily to anachronisms, but why rub it in?" And of Anna herself and her attempts at drama, Dale wrote, "emotion has not as yet found a place in the repertoire of her talents." He enjoyed her brief comic and musical scenes, but stated that when she was called upon to emote, she not only fell short but the effect on the play was jarring.

A less gentlemanly critic than Dale wrote that "the transplanted rose of M. Richepin turned out to be, in the hands of its present gardeners, a particularly large and offensive cabbage." While Dale merely found the show dull, others found it coarse and vulgar. Emergency surgery was performed: The show was shortened and certain vaudeville gags were taken out (such as referring to Napoleon and Josephine as "Boney" and "Josie"). Ever the trouper, Anna brightly called her *Mam'selle Napoleon* role "the best I have yet had. I love this part." Inadvertently, she pointed out the main flaw of the play while trying to praise it: "One moment I am all emotion," she stated enthusiastically, "another is all sympathy, and then again I am just gay, and I am Anna Held."

Ziegfeld spent another twenty thousand dollars to revamp *Mam'selle Napoleon* in December, borrowing from financier Jake Fields. He was deeply in debt now and saw no way that the show would come close to breaking even. All the rewriting, cutting, new songs, and more dazzling costumes had little effect ("Between gowns, the plot crept in," sighed one critic). Another trousers number was tossed in: Anna made her first entrance dressed as Gainsborough's *Blue Boy*, in tight satin breeches. She then slipped behind a screen (which covered her only to the shoulders) and changed into another costume in partial view of the shocked audience.

Shocked, maybe, but not titillated enough to buy tickets. And the critics continued battering the show. One fair-minded gentleman admitted that Anna was not to wholly at fault; she had already proven her talent in her previous vehicles. "The blame naturally, but most unfairly, falls on Miss Held's pretty shoulders," he said after the rewrites had their debut. "The book, which was not good originally, has become unutterably bad." "It is difficult to believe that so distinguished a poet and playwright as Jean Richepin is responsible for the cheap wit, slang, and variety acts that are the most salient features of *Mam'selle Napoleon*," read one typical review. "Costumes and scenery alone will not attract audiences, and Miss Held will have to find something more worthy of her sprightly personality." One critic even heard an audience member complain of Arthur Laurence, "That fellow looks as much like Napoleon as a Kilkenny cat!"

Anna came in for her share of personal insults as well. Her emotional scenes were dismissed as "pouts and purrs," and an anonymous New York reviewer seemed to delight in her failure: "She simply fell from the dizzy heights of ambition and the thud was heard for miles around. It merely proved once again that a dressmaker should stick to her stays." The same critic concluded, "Miss Held has a certain metier," then added nastily that "beyond this she may not venture without impressing upon us the fact that she is, after all, a clever little music hall performer who should remember that blood will tell."

It seemed the winter of 1903–04 conspired to keep people away from theaters. That winter was the coldest ever recorded in New York—for eighty days in a row, there was enough snow in Central Park for sledding. People stayed home and shivered at night; they didn't go out to see shows. And on December 30, 1903, the nation's deadliest theater fire changed entertainment business not only in the United States but the whole world. It occurred at Chicago's luxurious Iroquois Theater, where Eddie Foy was appearing in a holiday matinee of *Mr. Bluebeard,* Anna's predecessor at the Knickerbocker. The audience consisted largely of mothers and children.

The fire broke out during the second act, while the chorus was onstage singing "In the Pale Moonlight." A calcium lamp brushed against a curtain, causing a tiny finger of flame to skip over the performers' heads. "One of the stagehands first took his hand and then used a piece of plank to smother the flames," recalled audience member Emma Schweitzler. "It kept spreading." The chorus bravely danced on, to prevent panic, and Eddie Foy came out front to plead for calm. Foy called for the asbestos curtain to be lowered, and then a series of mishaps brought on tragedy.

The asbestos curtain caught halfway down, on a piece of machinery used to fly chorus girls overhead. The oil-paint covered canvas drop curtain was lowered and promptly caught fire. At that point panic was unavoidable. Most of the people in the orchestra section got out safely (as did the cast, with the exception of dancer Nellie Reed, the only casualty in the show itself). But when the cast members opened the backstage door to escape, the rush of cold air fanned the flames directly into the top two galleries. "The fire seemed to spread with a series of explosions," said Foy. "The smoke was fearful and it was a case of run quickly or be smothered."

"All at once a great ball of fire or sheet of flame—I don't know how to express it—shot out and the whole theater above us seemed to be full of fire," Mrs. F.R. Baldwin later testified. "Then there was a smothered sound as of a sighing by all in the theater." Those not incinerated in their seats raced for the exits, finding many of them padlocked. There were no exit lights, twisting hallways led into dead ends, and the ushers had long since run for their own lives. Patrons trampled each other by the hundreds, dying of smoke inhalation or being crushed to death in piles ten feet high. Survivor Albert Memhard stated, "The fire exits were all covered by heavy draperies that might readily be mistaken for simple decorations and were not marked or labeled in any way. Neither was there any one on hand to direct the crowd how to get out. The only light was the illumination afforded by the fire."

When firemen finally broke in, more than six hundred people lay dead;

many more died later in hospitals. One observer said, "I saw the great battle-fields of the Civil War, but they were as nothing to this. When we began to take out the bodies we found that many of the audience had been unable to get even near the exits. Women were bent over the seats, their fingers clinched on the iron sides so strongly that they were torn and bleeding. Their faces and clothes were burned, and they must have suffered intensely."

The reaction was immediate: Mayor Carter H. Harrison closed all Chicago theaters while city investigators updated ordinances and made plans to bring them into force. City governments and fire commissions all over the nation began padlocking questionable theaters and examining their own fire codes. New York's new fire commissioner, Nicholas Hayes, cracked down on theaters (as well as on schools and churches). Scandals broke out in Washington, Massachusetts, and Milwaukee as more potential theatrical deathtraps were uncovered. The panic spread overseas, as London, Paris, Berlin, and other capitals nervously updated their own fire codes and brought their theaters up to twentieth-century standards. The Iroquois was a Klaw and Erlanger theater, and those producers were forced to undergo some obviously warranted investigation. Many of their theaters were shut down and had to be rebuilt to fire code specifications. In the meantime, the up-and-coming Shubert brothers took advantage of this by promoting their new theaters as fireproof. Even so, theater attendance dropped starkly throughout the United States as the Iroquois horror lingered in everyone's minds.

Back in freezing New York, those few who couldn't live without musical comedy were attending the elaborate fantasies *Mother Goose* and *Babes in Toyland;* going to see Weber and Fields in *Whoop-Dee-Doo,* newcomer Fritzi Scheff in *Babette,* or comic Raymond Hitchcock in *The Yankee Consul.* But the seats at the Knickerbocker Theater got emptier and emptier. *Mam'selle Napoleon* was scheduled to start its tour with a month in Chicago, but word came that the Illinois Theater was "unavailable." Did its managers hesitate to stage a flop?

Ziegfeld huffily told reporters that the theater was being rebuilt to the new fire code specifications and simply would not be available in time. Was there any truth to the rumors that he would walk away from *Mam'selle Napoleon* and stage another tour of *The Little Duchess* or even *Papa's Wife?* Certainly not, he said. *Mam'selle Napoleon* would simply skip Chicago and go right to Baltimore— and he would be suing the Illinois Theater for lost ticket sales. Was it true that Ziegfeld was broke? He took ten one-thousand-dollar gold certificates from his pocket and waved them impressively in the reporter's face. "Does this look as if I were broke?" he snapped. Ziegfeld said everyone along Broadway was waiting for him to fail. "They all hope I will go broke and I wouldn't like to cause them displeasure. They've had me closing up *The Red Feather* company a dozen times, and now they are waiting for me to close *Mam'selle Napoleon*. Well, it won't close, and I won't go broke."

After an embarrassing five-week run in New York, *Mam'selle Napoleon* was to open in Toledo, Ohio, in early February 1904. But the show seemed to be cursed. On February 5 the company was involved in a minor train wreck in Hudson, Ohio. Their three baggage cars, two sleepers, and Anna's private car were hit by an engine and caboose. One actor suffered a broken nose, but everyone else was just shaken up. Special trains had to be sent out to replace the damaged cars, and the troupe went on its not-so-merry way. Meanwhile, the audience had been waiting in their seats from 8:15 till 9:10, fidgeting politely, when someone came out front to explain the situation.

The curtain finally rang up hours late, and at least one Ohio reviewer rather wished it hadn't. He hinted that the showgirls had gotten their training in department store windows, thought the costumes were "hideous," and dismissed Anna's "Flirty Gertie eyes . . . that do killing goo-goos for the undoing of the Unattached in the first rows. . . . Coupons should be attached to each ticket and every purchaser should be given three guesses on what he is watching and why." Clearly enjoying himself, this reviewer even approved of the train wreck, complaining that more noses hadn't been broken. "Where were those 'comedians' when the collision occurred?" he asked. "Wouldn't you like to hear them cr-un-ch under the wheels?"

As the tour limped along, the audiences shrank and the reviews were not any kinder. "The Worst Yet," one was ominously headlined, going on to call the show "the season's most colossal failure." Rodney Lee reported, "The performers have evidently been selected solely for their ability to wear expensive gowns, for they cannot sing nor act. . . . There are any number of girls who dance and cavort at their own sweet will with no attention to each other or to the orchestra." As for Anna herself, "Miss Held is in the spotlight pretty much all the time and does little else but work her eyes, a stunt that was rather effective when she first used it a good many years ago. Now it is exasperating. It makes one feel like throwing things."

The only fun Anna had at all on this tour was in Montana, where she alighted in March. She was a hit with the local cowboys and miners, who presented her with a pet burro (which she politely returned), as well as with a shower of hatbands and belt buckles. A photo was printed of Anna perched atop a very serene-looking "bucking bronco," surrounded by admirers. She even got an invitation to a hanging: "You are hereby invited to attend the Legal Execution of Louis H. Mott for the murder of Leah H. Mott," read the card from Harry W. Thompson, a local sheriff. "The execution will take place in the jail yard in the city of Missoula, Mont., on Friday, the 18th day of March, 1904, between the hours of 6 A.M. and 3 P.M." As much as Anna may have been in the mood for a hanging after more than three months of *Mam'selle Napoleon*, Ziegfeld thought it might not be good publicity.

The tour finally ground to a halt in early spring and Anna and her company skulked back into New York. Unlike the previous two shows, there was no thought of taking *Mam'selle Napoleon* on into a second season. Next year there would be no talk of Anna's dramatic possibilities, of Bernhardt or *Camille*. Anna was properly chastened at this tremendous failure and never again would attempt a serious role. From now on, she was simply to be "Anna Held." "If the public will not hear me recite Shakespeare, then I must dance the can-can, eh?" she sadly admitted. "In other words, I must sing my old songs." But still, she felt, it wouldn't help her career long-term if her act got stale. "We must always break our heads for something new. If you give the public chick-chick-chickens all the time, the public it will get sick."

Anna saw the future stretched out before her playing the naughty ooh-la-la-ing French soubrette, but that prospect didn't unduly depress her. True, she was a dedicated and ambitious actress, but she was also quite sensible and realized how lucky she was to have hit upon a salable commodity in her stage persona. She knew too many performers who labored for years and never quite found themselves a marketable schtick. If it took high-kicking and eye-rolling to make herself financially secure, that was a bargain Anna was more than willing to make.

She was also emotionally secure and smart enough to keep the private Anna Held separate from the public "Anna Held." She flirted and wore filmy low-cut gowns both onstage and for interviews, but in her own world she was known as a rather prim but good-natured housewife. She took great pride in her decorating and her cooking and dressed in modest, high-necked gowns when not on display (her rival Billie Burke called Anna "frugal" and "domestic"). Friendly and funny, interested in current events, Anna was popular among her coworkers—not only the producers and costars but also the chorus girls and carpenters. Playwright Harry B. Smith noted in his memoirs that "when not on exhibition as an advertisement for herself, she was unaffected and charming."

Despite his boasts to reporters, Ziegfeld was indeed in serious financial trouble. The losses of 1903–04 came to light the following year, when actor Dan McAvoy sued for his *Mam'selle Napoleon* salary. McAvoy had been hired to play a minor comic role in the show, took a salary cut, then had been fired during the December rewrites. In March 1905, after more than a year of trying to collect his salary, he took Ziegfeld to court for forty-four hundred dollars. After being fired, McAvoy complained, "I couldn't get any other engagement and had to go into vaudeville—a lower engagement—at three hundred dollars a week." During his testimony, McAvoy stated that Ziegfeld admitted to having lost sixty thousand dollars on *The Red Feather*, and another seventy thousand dollars on *Mam'selle Napoleon*. Ziegfeld leaped to his feet and insisted that he'd *invested*, not *lost*, that money. Judge Levintritt eventually ordered McAvoy to be paid his for his rehearsal time—but the word was out about Ziegfeld's losses (whatever he may have claimed about "investment"). Anna herself showed up to court ("looking smart in a brown walking suit, sable furs and a Frenchy green hat") but was relieved not to have been called to "that awful witness stand."

Anna and Ziegfeld desperately needed a break after the fiasco of *Mam'selle Napoleon*, and they took off in early June to see the St. Louis exhibition (best known today for inspiring the book, song, and movie, all titled *Meet Me in St. Louis*). But it was not a restful month. The press began leaking the first hints that all might not be well within the Ziegfeld marriage, perhaps inspired by Anna's career bump. Both Anna and Ziegfeld denied the rumors, and in fact their marriage was still relatively stable and happy at this point. "What do you have to say, Annie, about this story that we are to separate?" Ziegfeld asked joshingly at one press conference. Anna shot him a look and deadpanned, "Weellll, I say, Flo, we might separate *some*time, all right, n'est pas?" Ziegfeld quickly assured the reporter that she was joking.

Ziegfeld also began making plans for the fall of 1904 during his stay in St. Louis. While Anna saw the sights, Ziegfeld was sending his famous twenty-page telegrams to Joe Weber in New York. Weber was the same age as Ziegfeld but had been a star and a producer since the 1880s, when he'd teamed as a child with fellow New Yorker Lew Fields. They gained fame as roughneck "Dutch" comics and eventually headed their own touring companies. Fields was the tall straight man while the diminutive Weber, in a grotesque padded costume, played the put-upon (and frequently strangled or pummeled) stooge.

In 1896 Weber and Fields opened their Broadway Music Hall on Twenty-ninth Street. Their joint careers skyrocketed with the goofily named hits *Hurly-Burly, Helter Skelter, Whirl-I-Gig, Fiddle-Dee-Dee*. The high point of their shows was always a dead-on burlesque of a current Broadway hit, such as *Diplomacy* (renamed *Depleurisy*), *The Geisha* (*The Geezer*), *The Stubbornness of Geraldine* (*The Stickiness of Gelatine*). They even poked fun at Anna—while she was appearing in *La Poupée* in 1897, a Weber and Fields show introduced a living doll character named La Pooh-Pooh.

The team broke up in early 1904; Broadway gossips said that Joe Weber was tired of being Lew Fields's stooge. Additionally, the adventurous Fields wanted to branch out of burlesque into "book" shows, while the ever cautious Weber hesitated. "I believe it is a good thing to stick to success," he said, "and not go experimenting. Experience has shown us where our strength is. . . . Our style of show has made us a good deal of money and a big reputation. Why shouldn't we stick to it?" Fields begged to differ and began working on his own show, *It Happened in Nordland*, while Weber and Ziegfeld circled warily around each other. Lillian Russell, for one, thought Anna should jump at the chance to work with Weber. Russell had costarred in several Weber and Fields shows between 1900 and 1903: *Whirl-I-Gig, Hoity-Toity, Twirly-Whirly* (in which she introduced her theme song, "Come Down, My Evening Star"), and *Whoop-Dee-Doo.* Russell had thoroughly enjoyed her work, and the shows brought her down to earth as a broad comedy actress. Her ability to kid herself gained her good press and audience admiration. After the disaster of *Mam'selle Napoleon,* Russell suggested that Anna could use the same career boost.

Weber and Fields were well known for building new stars and reenergizing faded ones. Besides Russell, among their company were such famous names as De Wolf Hopper, William Collier, David Warfield, and Fay Templeton. "Never was a stage so cluttered up with high explosives of temperament," said Hopper (whose ingenue bride went on to become famed gossip columnist Hedda Hopper). "Half a dozen stars managed by two other stars! . . . I do not say there was no jealousy; that would be absurd. Had there been no jealousy, there would have been nothing remarkable in the harmony. The astonishing thing was that everyone kept a tight rein and curb bit on his or her envy." Anna felt that Joe Weber could provide a nurturing environment for her, as well as a good supporting cast. And Ziegfeld felt he could use Weber's money and goodwill on Broadway. Plans went ahead, and Weber began booking theaters for the proposed 1904–05 tour.

Without even realizing it, Anna and Ziegfeld had passed an important milestone: By March 1904, they had been living together as man and wife for seven years. According to the state of New York, that made them legally wed by common law. Neither of them even thought about it, and the subject didn't come up for quite a few years. Anna and Ziegfeld sailed to Europe for their annual vacation, promising to look for good costumes, settings, and chorus girls while otherwise enjoying themselves. But work took a back seat this year, as the couple motored happily around Europe, trying to put their last trying year behind them.

Long-distance automobiling was a dangerous and hazard-filled sport in the early years of the twentieth century. When C.S. Rolls (later a renowned and ill-fated aviator) took a similar trip through France in 1900, he had to deal with "joints of waterpipe gone, bad junction to be replaced, bad cut in tyre of front wheel, chain loose, burst of back tyre, mackintosh loose and wound up in shreds on pump, leaking cylinder, whole upper ends of cylinders red-hot, pump jammed, leaks in radiator pipes, ignition tube burst twice, oil on the brakes, another tyre burst." All this, of course, with no gas stations in existence, and Anna and Ziegfeld learning slowly out of necessity to become their own "pit crew."

Anna also had to dress for automobiling. Early cars had no windshield wipers—few of them had even windshields. So Anna had to cover herself neck-to-ankle in a linen duster (a rather attractive trench-coat type garment), a hat and scarf to keep her hair from getting wind-blown, and large functional goggles to protect her eyes from dust and gravel. "Those who fear any detriment to their good looks had best content themselves with a quiet drive in the Park," said the 1902 book *Motors and Motor Driving*, "leaving to the more ardent motorist the enchanting sensation of flying along the lanes and roads of our lovely country."

They soon learned a few tricks, taking a dozen extra tires with them and shipping gasoline ahead to their proposed stops (when using a gas-powered car). "My husband, Florenz, is the chauffeur sublime," the easygoing Anna told a reporter happily after the summer excursion. "We flew from Carlsbad to Paris. It took Florenz ten minutes for the trip. He say, 'are you ready?' I grasp my hat and say, 'oui, Florenz.' There is a zip! zip! and Florenz he say, 'get out, little girl . . . we got there while you were holding your breath.' Ah! That Florenz, he flies like a canary with that steam car" (it might be noted that Ziegfeld had been ticketed earlier that year for "flying like a canary" in New York). Anna and Ziegfeld also drove to Rouen and Germany that summer. Neither of them were overly impressed with the latter country—Anna because her French patriotism was put into high gear and Ziegfeld because "they are not kindly to Americans, the horses scare and one is in constant terror of knocking down a yokel."

Feeling they could now face anything, the couple returned to the United States on the *Deutschland* on September 2, 1904, to be met by Joe Weber and his company and crew. The welcoming party rented a small tugboat and band and greeted the ship playing "Won't You Come and Play with Me?" At this display of goodwill, Anna burst into tears. Once back in New York the Ziegfelds packed up and moved across town into the newly completed Ansonia, a luxury apartment building at Broadway and Seventy-third Street. Like their previous digs on Fifth Avenue, the Ansonia was surrounded by a growing community of huge, elaborate apartment buildings. Between 1895 and 1908 the Marie Antoinette, the St. Andrews, the Dorilton, the Spencer Arms, and the Apthorp all appeared in the same neighborhood. But the Ansonia was—and still is—the jewel of the Upper West Side, outclassed only by the Dakota a few blocks east. Designed by the firm of Grabes and Duboy, the Ansonia was the biggest and gaudiest building on Broadway when it opened. It boasted a garage, swimming pool, and several restaurants (a Palm Garden, Grille Room, Assembly Room, and so on). The lobby and suite interiors matched the extravagant beaux arts design of the building's exterior.

Over the years the Ansonia was to be home to such celebrities as Arturo Toscanini, Theodore Dreiser, Feodor Chaliapin, Igor Stravinsky, Babe Ruth, Jack Dempsey, and—according to neighborhood historian Peter Salwen—"several pre-World War I German spies, a deposed Mexican dictator, and a tidy selection of other eccentrics, gamblers, geniuses, hustlers, and con men." Long after Ziegfeld and Anna were gone, the Ansonia kept up its reputation for excitement: Ghosts were reported to haunt the premises, safe-cracker Willie Sutton was arrested there, and in the early 1970s Bette Midler and Barry Manilow entertained at the Continental Baths, a gay nightclub incorporated into the Ansonia's old steam rooms.

Ziegfeld rented the thirteen-room suite 41 on the tenth floor, and Anna decorated it in her favorite French style. It looked much like her home in Paris, scattered with blue-upholstered, gilded Louis XIV furniture, paintings, sculptures, and tchotchkes from their trips abroad. Anna's bedroom was done in tones of ivory and pale blue, lace and satin throws tossed over her bed. Her dressing room screens were covered in eighteenth-century bucolic scenes; the drawing room was in creams and yellows, setting off her famous piano (which was embossed with gold decorations, its keys made of mother-of-pearl). This piece of workmanship was pounded regularly by songwriters and rehearsal pianists and was replaced in 1911 when Anna bought another instrument at the estate sale of Belgium's King Leopold, this one inlaid with rosewood and bronze.

As soon as she'd settled in, Anna began throwing dinner parties for her friends, both in and out of the theater world. "What Miss Held can't do with an alcohol lamp and an ice box isn't worth writing about," noted one dinner guest, "and the things she accomplishes with a gas range—well, someday someone will write a poem about Anna's skillets and Victor Herbert will set her recipes to music." "Yes, I like to cook," Anna said. "I can cook anything but— what do you call them—pastries? My husband says nobody cooks like me." Turning to Ziegfeld (whose increasing girth attested to her skills), she asked, "Does anything taste like my French ragôut—the hardest of all to make—eh, Flo?" Journalist Amy Leslie noted that the glamorous star "keeps accounts, carries a bunch of keys, locking up everything from diamond tiaras and bank stocks to loaf sugar and patent flour. She rises at twelve and holds court with the chef, the butler, the maids, and tradesmen at her beck and call." Ziegfeld may have married a soubrette, but he found himself living with an old-fashioned European hausfrau, just like his mother.

By early September, everyone was hard at work on the new show, dubbed *Higgledy-Piggledy*. Written by Edgar Smith and Maurice Levy (with interpolated songs from a number of sources), *Higgledy-Piggledy* told the story of a trip to Europe by German-American pickle mogul Adolph Schnitz (Weber) and his daughter Philopena. Anna portrayed naughty French actress Mimi de Chartreuse, who attempts to seduce Schnitz; Charles Bigelow played a comic headwaiter, and Aubrey Boucicault was the requisite handsome leading man. While the actors were put through their drills by director Sam Marion, Ziegfeld and Weber oversaw the construction of the new Weber and Ziegfeld Theater. Anna picked her way through the planks and ladders with a reporter while the two coproducers haggled in the background. "Is it not beautiful?" she said of the house. "I love it so. I come here always. I cannot stay in the hotel. I cannot stay in the restaurant. I must come here." As Weber, in the background, complained about the cost of the forty-four chorus girls, Anna called out cheerily, "Discharge some. Keep the cream—ha! ha!—and throw away the milk!"

Weber noted proudly that the advance demand for tickets was higher than for any of his shows with Lew Fields and added, "There's going to be lots of money in this show. And we're going to have a regular plot, too. I don't know just how it comes out, because I haven't seen the finish yet." Recalling her recent debacle, Anna wryly chimed in, "Maybe we see our finish when the curtain goes up." From the start, Broadway insiders predicted trouble from the teaming of the risk-taking loose cannon Ziegfeld and the conservative, thoughtful Weber. The trouble wasn't long in brewing; it began while their theater was still being remodeled. Weber wanted to use a slice of the lobby for a remunerative concession stand, which Ziegfeld thought looked cheap and vulgar. The two disagreed on the theater's decorations (Ziegfeld wanted to spend as much money as possible, while Weber was eager to cut corners). The sets, as well, caused contention: Ziegfeld demanded that a backdrop of the French countryside be repainted, as it "looked like Hoboken."

For her part Anna thought her role was a bit small, though she was placated by having three good songs. On the whole everyone was optimistic, and Weber had already commissioned a burlesque of the popular show *The College Widow* (retitled *The College Widower*), to coproduce with Ziegfeld for Anna in the 1905–06 season. The Winter Garden in Berlin offered her $22,500 for three month's work in 1905, but she turned it down because of her new long-term relationship with Joe Weber. *Higgledy-Piggledy* opened out of town—Rochester, N.Y.—in October, and early indications were good. Anna's three songs went over well. She did a tribute to Gay Paree, sang "Little Nancy Clancy" to May MacKenzie (Anna once again dressed in a ragged newsboy outfit, as in *The Little Duchess*), and debuted her "Laughing Song," which she made a lifelong standard. *Broadway Weekly* called her "the personification of dainty grace," adding that "no foreign artist who has come among us to make her home in many years has entered into our affections as Anna Held." It seemed that *Mam'selle Napoleon* was safely in the past and all was forgiven.

But all was not well. The big hit of the show was Marie Dressler, portraying the loud, bumptious American daughter of Joe Weber. In her mid-thirties—like Anna—Dressler had become a star in 1896 and had turned in broad, successful comic performances in half a dozen shows since. When she made her entrance in *Higgledy-Piggledy*, bouncing onstage singing "A Great Big Girl Like Me," the show was hers. By the time *Higgledy-Piggledy* opened in New York on October 20, Anna knew she had a tough fight in store. *Theatre Magazine* praised Marie Dressler to the skies, commenting only that "Anna Held remains her usual self." Another reviewer (under the nom de plume Fannie Fair), called Dressler "the only genuine funmaker of the show," and went on to note that "Miss Held contributed a magnificent set of eyelashes to the entertainment. Such eyelashes have never been seen on Broadway except on Miss Held. They are not only long and curling, but each hair of them seems to have been subjected to an independent massage treatment which has resulted in an almost muscular development." One of the more upsetting reviews even compared Anna's appearance unflatteringly to that of Dressler. "Miss Held has not been so adroit as Miss Dressler in suppressing Father Time," it read. "Suspicious lines are growing around the actress's mouth, and this is a grave matter to the player who plays on beauty."

On October 27, a week after *Higgledy-Piggledy's* opening, New York saw a mass holiday for the opening of its first subway system. Anna felt rather superior, as the Paris Métro had been in service since 1900. But the New York opening was quite an event: Mayor George B. McClellan Jr. led some two hundred politicians and celebrities (Anna, alas, could not be among them) down the City Hall subway station into the five wooden cars. The train tootled along to One Hundred Forty-fifth Street in an impressive twenty-six minutes, and New York went subway mad. "Men fought, kicked, and pummeled one another in their mad desire to reach the subway ticket office or to ride on the trains," reported the *New York World.* "Women were dragged out, either screaming in hysterics or in a swooning condition; grey-haired men pleaded for mercy, boys were knocked down and only escaped by a miracle from being trampled under-foot." And thus was born the typical New York subway ride.

Goodwill seemed to reign in late December 1904, when Anna and Joe Weber (both of whom were Jewish, at least by birth) posed for a Christmas magazine layout in street clothes and sans makeup, clowning around and playfully pulling each other's hair over a pile of toys. They seemed to be thoroughly enjoying themselves. Anna hallucinated some heartwarming memories for the reporter. "You know, an old grandmother, like mine for instance, who is ninety-three years old, finds a family reunion at home on Christmas with all her children and grandchildren gathered about her, more satisfying than anything that money could buy." Warming up to her imaginary childhood, Anna continued, "My most appreciated gift was a Christmas stocking, from my aunts in America, filled with holiday goodies. It held so much more than a French sabot." It wouldn't be much longer that Anna could get away with this sort of tale.

While she may have not have attended the debut of New York's subway system, Anna witnessed the birth of a modern tradition on December 31, 1904, when Times Square was officially born. The *New York Times* Building was nearly completed by that date, and quite a sight it was: Modeled after Giotto's Campanile in Florence, it was generally acknowledged to be the most beautiful building in New York (and, at twenty-four stories, the tallest building by far in midtown). To celebrate 1905 and the building's opening, the *Times* sponsored a midnight fireworks display, complete with a band concert and some one hundred thousand fashionably dressed, cheering New Yorkers. Due mainly to the constant insistence of the *Times*, the neighborhood's nickname slowly began changing from Long Acre Square to Times Square (though the former name can still be spotted being used by competing papers as late as the 1920s). The New Year's celebration has continued annually since (with a blackout break during World War II), but the Times Building itself has been unrecognizable since the mid-1960s, when it was bought by Allied Chemical, stripped down, and entombed within an ugly marble sheath.

Holidays out of the way, Anna continued to labor in *Higgledy-Piggledy*. Her personal reviews weren't bad, just unenthusiastic. One paper, politely ignoring the current show, reestablished Anna's clout by mentioning in passing that she "has played New York more weeks than any other three stars combined and done the largest business." It was also brought up that she held box-office records in Philadelphia, Boston, San Francisco, and Chicago; and producer A.L. Erlanger called her "the Maude Adams of musical comedy." All this was very nice but it

Above left, Anna and her mother, Yvonne Held, around 1880. Courtesy of Martensen/Isola family. *Above right,* The young music hall star in 1890s. Wisconsin Center for Film & Theatre Research.

Anna's house (with wrought-iron balconies) from 1894 until her death, 86 rue Faubourg Saint-Honoré. Courtesy of Martensen/Isola family.

A demure Anna early in her career. Wisconsin Center for Film & Theatre Research.

Florenz Ziegfeld Jr., ca. 1900. Harvard Theatre Collection, The Houghton Library, Fredric Woodbridge Wilson, Curator.

Florenz Ziegfeld Jr. greets Anna on her arrival in America on October 15, 1896. Courtesy of Martensen/Isola family.

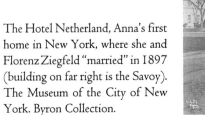

The Hotel Netherland, Anna's first home in New York, where she and Florenz Ziegfeld "married" in 1897 (building on far right is the Savoy). The Museum of the City of New York. Byron Collection.

Left, The bicycling enthusiast. Corbis/Bettman. *Below left*, Lillian Russell, Anna's theatrical predecessor and best friend. *Below right*, Posing for a face powder ad. Both from the Wisconsin Center for Film & Theatre Research.

On an 1896 vaudeville tour. Culver Pictures.

After being filmed by the American Mutoscope and Biograph Company in 1899, Anna posed for an advertisement for them. Culver Pictures.

In *La Poupee*, 1897. Corbis/Bettman.

Above left, Charles Bigelow, Anna's tempestuous and talented comic lead in five shows. *Above right*, Eva Davenport, the female comic relief in several of Anna's early shows. Both from the Harvard Theatre Collection, The Houghton Library, Fredric Woodbridge Wilson, Curator.

A Kate Carew caricature of Anna in 1901. The caption reads, "They like Anna Held so much in Eighth avenue that she will stay at the Grand Opera-House another week. It is said that Anna in private life has learned to speak Americanese so fluently that she is obliged to practise her broken French two hours every morning for fear she should forget it for stage purposes." Author's collection.

In her first American success, *Papa's Wife*, 1899. Culver Pictures.

Left, The famous salmon-colored dress from *The Little Duchess* (1901). *Below,* Anna (right) with Mabel Barrison in the "Pretty Mollie Shannon" number in *The Little Duchess.* All from the Wisconsin Center for Film & Theatre Research.

ANNA HELD

Left, Anna in her biggest flop, *Mam'zelle Napoleon*, 1903. Wisconsin Center for Film & Theatre Research. *Above*, The Blue Boy outfit from *Mam'zelle Napoleon*. Corbis/Bettman.

Above left, A candid snapshot of Anna playing hostess. Wisconsin Center for Film & Theatre Research. *Above right,* Joe Weber, Anna's costar and Ziegfeld's coproducer in *Higgledy-Piggledy* (1904). Harvard Theatre Collection, The Houghton Library, Fredric Woodbridge Wilson, Curator. *Below,* The Ansonia, on Broadway and 72nd Street, where Anna and Ziegfeld lived in the early 1900s—and where Ziegfeld also set up his mistress Lillian Lorraine. The Museum of the City of New York. Leonard Hassam Bogart Collection.

With Charles Bigelow in *Higgledy-Piggledy*. Harvard Theatre Collection, The Houghton Library, Fredric Woodbridge Wilson, Curator.

A sketch of Joe Weber, Anna, and Flo Ziegfeld at the time of the ill-fated *Higgledy-Piggledy*. Author's collection.

"Making her eyes behave." Wisconsin Center for Film & Theatre Research.

Marie Dressler, who stole *Higgledy-Piggledy* from under Anna's nose. Wisconsin Center for Film & Theatre Research.

Above, New York's Times Square in 1910. To the left of the 1905 New York Times Building is the still-extant Knickerbocker Hotel (1901); to the right is the 1904 Astor Hotel, where Ziegfeld met Billie Burke on New Year's Eve, 1913. The Museum of the City of New York. Print Archives. *Right,* Anna with her daughter, Liane Carrera, ca. 1907. Courtesy of Martensen/Isola family.

In the "living picture" scene of *The Parisian Model* (1906). Culver Pictures.

didn't keep Marie Dressler from stealing the show out from under Anna's nose every night.

Ziegfeld asked for rewrites, to punch up Anna's part. This, of course, did not sit well with Dressler. The *Morning Telegraph* made note of the dissension, saying that "Weber could not regard Miss Held with the same luminous glow of appreciation in which her husband found her resplendent." The success went to Dressler's head and she became so high-handed that comedienne Trixie Friganza was brought in as her understudy to throw a scare into her. It was not a happy backstage atmosphere. The last straw came in early February, when Anna saw the proposed script for *The College Widower*, the comedy in which she was supposed to appear the following season. She had all of twenty lines in the show and for once lost her temper, tossing the script aside contemptuously and refusing to even consider it. After her performance on February 11, Anna took a permanent leave of absence. Dressler's understudy Trixie Friganza took her place (the combination of Dressler and Friganza—both outsized, brassy comediennes—must have been overwhelming).

Years later, when Anna was long in her grave and Dressler could afford to be gracious, she wrote in her 1924 autobiography that Anna had been a "good sport." In this cheerful and unlikely scenario, Anna came to Dressler's dressing room, took her by the hand, and said, "I'm leaving, dear, but I have no hard feelings. Do you know what I did? I told Flo Ziegfield [sic!] if he didn't put you under contract for ten years he would make the mistake of his life." By this time, Dressler could say fondly, "I always loved Anna Held—she was a very fine woman." But temperatures in 1905 ran a lot higher.

By the time Anna left *Higgledy-Piggledy*, receipts were beginning to drop off anyway. To Joe Weber's dismay, his ex-partner's show *It Happened in Nordland* was a huge hit, and George M. Cohan had his first great success that year with *Little Johnny Jones*. There were also some notable debuts on Broadway in late 1904: The huge Hippodrome Theater opened with *A Yankee Circus on Mars*, and *Mr. Wix of Wixham* saw the New York bows of female impersonator Julian Eltinge and songwriter Jerome Kern. There were plenty of alternatives to *Higgledy-Piggledy*.

At the depth of Anna's career troubles, the specter of her past raised its head. Despite the fact that she'd been passing herself off as a native Parisienne and a Catholic since she'd arrived in the United States, there had been whisperings of her true origins. Before her first ship landed in New York, she was alternately described as a French chanteuse or a Polish Jewess. But on June 8, 1905, Anna was greeted by the kind of publicity she'd dreaded: That morning, the *Telegraph* carried an article by an anonymous reporter calling himself B.G.E., detailing for the first time Anna's background in Warsaw and the Yiddish theater. The reporter had been covering the recent New York successes of Jewish actress Berta Kalich and had gone to a deli on Second Avenue to chat with some of her coworkers. When they began reminiscing about Anna Held's days with Yisrol Gradner and Jacob Adler, B.G.E. sat up and took notice.

One of the actors present recalled "the pretty Polish Jewess" and her ailing mother anxiously checking out Gradner's company, as well as Anna's first big break: Jacob Adler had just lost several leading ladies in a row and took a chance on her. Her stage nerves and voice were tested by having her perform a French song at a postshow concert, after which she was given some small character parts and finally the lead in *Shulamith*. Other papers promptly picked up on this story; those who had been hinting that Anna might not be a Parisienne born and bred now crowed over her exposure. Theater critic Archie Bell—an up-and-coming rival to Alan Dale—said quite plainly that "Mlle Held is about as French as Bedelia Finnegan. She is a Polish Jewess and was born in Warsaw." Bell also tracked down some old associates and gave further details of Anna's early days. "No human being with her [lack of] experience could have assumed such a role on such short notice and achieved success without help," wrote Bell about *Shulamith*. "This came from old members of the cast, who stood about her and, fascinated by her effervescent charm, prompted her in her lines and allowed her to dazzle the audience by her beauty."

Horrified by all this, Anna continued to stonewall and deny point-blank that she was either Jewish or Polish. To her credit, she never made any kind of unkind remark against Jews; she merely denied that she was one. On the other hand, she never voiced any pro-Christian sentiments either. Religion was simply not a part of Anna's life. She educated Liane in French convents, but this was because her in-laws, the very Catholic Carreras, were willing to foot the bills.

Anna, of course, had good reason to be paranoid. She'd seen the pogroms of eastern Europe during her childhood, and had been in France during the depths of the Dreyfus case. Anti-Semitism was not as institutionalized in America as in Europe, however, and most editorialists thought she was being silly. Judaism, wrote one paper, "is not regarded in this country as carrying with it a crushing weight of odium. It might mitigate against her amongst the rude, unlettered sheepskin-clad barbarians of Russia, by whom the stoning of Jews is regarded as a national pastime productive of great hilarity at the mid-Winter fetes. But America makes no invidious racial or religious distinctions."

But Anna was a Frenchwoman, if only a self-made one, and her shame and fear of her Jewish background kept her in a full state of denial right to the end of her life. She was never able to quite explain her early fluency in Yiddish and never tried. Her Polish background was to be exposed once and for all in the next decade, but Anna could never bring herself to admit her Jewish heritage.

While Anna was being hounded by the press and licking the wounds inflicted by *Mam'selle Napoleon* and *Higgledy-Piggledy*, Flo Ziegfeld was going through his own career difficulties. After his recent failures, he badly needed another partner to help him produce his shows. Joe Weber was no longer an option, so he began looking around for other coproducers. This was walking on eggshells in the early 1900s because of the cutthroat competition between producing cartels.

It had all started in 1896 (quite a year for New York theater) when a powerful theatrical syndicate was formed by producers Abraham Erlanger, Marc Klaw, Charles Frohman, Al Hayman, Sam Nixon, and J. Fred Zimmerman. Before this, theatrical bookings were pretty much haphazard and informal. But within a few years those six men owned, leased, or otherwise controlled more than seven hundred theaters throughout the United States, and it was nearly impossible to book shows unless through them and their theaters. Smaller producers were all but frozen out of the business, as were acts who did not care to play ball with the Syndicate. The first real challenge to the Syndicate came in 1903, when the pugnacious Shubert brothers—Sam, Lee, and Jacob—found one of their bookings cancelled. The gloves were off, and Erlanger in particular was not a good enemy to have. A small Napoleonic man, he was a well-known terror in the business. Playwrights P.G. Wodehouse and Guy Bolton noted in their joint memoirs, "He's a bit of a Tartar. That's our expression. The Tartars, meeting a particularly tough specimen, would say that he was a bit of an Erlanger."

The Shuberts managed to lease or build theaters throughout the United States, bypassing the Syndicate houses (the dreadful Iroquois Theater fire of 1903 was actually a bit of a break for the Shuberts). Sam Shubert died in a 1905 train wreck while on his way to fight the Syndicate for a theater lease, and from then on his surviving brothers saw the battle as a holy war.

If Ziegfeld needed a moneyed and well-connectèd partner, he had to choose between the Syndicate or the Shuberts. He sent out feelers to both. In March 1905 he signed with the Shuberts to coproduce a show called *La Belle Marseilles*, but nothing came of this (despite a great deal of money invested by the Shuberts). As Anna packed her clothing and her hurt feelings for her yearly trip to Paris, Ziegfeld and Lee Shubert were mulling over another coproduction, an Anna Held extravaganza to be called *The Motor Girl*. This project was to simmer over the next year; as the Shuberts and Ziegfeld exchanged cables, Ziegfeld spent Shubert money—and was secretly in communication with their enemies Klaw and Erlanger. It would all blow up early in 1906.

But in spring 1905 Anna was determined to leave all clouds behind her. She sailed for Paris, with a proposed script for another show, *The Parisian Model*, tucked under her arm. Anna was still hurting from her recent debacles and not at all sure if she wanted to do this show. She and Ziegfeld took some time off to think over their futures. Ziegfeld played his double game, alternately wiring the Shuberts and the Syndicate, and even discussing with his father the possibility of returning to Chicago to take a position at the Musical College.

For her part, Anna did her best to forget show business. She put *The Parisian Model* aside and spent her time enjoying herself. She and Ziegfeld revved up the car and spent the summer and fall of 1905 driving all over the continent, reacquainting themselves with the small towns of France, Belgium, Germany, and Switzerland. And Ziegfeld reacquainted himself with the gambling resorts of Monte Carlo, Biarritz, and Trouville while Anna nervously looked on, mentally tallying the losses. Back in the United States, Eddie Foy, Fritzi Scheff, George M. Cohan, and Elsie Janis all enjoyed big Broadway hits. The first rumblings of the Russian Revolution grabbed headlines. But Anna and Flo Ziegfeld coasted through the year blithely ignoring these events, in their own little world. Anna turned down several music-hall offers, and as the theatrical season of 1905–06 opened, it was without Anna Held for the first time since 1896.

In February Anna appeared in the press for the first time in months, but it was only an article about great beauties of Paris. She shared the headlines with actresses and adventuresses like Jane Hading and Cleo de Merode, but there was no mention of Anna's current plans. In April Ziegfeld sailed back to the United States—his ticket paid for by Lee Shubert—after his lengthy breather, complaining about his gambling losses and admitting sheepishly that he might travel on to Chicago to help his father manage a new theater he'd constructed.

But Ziegfeld had bigger fish to fry, and once he was back into the swim of things in New York, his old instincts took over. With his blessings, Anna was being wooed by Lee Shubert, who offered her forty-five thousand dollars for a thirty-week season, sending her a forty-thousand-franc diamond horseshoe as a goodwill gesture. While Anna continued to study new drafts of *The Parisian Model*, Shubert was laboring under the delusion that *The Motor Girl* was all but a done deal. "Play *Motor Girl* great star part," Shubert wired to Ziegfeld. If that show fell through, Shubert wanted a signed statement by Anna that she would appear in Shubert theaters for the 1906–07 season.

Between March and May 1906, negotiations between Ziegfeld and Lee Shubert broke down, and Ziegfeld firmed up an agreement with Abe Erlanger and Marc Klaw to produce—through the Syndicate—the next Ziegfeld/Anna Held show. This was not to be *The Motor Girl*, but the same *The Parisian Model* that

Anna had been studying for nearly a year. Lee Shubert was enraged, and the Shuberts were as bad enemies to have as was Erlanger. J.J. Shubert in particular was known for his temper tantrums, physical violence, and long-running feuds, and Ziegfeld was now on his lifelong hit list.

In May 1906 Anna attended an unusual family affair, her daughter's first communion. It was the first time that Anna, Maximo, and Liane Carerra had been together in ten years and was probably the last. "I was so pleased that Mother and Father could be together with me," the affection-starved girl later wrote. "Flo sent me a present of a prayer book—of course the largest and most expensive in Paris." Liane remembered the yearly arrival of her mother as the great event in her young life. Now that she was old enough to be responsible and not too much of a bother, Liane was allowed to stay with Anna—for brief periods—in the Paris apartment. This spring Ziegfeld remained in New York, so Liane was permitted to share her mother's bed "instead of the little cot in the sewing room with which I had to be satisfied when he was there."

Inheriting Anna's talent for self-delusion, Liane claimed that "Mother had become fond of me and I was her constant companion. As soon as she arrived we would go on shopping orgies. She would never buy anything in America but would wait until she came home to replenish her wardrobe." While the shopping sprees were no doubt accurate, the relationship between Anna and her daughter was not as smooth as Liane would wish. The two got along and had fun together for brief periods of time, but Anna had no maternal talents and Liane delighted in pushing her mother's buttons. Often as not their time together was strained and punctuated by quarrels and recriminations.

Poor Liane didn't have much better luck with Maximo, who by now was suffering from advanced diabetes. "I was simply scared to death of my father," she later wrote. "It was an ordeal for me to go with him and the chaperon as far as the nearest patisserie whenever he wanted to treat me to a sweet. Poor Papa . . . most every day sat again on a bench in the Bois, thinking now of his past glorious days."

Ziegfeld sailed back to France to spend the summer of 1906 with Anna and perhaps to put as much distance between himself, Lee Shubert, and Abe Erlanger as possible. But this was not the carefree adventure that the previous summer's auto tour had been. This year the first major rift in their marriage appeared, and ironically it surfaced in a way eerily similar to what had occurred to Anna exactly ten years earlier. Both Maximo Carrera and Ziegfeld were addicted to gambling, and Anna was the one to pay for their habits. Ziegfeld, of course, was a gambler when it came to nearly everything (including his romantic life, though that would not to come to Anna's attention for some time). In show business, his "plunger" personality resulted in such long-shot successes as *Papa's Wife* and *The Little Duchess* as well as expensive flops like *Mam'selle Napoleon* and the Joe Weber fiasco. Anna was attuned enough to show business to accept this.

But when it came to actual casino gambling, Ziegfeld's obsession was getting out of control. He never went to Europe without stopping by the gambling resort of Monte Carlo, and he was dropping more and more money there each year. Once he and his friend Freddie Zimmermann arrived there flat broke. Zimmermann's father wired him five thousand dollars, and the two men went to check their hats and coats before entering the gaming halls. Zimmermann got into a brief conversation at the checkroom and turned to see Ziegfeld heading back out of the casino, having lost the entire five thousand dollars in a matter of minutes. His second wife, Billie Burke, recalled in her memoirs that Ziegfeld could easily gamble the entire night away. "His were the most spectacular stakes, naturally," she wrote with regret. "He would win or lose fifty thousand dollars in an evening, sitting dour-faced and silent at the roulette wheel hours after everyone else had gone home, determined to break the bank, determined to be the best. . . . Flo was just about impossible to reason with when these gambling moods were upon him."

Burke would yell and throw things, but Anna could not stand scenes. She enjoyed drifting through casinos when nothing was at stake: She might wager a dollar or two, watch others play, and go off to chat with friends. But she could not stand by while Ziegfeld got into one of his wagering fits. She would dine, go see the sights, try to unwind on the beach. This summer a nervous and frustrated Ziegfeld hit all the major gaming palaces in Paris, Monte Carlo, Nice, Biarritz, and Trouville. He had lots of gambling-acquired money and his credit was good, despite the losses he'd incurred in his last two shows. But in Biarritz in June, he managed to lose twenty thousand dollars more than he had. Ziegfeld then did something that is unforgivable in his world: He took off and reneged on his debts. Alfred Baulant, the proprietor of the gambling casino in Biarritz, had to take him to court. Anna was ashamed and appalled; one simply did not walk out on debts. In France, a wife was legally responsible for her husband's losses, so Anna (by this time Ziegfeld's common-law wife) saw her own hard-earned and -saved fortune imperiled.

This particular peccadillo eventually played itself out in 1910, when Baulant's lawyers finally caught up with Ziegfeld and tried to have Anna's belongings attached. Anna wrote a letter to him saying that Ziegfeld's "unfortunate gambling experiences in Europe at your place, where he lost millions of francs, left his financial matters in such a condition that they were placed in the hands of his attorneys . . . and he was practically forced into bankruptcy." She added hopefully that "he is doing the best he can and intends to pay every honorable debt that he owes, but you can't get blood out of a stone." That summer of 1906, Anna lost some of the trust and admiration she'd had for her husband. She still loved him, but saw him more clearly now. That "you can't get blood out of a stone" attitude was to remain hers when it came to his gambling: As long as it didn't effect her own savings, she would shrug her shoulders, put an "I told you so" look on her face, and keep her mouth shut.

On August 8 Anna and Ziegfeld hightailed it back to the United States. The newspapers reported that they were accompanied by twenty-four chorus girls recruited in Berlin, Paris, and Vienna, but these girls seem to have been a figment of some reporter's imagination. Anna and Ziegfeld attended the New York opening of the show *Marrying Mary*, her first public appearance in some time (her white dress and huge green feathered and beribboned hat took much audience attention away from *Marrying Mary*: "No one but a Held would dare to wear such a concoction," wrote a critic who was ostensibly reviewing the show).

There were other concoctions to be seen that summer, as well: The costumes for *The Parisian Model* had arrived and were photographed for the delectation of the press and public. The fashion houses of Worth, Paquin, and Callot had been raided to supply gowns for both Anna and her chorus, and these gowns indicated that *The Parisian Model* was to be more over-the-top and shockingly modern than any of her previous shows. By the time Anna and her company headed for Philadelphia in mid-September for tryouts, the papers were already hinting that *The Parisian Model* was a bombshell ready to explode on Broadway. They were right: If her last two shows had been notable flops, this would be a succès de scandale.

Ziegfeld was taking no chances with *The Parisian Model*; if this show wasn't a success, both he and Anna were washed up in New York. So he decided to fall back on the already tried and true adage that sex sells. *The Parisian Model* had a respectable cast, author, and a veritable gaggle of proven songwriters, but it was racier than anything ever seen on a major Broadway stage. Harry B. Smith was brought in to write the show and was instructed to make it far spicier than *Papa's Wife* had been. The plot concerned Ann, a Paris fashion model at Callot's, who inherits a fortune and a mansion from her aunt, provided she doesn't reveal its source until she weds. Ann's artist boyfriend Julien de Marsay (played by Henri Leoni) thinks she came upon it by immoral means, and she, angered, decides to act as cheap as he thinks she is. Finally she saves the day when one of his works is stolen and she poses inside the frame as a "living painting" for the critics. Charles Bigelow was brought back to play comic millionaire Silas Goldfinch, pursued by his nagging wife (Eva Davenport was unavailable for this role, so Mabella Baker filled in).

Also in the cast was Gertrude Hoffmann, who started out as a chorus girl but was soon promoted to a featured role because of her talent as a mimic. According to press releases, Hoffmann had been entertaining cast members with hilarious imitations of Eddie Foy, George M. Cohan, and Anna herself. When Anna caught her at this, far from being angry, she was amused enough to give Hoffmann a chance to show off in *The Parisian Model*. A very pretty story, but when Hoffmann left the cast (to go on to a successful career as a dancer and choreographer), she was replaced by Madalyn Summers—who was, if the papers are to be believed, discovered by Anna in the exact same way.

There were more than a dozen songs in the show, to be encored, dropped, or added to as audience reaction indicated. Some were written by Gertrude's husband Max Hoffmann, others by up-and-coming songwriter Gus Edwards, who later became famous for his Kid Kabarets, which provided early exposure for such budding stars as Eddie Cantor, George Jessel, and the Duncan Sisters. But in 1906, he provided a song that was to eclipse "Won't You Come and Play with Me?" as a theme for Anna.

Anna's expressive eyes had been her trademark since early in her career, and she tried to have an "eye song" written for every show. Thus far, none of them had really clicked with the music-buying public. When the ambitious Edwards approached Anna with some recently written songs, she challenged him to come up with a really effective "eye song." Later accounts had him sit down at her piano in the Ansonia and write his masterpiece in a matter of moments, but this is no doubt an exaggeration. What he eventually presented Anna with was a clever, bouncy little number, detailing the comic misunderstandings caused by her flirtatious eyes. Edwards even managed to work the title of her previous theme song into the chorus:

> I just can't make my eyes behave;
> Two bad brown eyes, I am their slave.
> My lips may say, "run away from me,"
> But my eyes say, "come and play with me!"
> And you won't blame poor little me, I'm sure—
> For I just can't make my eyes behave!

Both the music and lyrics were more sophisticated than those of "Won't You Come and Play with Me?" (which was, essentially, a roughly translated children's song). "I Just Can't Make My Eyes Behave" put that former number in the shade, and became to Anna what "Over the Rainbow" was to Judy Garland and what "Falling in Love Again" was to Marlene Dietrich. Restaurant musicians played the tune when she entered, audiences demanded it as an encore; when theater orchestras played a chorus, everyone knew whom to expect and began applauding. Anna sang several other catchy songs in *The Parisian Model* ("La Mattchiche," "A Lesson in Kissing," "A Gown for Each Hour of the Day"), but it was her new "eye song" that people whistled as they left the theater.

To oversee the cast of *The Parisian Model*, Ziegfeld hired Julian Mitchell, one of the most eccentric directors Broadway ever saw. Mitchell, who was fifty-two when he first worked with Anna, was the nephew of Civil War-era star Maggie Mitchell. A successful dancer, he lost his hearing in the early 1890s. This would have discouraged most people, but Mitchell, bizarrely enough, decided to become a director. He excelled at this task, which must have been exceedingly difficult both for him and his casts. He successfully helmed such hits as *A Trip to Chinatown* (1891), several Weber and Fields shows, and the huge 1903 extravaganzas *The Wizard of Oz* and *Babes in Toyland.*

Mitchell used his senses of sight and touch, taking off his shoes to "hear" the beat of the music and the chorus dancers. A joke current at the time had a piece of scenery crashing to the ground, and Mitchell yelling, "Which one of you girls is off beat?!" P.G. Wodehouse and Guy Bolton recalled him as "an independent spirit who truckled to no one. He would fight manfully against any suggestion, even from the All Highest, that was in his opinion bad for the show. He knew his job, he did his job, and he was not going to have anyone telling him how to do it."

Just as *The Parisian Model* embarked for its Philadelphia tryouts in late September, Anna was faced with another invasion of privacy—though she herself had a hand in this episode. On September 25, The *Chicago News* broke the story of Liane Carrera's existence, though not of Anna's first marriage. The story was written by forty-five-year-old Amy Leslie, the country's first successful female drama critic. Not as acerbic as Alan Dale or Archie Bell, Leslie (an ex-actress herself) tended to befriend show people and went out of her way to be nice to them in print.

Anna and Amy Leslie became lifelong friends, which indicates that the two collaborated on these latest revelations. That also makes all the errors in the story harder to understand. Headlined "Her 'Child' Adopted," it told how Anna and her "admirer" Monsieur Carriere [*sic*] had adopted Lillian [*sic*] when she was abandoned by her mother. This tale sounded highly suspect even in 1906. "There was never any sensational claim that [Liane] belonged to Miss Held, either by marriage or romance," Leslie assured her readers.

Maximo Carrera was described as an "irascible, bituminous, quarreling old man" who took little interest—emotional or financial—in Liane, leaving Anna to raise her. Dancing around whether or not Carrera was Liane's natural father, Leslie went on to claim that "Lillian is a countess in her own right" and "the living image of her father, who was not especially handsome." Liane was further described as "a stocky, handsome child, dark, piquant and fascinating, nearly as large as Anna, whom she called 'Anna' or sometimes in fun and petting 'Petite maman.'"

Anna's love and attention to "Lillian" were dwelt upon. "Anna overwhelmed her with gifts and money and every affectionate testimonial," wrote Leslie, adding that in 1904 Carrera—who was actually still alive, though ailing—"went mad and died raging, raving about gambling, picturesquely, in close confinement." As of 1906 Liane was, it seems, "raised like a princess to command, to spend money furiously, to be obeyed and provided for sumptuously."

The public at large had known nothing of Liane or Maximo Carrera up till this point; everyone was amazed and laughed off the story about Liane not being Anna's natural daughter. Anna knew it was only a matter of time till Liane's existence became known, and she wanted to stage-manage that herself, with Amy Leslie's kind assistance. Liane was described as "about 18" in this piece, which cannot have had Anna's approval, as Anna later claimed 1900, then 1895, as Liane's year of birth. But Maximo was failing rapidly, and there was no telling when he might die. Once he was out of the picture, Anna realized, she would have to become more of a mother to Liane who, at about twelve, would soon be too old for school. This clumsy attempt at explanation, though, merely made Anna look silly and duplicitous and further damaged her relationship with her daughter. Liane found the story understandably hurtful, as her mother collaborated in denying her very parenthood. Liane never quite forgave Anna for this episode.

—5—

A Lucky Star

The *Parisian Model* had an unusually long tryout period, spending more than two months in six cities before heading to New York. There were several reasons for this, the two most troublesome being the show's raciness and the misbehavior of Charles Bigelow. The Philadelphia opening had to be delayed for a week because Bigelow showed up late for rehearsal and hadn't yet learned his lines (despite having been contracted back in March). Indeed, he hadn't worked for some time because of his alcoholism and erratic behavior, but Ziegfeld was always willing to put aside personal considerations if the person were the best for the part. Anna wasn't quite so sure and came to a slow boil over her costar's antics.

The show's naughtiness was a mixed blessing, one that became obvious during the earliest tryouts. A writer in Chicago huffed that Anna's plays "are always more or less indecent, and Miss Held herself seems to think that the nearer she comes to the borderland of outright vulgarity the better she will please the American public." Even respected critic Burns Mantle felt that there were things in *The Parisian Model* "which press the limit of decency and should not be permitted even in a burlesque house where men only attend." Then he went on to admit, "But every time that much is written, the line at the box office grows longer. So what's the use? The annual Held revels are beyond our controlling." Another reviewer primly summed up, "In an effort to avoid prudery Miss Held's stage performance runs occasional risk of going to an opposite extreme."

There were several lines that skirted propriety, but several musical numbers in particular were hissed by moralists and cheered by the audience. Anna's first song, "A Gown for Each Hour of the Day," involved her changing costumes several times, using the outstretched arms of her chorus girls as a peekaboo screen hiding her from the audience (these quick changes were no easy matter in the days before hooks and eyes were replaced by snaps and zippers). The "Artists and Models" number featured six chorus girls and six artists. The girls stepped behind large canvases and dropped their robes, their exposed shoulders and legs hinting that they were perfectly nude. Later in the number, they stepped out—to expectant gasps—and revealed themselves in shoulderless gowns, their skirts tied up.

Anna danced to a catchy tune ("La Mattchiche") with Gertrude Hoffmann, who was in male drag. The "Bells" number featured fourteen chorines with sleighbells attached to their legs and feet. At one point they lay on the floor and kicked their black-stockinged legs in the air, playing a little tune. And the last number took place on roller skates (the stage of the theaters where the show played had to be refloored in hard, smooth wood for this). Anna, her short-skirted chorus, and Earle Reynolds (billed auspiciously as "The Champion Skater of the World") rolled noisily around the stage for the grand finale. Neither Anna nor her chorus were champion skaters, and one writer noted eagerly of this number that "if you wait attentively you will observe the falls, and they are more startling than Niagara."

But from the very first preview, it was obvious that Anna and Ziegfeld had surmounted their *Mam'selle Napoleon* and *Higgledy-Piggledy* problems and produced a potential blockbuster. The Philadelphia opening played to a turn-away crowd, and Anna was brought out for repeated curtain calls after each act. Those curtain calls were carefully monitored by the star. If the applause began to die down after her sixth appearance, Anna would bump into the curtain, waiting to see if that visible jostling brought more expectant applause. If so, she'd step out for another bow. If silence or the sound of people rustling their hats and programs was heard, she would retire to her dressing room.

"Why go to Paris when Mr. Florenz Ziegfeld will bring Paris to you?" asked one paper. Another raved, "The show went with a spirit that never lagged. . . . Nothing so gorgeous as *The Parisian Model* has probably ever been presented by a traveling theatrical company." It played to standing-room-only crowds during its Philadelphia run, and tickets for future cities sold out within hours of being offered. "I Just Can't Make My Eyes Behave" became an instant hit and was encored repeatedly (new verses had to be hastily written for future performances). As the pre-opening tour got up steam, Anna complained wearily about the trains. Seeing the American countryside was no longer a novelty to her, and the inconveniences seemed all the more annoying. "It is so dirty, these trains," she groused to a reporter as she awaited a connection. "They have so much smoke, and one does not sleep, because the portier [*sic*] will close the windows and conspire with the engine-man to have all the heat. The scenery rolls by sometimes when you can see it and at other times the smoke is all over." Hardheaded businesswoman that she was, though, Anna sighed, "Yet one must go from place to place for the dollars—non?" So the tour ground on.

Still, Anna ran a happy and contented troupe. Not all stars were appreciated by their chorus girls, and vice versa. But Anna poured all the motherly affection into her cast that she never wasted on her daughter. The "Anna Held Girls," as they were known, were better paid and better dressed than the casts of other Broadway shows. Additionally, the *Cleveland News* noted, "Miss Held is reputed to be very liberal in giving her subordinates a chance. Any symptom of talent is said to be rewarded with an early opportunity for development. More chorus girls have graduated to speaking parts from Held companies than from those of any other star, according to all accounts." The contented and well-trained girls in *The Parisian Model* also got good notices, which reflected well on the show as a whole. "Each girl seems to take a special interest in her work and to feel as if the burden of the entertainment was on her shoulders and it was her duty to make the piece a success," read a typical review. "The fact that Mr. Ziegfeld can maintain such enthusiasm among his people speaks volumes for his sagacity and tact."

Anna simply had little professional jealousy, unless someone like Marie Dressler actually strolled in to steal a scene out from under her. Anna knew she was not a great beauty or a brilliant talent, but she was secure in the knowledge that she excelled in her particular niche. She surrounded herself with talented casts, as she knew that would make the show—and her—look better. She sought out lovely showgirls, in particular, because she felt safe that none of them was about to steal her career: Anna, at barely five feet one inch, picked the tallest girls she could find, setting herself off like a tiny flower amongst the mighty oaks.

All her lies were bound to catch up with her sooner or later. Not so much the prevarications about her birth (many actresses stretched the truth a bit when it came to hometowns and birth dates), but press stories about Anna's milk baths, runaway horse rescues, kissing contests, and automobile races had earned her a reputation as someone whose word was not to be taken seriously. This all blew up in her face in October 1906 during out-of-town tryouts for *The Parisian Model*. Anna was the victim of a bizarre crime that not only made her a laughingstock but also severely shook her marriage for the second time in less than a year.

On October 21 she and Ziegfeld—along with the rest of the company—were en route from Baltimore to Cleveland, where they were booked to play the Opera House. Before they left Baltimore, a man approached company members Libby Diamond and Claudie Rogers and asked if Anna Held were traveling on the train. Thinking him a star-struck fan, they told him she was. Anna and Ziegfeld ate in the dining car that night, locking their stateroom. In that room was a small satchel, wrapped in a blanket, containing Anna's jewels and a large amount of cash. Estimates of the value ranged wildly as the story spread: anywhere from $120,000 to $297,000. Pullman porter Edward Ridgely had tried to help Ziegfeld with the bag, but he'd pulled away nervously; Ridgely assumed the couple was sneaking one of Anna's now-famous lapdogs into their compartment and backed off. Ziegfeld and Anna retired to bed around ten o'clock that night.

On the morning of October 22, they dressed, checked on the bag, and went into the next compartment to chat with company members. Ziegfeld later said that a large, gray-haired, middle-aged man came into the car, blocking his view of the door to their own compartment. When the train stopped at the Euclid Avenue station, he was seen getting off with a "small, ferret-looking" man. Shortly thereafter Anna got up and went into her compartment: Her satchel was missing. By the time they'd arrived at their Cleveland stop, Anna was in a state of hysterics, a lifetime collection of jewels gone. She wore the larger and more sparkling pieces as part of her act, the smaller ones to dinners and interviews. Ziegfeld contacted Opera House manager Kingston who, oddly, called Cleveland's mayor. Mayor Johnson sensibly suggested they notify the police. Ziegfeld and Kingston led a sobbing Anna to the police station, where Chief Kohler took her statement and tried to hold off reporters (Ziegfeld had made a few other calls as well).

Right off the bat everyone assumed it was all a publicity stunt. Kohler assigned a bunco squad man to the case, intending to prosecute if it turned out that Ziegfeld was using his police force to promote *The Parisian Model.* Inspector Rowe and Sergeant Doran were brought in to hear Anna's story, and within a few hours were convinced that she, at least, was being painfully up-front. Crying hysterically, she managed to piteously choke out, "All these years that I have worked, oh, so hard. All my savings gone, everything I had was in that bag. . . . How shall I ever live again? I've done my possible all my life, but now I feel that I can never play again. Mon Dieu!"

It took Ziegfeld and Kingston an hour to convince Anna to go on that night, sans jewels. She had no understudy, and her professionalism forbade her from closing the theater. She somehow managed to get through the show, then was led back to her hotel and sedated. "We have had no sleep," said Ziegfeld, "but she'll surely go on with her part."

Newspapers the next day were far from sympathetic, still smelling a rat. "Anna will find ample compensation for her 'jules' in the sympathy of her audience this week," said one, "and if her hubby wants to cheer her up he should flash the box-office receipts before her eyes." In an (unsuccessful) attempt to get her name into the papers, a chorus girl at a competing show claimed to have found the jewels. Even Chief Kohler still sounded somewhat dubious. "I am really at sea on this proposition," he said, obviously bewildered by the crush of reporters and wildly emotional show folk. "It is no more than natural that we should be suspicious of press agents' diamond robbery tales. This little woman, however, appears to be sincere. She certainly did weep real tears, and I firmly believe that her emotion is genuine. That the satchel was on the train I am positive, and that it is missing at this time, I am convinced." Kohler later added, "Whether it contained five cents or $200,000 I cannot say and do not know."

The police were overheard to marvel at Anna's acting skills and to half-admire the audacity of the stunt, which only prompted a fresh burst of tears. "I am sleepless, I am near insane," Anna told the assembled reporters the next day. Her Philadelphia attorney, S.L. Shields, offered a reward of $11,800 for the jewels and cash, no questions asked. Theater manager Kingston blamed the Pullman company for not providing better protection. A list was released of the missing items, which included both French and U.S. currency, checkbooks, life-insurance policies, and keys, along with thirty-six pieces of jewelry, the most impressive being a diamond and emerald "corsage piece"; a diamond, pearl, and ruby necklace; a diamond and pearl dog collar; a brooch of four pear-shaped diamonds with a ruby in the center; a pearl elephant with diamond feet (Ziegfeld was a lifelong collector of elephants); and a sapphire and diamond-encrusted purse.

"They were rare trinkets," said Ziegfeld, "and Miss Held so loves her jewels. It is pain for her to appear on the stage without rings and bracelets and necklaces." "It is!" Anna pathetically squeaked from behind her husband, breaking anew into sobs. Angrily denying rumors of a stunt, Ziegfeld insisted, "It is nonsense. We don't have to stoop to such things. Look at Miss Held—that ought to tell you whether it is true or not," he finished, gesturing toward his sniffling, red-eyed wife.

Days passed without much being accomplished, though police sent out agents to various cities in pursuit of the mysterious ferret-faced man and the gray-haired man. Anna went on with her show, bitterly complaining that if the Cleveland police had spent more time pursuing the criminals and less time questioning her veracity, her property might have been recovered by now. Her hopes were raised on October 31 when a reporter stopped her to say that the thieves had been caught in Toledo. "Merci, can it be true?" she asked the bearer of good news. "Oh, I hope so, I hope so! Only a short time ago the detectives told me they would arrest the men, and bid me be calm and cheerful. I have tried to be patient, but it is so hard." Having tricked her into this personal interview, the reporter rushed back to his paper. The harshest jab came that same week, when the *Cleveland Press* published an amusing little poem in her honor:

> Tell us, Anna, tell us truly, was it all a little fake?
> Have you, honest, wept so madly? Is your heart about to break?
> Did you really split your corsage with the sobs you loudly sobbed?
> Was it advertising, Anna, when you told us you were robbed?
>
> It was clever, Anna, clever, even though it wasn't new
> Many other folks have tried it, but the mustard's all to you
> In a thousand daily papers on the front page up it bobbed
> Was it advertising, Anna, when you told us you were robbed?
>
> Anna, if you dare to find those diamonds Monday a week,
> Don't you smile at us, we won't care to stop and speak
> For we'll know you bluffed us badly when the Opera House we mobbed
> Was it advertising, Anna, when you told us you were robbed?

Anna got on with the tour, and on with her career, as hope slowly faded for her property's recovery. The worst part was being laughed at: Genuinely shaken by the invasion of her stateroom and the specter of poverty—as well as the loss of some treasured objects—Anna felt slapped in the face by the cynical lack of sympathy shown to her. Her relationship with the press was never as open and jovial as it had been before this incident.

The great jewel robbery episode was finally wrapped up at the end of November 1906, shortly before *The Parisian Model* opened in New York. Anna was reported to have recovered her jewels—though not the cash—through some mysterious agreement with the thieves. The details were never made public, but Anna's daughter later wrote a revealing version in her unpublished memoirs of the 1930s. According to Liane, Ziegfeld told Anna that he'd received a message to reserve two adjoining rooms in a hotel. He was to put a large amount of cash in one room and sit in the other for two hours; he would be covered at gunpoint the whole time. At the end of the two hours, Ziegfeld found the cash gone and a baggage-claim check in its place. In the hotel checkroom he found a brand-new satchel containing all of Anna's missing jewels. The stolen money and the ransom were gone for good.

According to Liane, Anna didn't know whether to believe this melodramatic tale or not; it sounded suspiciously like the plot of too many Broadway shows. "She was never quite satisfied with Flo's explanation," said Liane, "and she suspected that there was more to it than he admitted." True, Liane resented Ziegfeld and would do anything to blacken his name. But it's also true that this story is too convenient to be believed. Why would thieves who have gotten away scot-free return Anna's jewels, which could be broken up and sold for huge amounts of money? And why were the police not involved in the recovery?

Ziegfeld was in desperate need of cash in late 1906, and had never scrupled to promote the most outrageous stunts. While the theft was given a huge amount of newspaper space, Ziegfeld made sure that the jewels' recovery received as little public notice as was possible. Was Anna made an unwitting accomplice to fraud and the theft of her own jewels? Did Ziegfeld have a change of heart after seeing her genuine distress and backtrack, coming up with this transparent way to not only "retrieve" her jewels but also wangle the ransom money from her? Of course Liane's version of events must also be questioned closely. When her rewritten memoirs were published in the 1950s, her story had changed, using dates and amounts of money that are clearly contradicted by newspaper reports. Anna never mentioned the jewel robbery in public again, but from late 1906 one more wedge of distrust and suspicion was thrust between her and her husband.

The Parisian Model spent much of November in Chicago, where Anna and Ziegfeld had a nice long visit with his parents. Anna had always gotten along famously with her in-laws, who became the only parental figures she had. She was especially fond of her mother-in-law, Rosalie, who had been born in France. The elder Mrs. Ziegfeld was thrilled to have a daughter-in-law who was anxious to trade recipes and housekeeping tips and who was an old-fashioned European cook and hostess. But with Anna on the road and Ziegfeld Sr. busy with his college, Anna rarely had time to see the couple.

Florenz Ziegfeld Sr. gave his daughter-in-law the nicest gift possible at this difficult time by inviting her to lecture on acting at his Chicago Musical College. As nervous as she was about addressing a serious crowd of hopeful performers, Anna was thrilled at being considered professional and intelligent enough to give these students good, useful advice on their careers. After being made such sport of in Cleveland, Anna took her lecturing duties very seriously. She rose to the occasion brilliantly, speaking off-the-cuff in a "terse, sensible, matter of fact way," according to one member of the crowd. She admitted to the students that she suffered from stage fright, adding that "unless one suffered from this nervousness one could not do conscientious work in the presence of the public," and that "nervousness was not only an index to good work but an absolute necessity." The reporter in attendance added that Anna said her own performance was affected by the mood of the crowd, and that "if the audience was cold it would always take her at least 15 minutes to get into the part she was playing, but if the audience was sympathetic and responsive, she could, as it were, jump into the part immediately."

Anna told the students the importance of punctuality (thinking, no doubt, about Charles Bigelow) and referred to the stage as a club akin to a fraternity, where gossip is rife and a bad reputation spreads quickly. There was no excuse, she emphasized, for ever giving a weak or lackluster performance, no matter how few people were in the house. "The poor little fellow who has saved his 25 cents and has spent it for a seat in the second gallery that he may see my performance is of just as much importance to me during the performances as are the more fashionable and richer people who sit in the boxes. Indeed, the little fellow deserves the greater consideration, because he cannot afford to spend 25 cents as well as the others can two dollars."

The aspiring actors and musicians got more practical help from Anna in that one day than they could have from a year of more esoteric lectures, and much of her advice holds just as true today as it did in 1906. "If you feel you have a specialty," she said, "such as singing or dancing, develop it. If you find that your forte is comedy or tragedy, devote your attention to that to which you feel you are best fitted. At all times show your true self to your instructor. Do not be artificial in his presence. The more natural you are with him the better able he will be to feel and estimate your personality, and the better will be the result of your instruction."

Asked about the importance of beauty versus talent, Anna admitted that her own plays were sometimes dismissed as girlie pageants, but said that she herself would rather employ a plain but talented chorus girl than a vacuous beauty. She spoke of hours before her mirror rehearsing, "rounding off the rough edges of expression, so that there might be nothing to displease anybody. . . . Do not make a gesture unless you absolutely feel it and imagine that it is necessary." Anticipating the acting style of certain screen stars, Anna advised, "Always watch your facial expression and when you feel that you must cry on the stage, cry beautifully. Never make a facial expression which is not pretty. Avoid making grimaces."

Whatever one may think of Anna's appearance-conscious acting tips, it is obvious that she devoted deep thought and hard work to her profession. For once, a lecture hall full of serious students was paying great attention to her: not to her legs or her rolling eyes but to her thoughts. Thanks to her father-in-law, Anna's spirits revived somewhat on this trying tour. She still managed to leave Chicago under a cloud of bad press, though, with a trail of unpaid bills behind her. Marshall Field and Company sued Anna for thirty-five hundred dollars worth of hats and lingerie, for which she'd neglected to pay. The litigious Ziegfeld in turn sued them for defamation of character to the tune of fifty thousand dollars. It was all settled out of court.

Anna's stopover in Detroit was marred by more silly press-agentry: Ziegfeld's minions released a story to the press that Anna had toured the local insane asylum, "where people with plaster loose in their garrets are sheltered and safeguarded." An already old joke was revived with Anna as the straight woman. She was conversing, it was said, with an apparently sane inmate. When she departed, the man asked her to shake hands carefully as he was made of glass. (The same tired story resurfaced sixty-six years later in comedienne Beatrice Lillie's autobiography, only this time the gentleman in question had a "glass ass.") After her experience in Cleveland, Anna had little patience left for this kind of story, and asked Ziegfeld that his staff tone down their efforts for a time.

The Parisian Model company landed back in New York in late November, stopping off in Syracuse to pick up the two-year-old baby of one of the chorus girls, to the oohs and ahs of the more maternal in the company. By this time it was obvious that the show was to be an even bigger hit than *Papa's Wife* and *The Little Duchess* had been. Chicago's Amy Leslie had, of course, given it the full treatment. Anna was "more delicately lovely, chic and special than ever. . . . It is a noisy, brilliant, dazzling, and tuneful romp, all whirls of dance, melody, and revolving pictures." There were continued squeaks of alarm from the easily shocked, such as the indignant Chicago critic who wrote of Anna, "I have never heard anyone say during the whole time she has been foisting her vulgarities upon the stage that he liked her."

The Parisian Model opened at the Broadway Theater on November 27, 1906, with Anna's friend Lillian Russell in attendance (Russell had the night off from her own first nonmusical play, *Barbara's Millions*). Built in 1888 on the corner of Broadway and Forty-first Street, the theater was an impressive brick and brownstone structure that had housed such respectable dramas as *Little Lord Fauntleroy*,

Edwin Booth's *Hamlet,* and the biblical hit *Ben-Hur. The Parisian Model* must have shaken it to its foundations.

As at all openings, Ziegfeld stood backstage, unnervingly calm amid all the frenzy. Cast members rushed to and from their dressing rooms, prop men shifted scenery, lighting crews scurried around the catwalks, but Ziegfeld stood "as if he were alone in the theater," according to Eddie Cantor. Everyone else wore evening clothes, but Ziegfeld was comfortably attired in day wear. For someone known for producing high-fashion shows, he dressed appallingly, often wearing brown shoes with a gray suit, an unlit cigar clamped between his teeth (though no one but Anna and his valet knew it, Ziegfeld also wore pink silk-and-wool long johns, day and night). During intermission he would slip into the box office to see how receipts were piling up and would make sure a box of flowers was delivered to every chorus girl and a letter or telegram to every principal cast member.

A night or two before the opening, Anna had professed herself to be nervous; it had been a full five years since she'd opened in a hit. "I do not know how I am to be received," she charmingly admitted to the New York press. "I have been away, and perhaps I am forgotten. I take a great interest in my work and I want to please, and I am afraid I will not. But everybody has been charming to me. They say all kinds of nice things about me—that I am prettier than ever, that I sing better, that I act better." If she was fishing for compliments, it worked: People did say all kinds of nice things about Anna when the show opened in New York. Archie Bell admitted that yes, the show was "naughty— real Parisian naughty, in spots. . . . But nobody fainted. Nobody was shocked. Everyone enjoyed it thoroughly. . . . The whole show is a giddy vaudeville. Don't miss it."

Not only Anna, but everyone in the show, got good notices. The chorus line "makes all of Constantinople look like 30 cents," Gertrude Hoffmann was called out for several encores, a number of songs were called potential hits, and the extravagant costumes and sets were applauded on sight. The troublesome Charles Bigelow made a hit, one reviewer saying, "His clever work is adding new laurels to his already excellent reputation as a comedian." Even the frequent falls during the skating number were as appreciated and cheered as much as perfection would have been—perhaps more so.

Except for the complaints about the show's raciness, there was not one discouraging word. The show was not great art or drama; it was a silly, enjoyable, and brainless evening at the theater. One New York reviewer summed up audiences' popular opinion by saying *The Parisian Model* was "dazzling with costumes, a riot of color effect, and with the finest collection of showgirls we have ever seen. While the piece is very Frenchy, it is still Americanized enough to make it wholesome from start to finish." Writer W.E. Anderson, while feeling more strongly how risqué the show was, called it "a new epoch in American musical comedy."

As for Anna herself, she was crowned "the past-mistress of the art of depicting delicate, languorous wickedness." Irving Lewis wrote, "She delights with her smiles and her dances, her roguishness and her alluring style; she is wonderfully pretty, bewitching; a Lorelei set to music—oh, you can think of many adjectives to apply." But along with the praise came some hints that Anna was no longer the cherished new darling on the block. She had been a star for nearly a decade now and had begun to slip into some hardened mannerisms, which her public found endearing and her critics annoying. There was her renowned eye-rolling, of course. And her singing voice was variously described as "insinuating" and "nasal."

Then there was the Anna Held walk. Now lost to posterity, it was described by one impatient critic as "sort of a half-stooping walk, suggesting the indolence of lotus-land and the grace of the Parisienne. There are times when you feel that you should like to see her straighten up into a normal position just once—to rest and take a fresh breath for further exertion, but Miss Held recognizes the full stage value of that walk, and never does she relax the position." Anna was even spotted in her loping stroll with Ziegfeld outside the theater, indicating it may have been due more to high heels than any stage presence.

Anna's posturing and posing struck many as too calculated and precious, though in the days of Delsarte acting, Anna was—if anything—refreshingly natural. This outmoded school, popularized by French acting coach François Delsarte, taught specific poses, expressions, and postures to telegraph emotions. Acting books showed models registering "hope," "horror," "coquetry," and other poses. Talented performers were able to use this to their advantage as a launching pad, but amateurs and less-gifted professionals soon made such stilted methods a laughingstock.

Anna did "pose," but she did so with a dancer's grace. "There are few actresses of the day who understand as well as she how to get the best possible results from any given pose," said one New England critic. "Again and again she makes a posture of herself that an artist would be only too glad to paint could he have the opportunity." Admitting that these poses were studied and inherently fake, the writer went on to add that "they appear for the moment so natural and unaffected as the limelight strikes the figure of the star that the playgoer goes away with the impression of a picture gallery full of beautiful portraits."

Ziegfeld himself warned Anna against becoming a caricature of herself. She told one reporter Ziegfeld often said to her, "'Do you not think you are a little broad? Do you not think you could modify some things a little bit?' I always reply, 'When *I* do things they are chic—they are different—they are— Anna Held! If I modify myself, what will I be? Nobody! The same as hundreds of others!'" The crowds of stage-door Johnnies and gallery girls outside the theater door every night, the curtain calls, the flowers tossed onto the stage (many of them actually not paid for by Ziegfeld), the full houses, assured Anna that all was forgiven and she was again the queen of Broadway musicals. *The Parisian Model* broke all house records at the Broadway Theater, taking in $2945.75 in a single night.

Determined to advertise the show's success in whatever way he could, Ziegfeld ordered a huge electric sign to be placed outside the theater. By 1906 the recently renamed Times Square area was already becoming the Great White Way, with sparkling electric signs lighting up the night. Maxine Elliot was actually the first actress to have her name in lights, over her eponymous theater. The *Florodora* Girls of 1900 were depicted in a clever moving electric sign, dancing outside the Casino Theater. Anna's contribution was to be a set of huge electric-bulb eyes, which were supposed to roll engagingly.

It took till Thanksgiving to set the sign up, but the eyes kept shorting out instead of rolling; sometimes one would work and not the other, resulting in giant crossed eyes atop the marquee. "Have you seen those misbehaving goo-goos?" laughed one paper. An electrician, trying to rewire the sign, fell off his ladder, bringing down with him a tangle of wires and bulbs. The sign was put back up but never really worked right. By December 14 it was finally taken down in disgrace.

On December 2, 1906, the *New York World* and the Reverend Dr. Madison J. Peters inadvertently threw Anna another publicity bouquet. After seeing *The Parisian Model,* Peters dashed off a two-page editorial that was nearly incoherent with rage. First getting up steam for a few paragraphs discussing how elevating the stage should and could be, the good reverend got down to business: "I believe if the Bowery so transgressed public morals by presenting such a travesty on decency, the police would step in to preserve the public from such contamination." Latching onto the popular "La Mattchiche" number, he thundered, "[Anna's] lascivious contortions and advances towards her partner in the convolutions of decency are worthy of Coney Island in its palmiest day." Had Peters realized that Anna's partner was actually Gertrude Hoffmann in male drag, he no doubt would have added a few more choice words to his condemnation.

The popularity of the play, Peters sighed, "is confirmation strong and proof of Holy Writs that New York is becoming more wickedly Parisian than Paris." Leaving the play behind, he got quite personal about Anna, complaining that she "gets her money by pandering to the animalized and depraved passions of a sin-slaved public." He quoted a rather cute line from the show ("I was a good girl for 20 francs a week; now I am going to be good for nothing!") and declared that Anna was in fact "good for bad, a potent force for moral corruption." It's hard to believe that the Reverend Peters didn't realize what great advertisements such phrases as "mind-corrupting, soul destroying pollution" and "lewdness, ribaldry and indecency" were for the box office. The newspapers all thought this was hilarious and gave him full play; Ziegfeld must have been tempted to add Peters to his payroll.

Peters wasn't the only New Yorker who felt that both Anna and her show overstepped the bounds of decency. "The play cannot be said to smell vilely," another critic wrote, "but it exudes an unpleasant odor as of excessive perfumes." It was also noted with some alarm that other Broadway shows began inserting spicy jokes in order to keep pace with *The Parisian Model*. Anna had little patience for such prudery, having cut her teeth in the French music halls. "Every country has its own ideas and appreciations," she said when this latest scandal broke. Casting herself patriotically with her new homeland, she continued, "You see, we over here in America are young, and they over there in France are old. The French people, especially the people in Paris, have had so much longer to get used to things. . . . America is much more prudish, but I think it improves every year—yes, every month! It is youth, and youth is ever a beautiful thing— also it is a fault from which we all too soon must recover."

Anna shocked in the same way that Mae West did a generation later: She laughed at sex. This infuriated people who felt that sex, love, and the family were no laughing matters. The characters Anna portrayed were not serious Ibsen heroines or the nice Salvation Army lasses and good little shopgirls of other musicals. They were actresses, models, lighthearted adventuresses who delighted in flirtation, could meet their leading men kiss for kiss, and winked knowingly at the conventions of the day. Like West, Anna subverted the sex roles and often took the lead. Even when she played innocents, they were faux innocents, ready and willing to be led into the world of the demimonde. Most musical comedy actresses of the day were broad and sexless: Marie Dressler, Marie Cahill, May Irwin. The prettier ones were petite and ladylike (Edna May, Elsie Janis). The only actresses to bring anywhere near the sexual electricity as Anna did to the American stage were Fritzi Scheff, Fay Templeton, Fannie Ward, and the up-and-coming vaudevillian Eva Tanguay.

Tired businessmen, college boys, and society matrons attended Anna's shows in droves, true. But the majority of her fans were actually middle-class housewives. One particularly perceptive writer noted the release Anna provided for these lonely, "unliberated" women across the country: "Slaving away their lives within the narrow confines of virtue, whether at afternoon bridge parties or over the kitchen stove, they long to gaze, just once a season, on vice, when it is well dressed and glitters. . . . Then they return to their homes tingling with the sights and sounds of the dazzling, whirling world, and settle down in loving faithfulness to the prosaic duties of their own unspangled lives."

The Parisian Model continued selling out every performance. Anna capitalized on one of the most popular numbers by giving a roller-skating party at the Metropolitan Roller Rink on December 8. Inviting her own company and the cast of *The Belle of Mayfair,* Anna professed to enjoy her skating finale, calling it "the grandest of sports. . . . It is a healthy pastime. Of course, it may be hard at first. We all have our troubles when we begin. I had quite a fall when I first tried to glide."

Like most of Anna's shows, *The Parisian Model* was so loosely constructed that tossing in a new musical number every month or two merely freshened up the mix without disturbing the minimal plot. During the show's two hundredth performance, on February 27, 1907, the song "Won't You Be My Teddy Bear?" (no relation to the Elvis Presley hit of the 1950s) was added. Capitalizing on the Theodore Roosevelt teddy bear craze, the number featured six chorus girl astride fake bears, as well as two small children attired as tiny teddies. The number scored another hit and was published as cowritten by Anna herself (this was a common ploy at the time; writers often agreed to share credit with stars to help get their own work published). In an ill-conceived ploy for publicity, Ziegfeld sent out postcards of Anna leading the child "bear cubs" in a kind of conga line, with a tagline about her having a "little bear behind." This tribute from a husband to his wife most definitely crossed the line of early-twentieth-century decency.

"The card is so brilliant an example of execrable taste that it cannot pass unnoticed," read one typical editorial. "Applied to a prominent actress, or any woman, for that matter, it is not exactly the sort of literature one would ordinarily circulate with the expectation of enhancing her dignity, even in an East Side burlesque theater." Ziegfeld admitted his overzealousness, apologized, and withdrew the offending cards. Still the teddy bear number remained, one of the new hits of the show. A fan sent Anna a mechanized teddy bear doll possessing eyes that, when its front paw was squeezed, lit up with little red bulbs. Anna encountered William Gould walking his dog outside the theater one night and squeezed the bear's paw as a greeting. Gould's dog went ballistic and tore the bear to shreds. "I always knew he was a bulldog," said Gould proudly, "but I never knew he was a bear dog." Whether the story was true or simply more publicity fluff, it kept Anna and *The Parisian Model's* new number in the public eye.

Up till this point in their careers, Florenz Ziegfeld was merely a dim satellite of Anna Held. His name was still misspelled in the press as often as not, and when he was mentioned, it was always as the husband and manager of New York's brightest star. She appeared on the cover of theater magazines and sheet music, on postcards and cigar bands. She couldn't walk down the street or into a restaurant without being mobbed. Ziegfeld, if he was noticed at all, was seen only in the reflected glare of her light. But in the summer of 1907, Ziegfeld took the first step that would skyrocket him to his own brand of fame, one outlasting that of Anna.

The *Ziegfeld Follies* were, everyone agrees, Anna Held's idea. None of his shows had been great successes unless they starred his wife. *The Red Feather* had been his last non-Held production, back in 1903. With the success of *The Parisian Model* assured for the next year or two, Ziegfeld wanted to break free and try something new. Anna knew theater: It had been her whole life. She knew what drew audiences and she knew the sort of dazzling, mindless spectacle at which her husband excelled. So she suggested an American version of Paris's popular Folies-Bergère: part girlie show, part fashion show, with some comedy thrown in.

Ziegfeld saw the genius in her plan. There had been such variety shows before, but not with what would soon be known as "the Ziegfeld Touch." He began choosing the most beautiful chorus girls in New York for his *Follies of 1907* (he didn't dub them *Ziegfeld Follies* until 1911). In the Broadway Theater, Ziegfeld, Anna, coproducer A.E. Erlanger, and financial advisor Jerry Siegel sat and watched hopeful showgirls parade up and down the stage, judging their good and bad qualities and stage presence. It was decided to dub the chorus the Anna Held Girls.

Ziegfeld rented the rooftop garden of the New York Theater, which he elegantly renamed the Jardin de Paris. This was to be the *Follies'* home for its first five seasons. The name *Follies* was, it turns out, lifted from Ziegfeld's ex-partner Joe Weber, who had imported the *London Follies* to New York in 1906 (there were still some hard feelings, and Weber did not take this larceny with good humor). Ziegfeld's first *Follies* opened on June 8, 1907 at the Jardin de Paris, with Anna in attendance. This first show gave little indication of what a phenomenon the *Follies* would become over the next twenty years. Only one of the comics or singers featured gained lasting fame: the great Nora Bayes. The rest of them (Harry Watson Jr., George Bickel, Grace Leigh, Mlle Dazie, May Leslie) have pretty much faded from history. The only one of these first Anna Held Girls to go on to fame was Helen Broderick, who later became a successful character actress and the mother of actor Broderick Crawford.

The rooftop Jardin de Paris did not live up to its swanky name. The stage was small and shallow, so, Ziegfeld recalled, "we spilled our attractions a good deal over the theater. This was something of an innovation then and was much commented upon." Later *Follies* star Eddie Cantor added that "it was unbearably hot on the roof, particularly as the theater had a glass dome which intensified the rays from the sun like a lens." When it rained, the dome leaked. Still, Ziegfeld found himself with a nice little hit on his hands (perhaps because there was very little competition in the summer, when most shows had closed down or gone on tour). The first-night reviews were promising: "Mr. Florenz Ziegfeld, Jr., has given New York quite the best mélange of mirth, music, and pretty young women that has been seen here in many a summer," read one. "There is not a dull moment in the entire show." The first *Follies* cost $13,800 to stage and $3800 a week to run; it wound up with a profit of $120,000. Ziegfeld already saw his 1907–08 season laid out before him. The phenomenally successful *The Parisian Model* would be good for at least one more season, and his new *Follies* was enough of a hit to try again the next year as well.

While Ziegfeld was preparing his *Follies,* Anna continued her unprecedented run of *The Parisian Model* in New York. The show was doing such good business that it never went out on tour that spring but stayed at the Broadway Theater through early July, a record-breaking thirty-three weeks. All was not running smoothly with the show, however. There was continuing trouble with Charles Bigelow, for one thing. Playwright Harry B. Smith recalled that at one performance during the Chicago tryouts, the actor didn't show up onstage for his cue. "Finally he was discovered in a adjacent barroom," Smith wrote, "buying liquid refreshment for all comers and causing much innocent merriment, as he was dressed as a ballet girl, and with his bald head and bulbous nose would have made the Sphinx laugh." He didn't make Anna Held laugh, though. She ran a tight ship and this kind of behavior infuriated her.

It all blew up on June 21. Bigelow had signed a contract with Ziegfeld's enemies the Shuberts, which he hoped would advance him from character player to star. As he stood backstage, Anna brushed past him and snarled, "You couldn't become a star if you stayed in the business 5,000 years." The two then took their quarrel onstage. After Bigelow's comic yodeling song, Anna's character remarked, "Grand opera for yours," to which he replied, "Yes, at the Dewey." Dropping her character, Anna cracked, "And with the Shuberts next season."

This was actually pretty clever and fit into the real dialogue so well that the audience didn't notice anything amiss. But Bigelow stormed offstage, removed his makeup, and left the theater. His understudy, Clyde McKinley, took over for the third act. By the time he woke up the next day, Bigelow realized what a hideous mistake he'd made and called his lawyer, Henry Staton, to help him salvage his career. "Tell him to come around and see me at noon tomorrow," Ziegfeld told Staton. The three met the next day, along with the Broadway Theater manager, Sandy Dingwall. Anna, still fuming, stayed home. Bigelow apologized profusely. "I made a mistake, I know," he pleaded. "I am willing to go back on the job." "That may go for Ziegfeld, but it don't for me," replied Dingwall. "It will take more conversation than that to get my consent! How are you going to excuse your conduct to your audience? You know they paid $2 to see the regular cast, and you arbitrarily make them accept an understudy."

As the show only had a short time left to run, Bigelow was dropped from the cast and replaced by McKinley. When *The Parisian Model* reopened the next season, his role would be played by Otis Harlan, a comedian broad in both physique and technique. Bigelow took his case to the press. "I left because I was not treated as a gentleman should be treated, because I was not accorded the ordinary professional courtesy that anyone on the stage has the right to expect." Anna, he added, "treated me in such a mean manner that I could endure it no longer." This came as a shock to everyone who'd worked with her; Anna was well known as one of the most democratic and easygoing of stars. When *The Parisian Model*'s first season ended, Anna felt that she'd seen the last of Charles Bigelow, but the two were to cross paths again.

Anna turned down an eight-week vaudeville offer so she could rest up over the summer of 1907; she also sent her regrets to an auto hill-climbing contest to be held in Wilkes-Barre, Pennsylvania. She had wanted to return to Europe in May, as usual, but her contract kept her with *The Parisian Model* until July. When the show's first season closed, it was announced that *The Parisian Model* had scored the biggest financial success of any musical starring a woman in the recorded history of theater. Despite some publicity mishaps (or perhaps because of them), Anna had made a comeback of unprecedented proportions.

She spent only two months in Paris during the summer of 1907, as Ziegfeld wanted to open *The Parisian Model*'s second season in September rather than the usual late October. Anna traveled with her friends Mr. and Mrs. Frank McKee, paid a flying visit to Liane, and made a charity appearance in Trouville, singing her old hit, "Won't You Come and Play with Me?" Her return to the United States on September 9 was marred by a dustup at customs. After Anna disembarked from the *Kronprinzessin Ceclie*, her twelve trunks were held for duties;

foreigners were not allowed to bring that many trunks into the United States. Anna claimed citizenship through her marriage to Ziegfeld but, of course, had no marriage certificate to show. "I was never so treated in all my life," she sputtered indignantly. "Here I have been crossing the Atlantic for ah! many years, and never before were my trunks held up."

It took several days for Anna's luggage to reach the Ansonia, and not a moment too soon. They contained dazzling new frocks for *The Parisian Model*, scented fans (orange blossom for her white fan, forget-me-not for her blue, and so on), and her shoes, carefully packed by Beatrice in Spanish leather. There was also a Russian sable coat that received more publicity than her own daughter had up to this time. The floor-length cloak, which cost twenty-five thousand dollars, was made of 110 skins, designed kimono-style; the white satin lining was embroidered with pale blue wisterias. "I was simply crazy for it," said Anna, "but I really don't know why I bought it. I have never had occasion to wear it. About the only place one could use it would be in an open carriage. It is too expensive for an automobile." The cloak did not go to waste, though; Anna dragged it to the photographer's studio and posed happily draped in it.

The Parisian Model reopened on September 30, 1907. The show did extremely well in its second season, outdrawing nearly every other musical comedy (Anna's box-office receipts never dropped below thirteen thousand dollars). Only the Franz Lehar operetta *The Merry Widow* made a bigger impact on Broadway. That show, with its timeless, lilting waltz, was the inspiration for hundreds of lesser operettas over the next two decades. Broadway was soon swamped with mittel-European schmaltz, baritone Cossacks, soprano princesses in distress, and choruses of comely peasant girls. From Anna's viewpoint, *The Merry Widow* was notable mostly for introducing the Merry Widow hat, a huge wilting tea tray topped by ostrich plumes.

The Parisian Model also competed with Lew Fields's *The Girl Behind the Counter* and the all-black musical *Bandanna Land* in the 1907–08 season. But the biggest threat to its run was the nationwide financial panic that began in October. The Knickerbocker Trust company failed that month when it couldn't meet its depositors' checks, and runs on other banks followed. This currency panic— which was largely responsible for the formation of the Federal Reserve System in 1913—resulted in a business depression and a subsequent political shake-up. Banks and businesses throughout the country failed, and of course people did not spend as much on frivolities like the theater. Anna bizarrely blamed the whole crisis on free-spending American wives. "In no country in the world are women as careless of their money as they are here in the United States," she said, in an interview seemingly calculated to alienate her biggest fans. "The wives of the rich are living on planes today which would astonish the rulers of ages ago who were famed for their extravagance. . . . American women of only average means are gradually driving their husbands to desperation."

Despite the financial crisis and Anna's less than astute evaluation of it, *The Parisian Model* continued to do bang-up box office throughout the country (one reviewer suggested that the chorus girls' somewhat bedraggled costumes could have used a dry-cleaner by this point, though). The show went out on tour after only a month in New York, as more money could always be made on the road. Ziegfeld even used the panic as an excuse to brag: When *The Parisian Model* broke all records at the Olympic Theater in St. Louis during the first week of February, he placed an ad in a trade journal crowing, "STOP CRYING HARD TIMES—GET BUSY AND YOU WILL DO AS WELL AS ANNA HELD." They made more than twenty-one thousand dollars that week, despite a blizzard on February 4.

There were a few minor changes, including some new songs and costumes. Otis Harlan and the rehired Charles Bigelow alternated in the role of Silas Bullfinch, depending on Bigelow's delicate state of physical and emotional health. A "wonderful little Arab acrobat" named Tiutiu was added to the teddy bear number. A "Merry Widow Waltz"-type number was also incorporated, just as a little extra insurance. The biggest problem on tour turned out to be the popular roller-skating finale. The regional stages were smaller than that of the Broadway Theater, and many of them were bumpy and more steeply pitched toward the audience. It took a lot of rehearsal and athleticism to keep the chorus from rolling headlong into the orchestra pit.

Through the winter of 1907 and into the spring of 1908, Anna traveled her usual route through Boston, Cleveland, Cincinnati, Chicago, Detroit (where an old neighbor from Poland inconveniently gave interviews to the local press), and other points large and small. Boston proved to be rather unfriendly, its staid *Tribune* calling the show "stupid, vulgar and . . . swinish." Anna was also taken to task for her "ogling of the audience, her self-conscious and perpetual winding up of her thin skirts around her form, her feeble and tuneless singing, her drawling speech." The only kind word was for one of the children playing a teddy bear ("with genuine skill"). The same city's *Telegraph* also hated the show but noted with a sigh that "Bostonians are stumbling over one another in the clamor to take a chance of having their moral sense shocked." Bostonians stumbled over each other for three weeks, to the tune of forty-five thousand dollars. A Pittsburgh newspaper, the *Leader*, cooperated in a publicity stunt that had Anna "taking over" editorial duties for the December 12 issue. Snippets supposedly written by her on hairstyles, bridge, exercise, and recipes were printed, along with engaging photos of Anna cheerfully struggling with the Linotype machine, setting type, and preparing her copy (among her snippets was the startling news that "hatpins with little furry animal heads are to be worn this winter").

At the same time Anna was playing Pittsburgh, James O'Neill was enacting *The Count of Monte Cristo* and *Julius Caesar* for the highbrow set. The *Pittsburgh Gazette* noted that Anna beat out O'Neill every night at the box office. Annoyed at the *Leader's* scoop, perhaps, the *Gazette's* critic—who admitted he'd not even seen *The Parisian Model*—thundered, "Why should we pay to see in a theater what we wouldn't dare permit in the sacred privacy of our own homes?" He went on to "pity" the patrons who would go see such "evil and unclean sex passions."

Ziegfeld fired off an angry letter to the *Gazette*, pointing out quite rightly that "for a dramatic critic to write an advance notice of a show based on hearsay purely is certainly unjust," adding that the huge receipts indicted that the citizens of Pittsburgh begged to differ with his opinion. Not one to let Ziegfeld have the last word, the *Gazette's* critic shot back: "If Mr. Ziegfeld can justify the dance of Miss Held in the first act of *The Parisian Model*, of the spirit of the studio scene, with the accompanying song, before any audience of clean-minded American men and women, I will retract my criticism."

Things went much better for Anna in Cincinnati, where she was greeted with open arms not only by the public but by a much more sympathetic press. The *Examiner* compared her favorably with other, more respected, stars who were enjoying successes in Ibsen and Shaw plays. "The artist making a great deal out of this flippant airy nothingness of musical comedy does more than the player whose every detail has been outlined for him," said that paper's dramatic columnist. "Anybody who can make what she does out of *The Parisian Model* has initiative, talent, and tremendous individuality."

While in Washington, D.C., Anna got to meet President Theodore Roosevelt. Illinois senator Hopkins happened to be related to Maybelle Baker of *The Parisian Model* company, so the two women were treated to a private tour of the White House. Roosevelt, greeting Anna with his signature "dee-lighted!," told her, "I gave a little bear dinner here last night, but I suspect my guests would rather have been down at the theater to have seen you and your little bears."

Less happy was Anna's experience in Philadelphia, where she was felled by the flu and missed several performances. Running a high fever, she fainted in her dressing room and was confined to her room at the Hotel Majestic while Ziegfeld fretted and tens of thousands of dollars in advance business was lost. Her room was filled with violets and roses (the overpowering scent of which probably did nothing to speed her recovery), and it was two weeks before she was well enough to resume the tour. She was sufficiently recovered by New Year's Eve 1907 to attend a party with the casts of *The Parisian Model* and the 1907 *Follies,* whose tours intersected in Cleveland.

Ziegfeld, meanwhile, was busy overseeing the January 1908 opening of *The Soul Kiss* (sort of a combination of *Faust* and *Pygmalion*). This lavish musical starred British dancer Adeline Genée and enjoyed a respectable one-season run at the New York Theater. Anna returned to New York state in the spring to play in Brooklyn and Poughkeepsie, finally closing the show once and for all on May 23, 1908. Exhausted, Anna took off for a short break at the Maine cottage she and Ziegfeld still maintained. The two didn't get a chance to see much of each other that season, but their public image, at least, was still that of a contented couple. Montgomery Phister in the *Cincinnati Herald* wrote that "their intimates and those of their company report very favorably as to the blissful relations of the twain."

There were plans to bring *The Parisian Model* to London for the summer of 1908, but this fell through when a fire at the Drury Lane Theater rendered it uninhabitable. Charles Frohman later offered to take the show overseas, but by that time Ziegfeld was mired in his *Follies* commitments and turned the chance down. Anna was just as glad for the rest. She sailed on the *La Savoie* on May 28, looking forward to her first extended stay in London since her teenage years. She had not been feeling her best through the end of *The Parisian Model* tour, suffering from painful rheumatism in her shoulder. Ziegfeld had written to his lawyer, Charles Hanlon, in late April that "I have tried to persuade her to go to some sort of a cure or go fishing and get some good fresh air and a rest before going to those all-night cafes and gambling places of Europe. Of course she has got no sense and there is really no use talking to her." Fishing in the chill of Maine had no charms for Anna, and she felt that the warmth—both physical and emotional—of Europe would be much better for her pains.

She spent the summer in Paris and London without Ziegfeld, while he oversaw the 1908 *Follies,* which opened on June 15 and featured Nora Bayes singing "Shine On, Harvest Moon" with her husband Jack Norworth. That edition also featured what must have been a hugely entertaining number, with chorus girls dressed as "light-hearted mosquitos" emerging from the subway and singing about their commute from New Jersey ("we travel in bunches/we carry no lunches/for we find lots of food over here!").

Anna stayed in the Hotel Cecil London for a few weeks, then went to Paris to take care of some very pressing family business. On April 23, 1908, while Anna had been deep in her nationwide tour, Maximo Carrera had died of diabetes in his attic room at the Hôtel Gilet. The day that both Anna and Liane knew was coming had arrived—their shaky mother-daughter relationship was to be put to the test. Liane hardly knew her mother and was conflicted about the way she earned her princely living. With her strict religious upbringing, Liane later wrote, "I was made to understand that the stage was something bad. I was ashamed of any family connection with it. This feeling was so deeply instilled in me that perhaps it is one of the reasons I never gave my mother as much credit and admiration as she really deserved." In 1908 Liane was a bit of a prig. Socially awkward and incredibly naive for a fourteen-year-old, she also lacked the beauty and grace that might have won her mother over. Passing through a difficult stage, she was not a pretty teenager. Plump, with protruding eyes and a receding chin, she was not a prize for Anna to proudly show off.

For her part, Anna was a stranger to Liane. Worldly, beautiful, accomplished, and witty, she terrified the sheltered and self-conscious youngster. As warm as Anna was with her friends and coworkers, she was at a loss as to how to act around her daughter. She made an effort that summer; she and Liane shared the rue Faubourg Saint-Honoré house, going out to dinner and shows, shopping for clothes, and strolling the boulevards of Paris. This early in their relationship, both were determined to make it work.

In early August Ziegfeld joined the two in Paris, with the script for Anna's next show, *Miss Innocence.* "I do so disgust to study one new part!" she cried, her English skills deteriorating in her distress. Later in life, Liane claimed to have hated Ziegfeld from the first. She had to share a bathroom with him and recalled with distaste that he was afflicted that summer with tapeworm. "He had to take some medicine the effect of which was rather repulsive," she wrote, "but Mother attended to this unpleasant task until he was cured." A cured Ziegfeld, along with Anna and Liane, returned to the United States on September 1, on the *Kronprinz Wilhelm.* Also accompanying them were Beatrice, Anna's new white bulldog Bill Taft, and Ziegfeld's professional acquisitions: a performing police dog, the Spanish dancer Faico, and a bevy of showgirls.

This was Liane's first introduction to the American press, and she was petrified. Anna and Ziegfeld packed her off to the Ansonia and kept her under wraps while they tried to figure out a proper "unveiling." Liane never joined guests at dinner but was tended to by a French maid while she polished up her English skills with the help of a tutor. With the opening of the school year, Liane was enrolled at the Comstock School and was ushered to and from classes by a maid or butler while Anna either slept or rehearsed. "But when the press began to be more and more aggressive and tried to bribe the servants to let them in the apartment, Flo and Mother decided that perhaps it would be best to invite them in to meet me," Liane recalled.

Ethel Lloyd Patterson of the *Philadelphia Telegraph* was one of the first reporters introduced to Liane, who was, by this time, as tall as her mother. Anna
was trying—with no success whatsoever—to pass Liane off as eight years old.
"She is so BIG for her age," Anna kept repeating hopefully in interview after
interview. Anna also dismissed the furor about her motherhood, denying that
she'd ever tried to cover it up. "Just because people who do not know my private
life suddenly found out I had a daughter. All my intimate friends knew it. It was
no surprise to them."

Anna tried to defend her minimal parenting skills. No, she had not seen
much of Liane over the years, she admitted. "How could I, with rehearsals and
matinees and evening performances? I could not have given her any care. She has
been in a French convent. . . . That is the best place—the best life—for a little
girl." She then went into paroxysms of maternal bragging, claiming that she'd
longed for each summer, as it gave her the chance to see her beloved Liane.

"My mother heart yearned for my Lilly, my daughter," Anna emoted. "I
would fly and open my Paris house, so that I might have my child with me.
There I would stay until I was forced to return, by the demands of my art."
Brushing off the emergency of Carrera's death, Anna claimed that it was Ziegfeld
who had asked her to bring Liane back to the United States, so the loving
threesome could be together. "Now he is happy," she concluded. "He smiles.
He knows that I will not have to leave him when the season is over."

But even with Liane in the United States, Anna saw little of her. By the
time she returned home from school, Anna was either in rehearsal or performance, arriving home after Liane's bedtime and awakening after she'd gone to
school. Only on Sundays did Anna, Liane, and Ziegfeld take day trips, see the
New York sights, and try to mold themselves into some semblance of a family.

There were rumors as Anna prepared for her new show that she was running
low on money and had sold her famous sable coat. The fact that she sold her
name to the Anna Held Beautifier Company (makers of face creams) and E.G.
Murray and Co., manufacturers of Anna Held petticoats (a pricey five dollars),
helped perpetrate those stories. "Broke, am I?" Anna laughed. "Well, that is
news, indeed. Selling my furs? Goodness me! I just ordered another beautiful
set. Oh dear, what horrible tales Broadway gossipers do start!"

Ziegfeld was a bit more acerbic when confronted with these rumors. For
several years now, money had been a sore spot between the couple, what with
Ziegfeld's gambling debts and the still shadowy jewel robbery. Anna carefully
banked her salary in Paris and made sure that Ziegfeld could not get his careless
hands on it, and this rankled him. "I wish I were no nearer being broke than

Miss Held," he said somewhat bitterly in September 1908. "Just you call up her bank or go down and take a look at her big automobile waiting for her downstairs, and if you want a little more corroboration as to Miss Held's prosperous financial condition—but oh, what's the use of talking about it? Why, she just put $45,000 in gilt-edge bonds that are paying 7 percent dividend."

Both Ziegfeld and Anna agreed that the new show did not need the added raciness that both had put *The Parisian Model* over the top and had caused such notoriety. *Miss Innocence* would, of course, be as modern and full of double entendres as any popular musical, but would also incorporate a fairy-tale atmosphere. The huge success of the childlike musicals *The Wizard of Oz, Babes in Toyland, Happyland,* and *Mr. Bluebeard* pointed out a new avenue for Anna.

Harry B. Smith was brought back to write the script, and Ludwig Englander's light-as-air music was thought perfect for the new enterprise (Gus Edwards and Joseph Stern also contributed a song or two). The no-nonsense Julian Mitchell was again hired to direct. The stage manager was out-of-work actor Caro Miller, whose daughter Marilyn would, in the 1920s, become a major Ziegfeld star and a major heartache to his second wife. Smith's script combined a rose-petal preciousness with the usual Anna Held naughtiness. Anna portrayed "Anna," a pupil at a girl's school on the Isle of Innocence, presided over by a comic old maid with a past. An arch detective comes looking for Anna, believing her to be a missing heiress; she flees with him to Paris and meets Lt. Brissac of the French Navy and Captain Mountjoy of the First Life Guards. Her eyes are opened to the delights of the big city—as well as to the delights of Capt. Mountjoy. It all winds up happily in "The Land of Peach Blossoms" (backdrop "painted by Ernest Albert," according to the program).

Angular comedienne Emma Janvier was cast as Miss Sniffens, the school's proprietress, and the romantic leads were taken by Lawrance D'Orsay (as Mountjoy) and Leo Mars (as Brissac). For the important comic role of Ezra Pettingill, "the Greatest Detective in the World," Ziegfeld amazed the theatrical world and hugely annoyed Anna by casting the disgraced Charles Bigelow. Ziegfeld was known for putting personal likes and dislikes aside for the good of his shows. He frequently couldn't see the humor in such stars as Will Rogers, W.C. Fields, and Eddie Cantor—but if the audience laughed, that was good enough for him. Ziegfeld was often, unfairly, called humorless, but he actually loved practical jokes and costume parties—the goofier the better. However, he admitted, "I don't have a very quick sense of humor. Half the great comedians I've had in my shows and that I paid a lot of money to and who made my customers shriek were not only not funny to me, but I couldn't understand why they were funny to anybody. You'd be surprised how many of my expensive comics I've run out on and locked myself in my office when they were onstage." Bigelow drew the crowds, and he and Anna made a good team onstage, if not off. Actor William Powers was hired as Bigelow's understudy and was told to be ready to take his place at a moment's notice, even in midshow if need be.

As the *Miss Innocence* prepress geared up, humorist Clarence Cullen suggested a few possible stunts Anna might pull to publicize the show: "Take giraffe's-milk baths; refuse to live at the Chicago hotel that declines to receive her nine pet hippopotami; wear a hooded cobra as a corsage ornament; minister nobly unto the wounded and dying when she gets into a railroad wreck; almost fall from the rear platform of her private car into a Rocky Mountain gorge seven thousand feet deep."

But, if later rumors are to be believed, Anna had more than Charles Bigelow to worry about as *Miss Innocence* neared its November opening. One must be very wary of believing or perpetuating ages-old theatrical gossip and unverified rumors, but the story of Anna's supposed pregnancy and coerced abortion in late 1908 has been repeated in nearly every biography of Florenz Ziegfeld and has become part of Anna's legend. The one and only source for the story is Liane Carrera, and she proved to be less than accurate on many facts of her mother's life and career. In her unpublished memoirs of the late 1930s, she claimed that Anna and Ziegfeld mutually came to the decision to abort the fetus. Always anxious to demonize Ziegfeld, Liane recalled her mother saying to her, "Lili, he was simply horrid and a beast. He said, 'You can't have a baby now. All the money I could borrow is tied up in this new production and I can't back out now.'"

In Liane's first story, Anna agreed to the abortion, but "for fear of scandal Flo did not permit her to go to a hospital. They operated on my mother right in the dining room on the table." Liane has Anna sobbing to her years later, "Flo and I—we committed a murder together. I can never love him again." The story got even more melodramatic in the rewritten memoirs Liane published in the 1950s, which were fashioned to be Anna's autobiography. When Ziegfeld insists on an abortion, Anna bursts into tears: "Never! Do you understand me? I'm going to keep the baby! He's mine!" "We'll see about that, my dear," growls Ziegfeld, exiting stage left and all but twirling his mustache. "I kept Liane close to me, as if her presence protected me against the evil spells that I sensed were all around me," Liane modestly has her mother say.

In this latter-day story, Ziegfeld pays a gin-soaked quack to force Anna onto the dining room table, as she screams, "I beg you Flo! Have some pity!" Ziegfeld "laughed mockingly. An evil gleam made his pupils seem larger. I began to scream, 'No! Don't do it! Don't do it!'" The next day, Anna supposedly sobbed to her husband, "What kind of slime is your heart made of, anyway? You've killed our love. Now I hate you!" All that was missing were the bloodhounds nipping at Anna's heels as she fled over the ice-covered river.

Liane Carrera's blood-and-thunder version of Anna's purported kitchen table abortion hardly seems likely. A relatively safe abortion would have been easily obtainable for a wealthy woman like Anna in 1908. According to social historian Harvey Green, "Abortions were inexpensive and common in the late 19th century: Ten dollars was a standard rate in New York and Boston; and in 1898 the Michigan Board of Health estimated that one-third of all pregnancies were artificially terminated."

Although hospitals were not widely used for such operations, rest homes and privately owned sanitariums were available for those who wished to avoid seeing family or friends. Many show business people went to these places for abortions, to dry out, to recover from surgeries, or simply to rest and get away from it all. After Anna's hectic schedule, no one would have suspected anything out of the way had she retreated to one of these "country cottages" for a brief rest. And, who would suspect a happily married woman of having an abortion?

Liane's overwrought dialogue and accusations also do not fit in with what we know of Ziegfeld and Anna. For one thing, all of Ziegfeld's money was not tied up in *Miss Innocence:* His 1908 *Follies* were still playing on the road, and if Anna had really wanted to have this baby, Ziegfeld could have simply hired another actress for the part. Scores of female stars—some of them just as right for *Miss Innocence* as Anna—would have flocked to Ziegfeld for the opportunity if Anna had been willing to secede from the role for at least one season.

Additionally, the parental instincts of the couple suggest that Anna herself, rather than Ziegfeld, would have been more likely to rush to the abortionist's office. She never had an ounce of maternal feelings for Liane (this, of course, would not have been noted in Liane's own book). The real question is not why Anna may have had an abortion in 1908 but rather why didn't Anna abort Liane back in 1894? She'd never shown much interest in her daughter, even denying her existence at times. Anna's career was much more important to her than any baby. As far as religious objections to abortion, even Liane doesn't bring those up. Despite her nominal conversion to Catholicism, Anna never mouthed any religious sentiments.

As far as Ziegfeld, his devotion to his daughter Patricia (born in 1916) is well known. If anyone would have put parenthood ahead of money and career, Ziegfeld would have. And his biographer and cousin Richard Ziegfeld notes, "Carrera's claim of overt physical cruelty to a woman simply does not fit Ziegfeld's reputation for being soft-spoken and gallant with women." Richard Ziegfeld also writes that information from Liane's estate executor, Dr. Alexander Hegedus, adds another mystery to the equation. Hegedus told Ziegfeld that Liane herself had undergone an abortion, probably in the 1920s. With her intense identification with her mother and her equally virulent hatred of Ziegfeld, Richard Ziegfeld wonders if Liane didn't take her own experiences and project them back onto her mother. Making Liane's story more suspicious is the fact that her unpublished 1930s memoirs and her 1954 book do not agree. In her first account, Liane knew nothing of the abortion until years later, when Anna confided in her. But by 1954 Liane was being held close to her mother at night after the trauma. Fourteen at the time, Liane was surely old enough to sense something going on—had something indeed been going on.

Still, there is evidence that Anna was suffering from some sort of ailment at this time: A November 8, 1908, letter from Ziegfeld to his lawyer states, "Madam has been very ill and for the past ten days has been in bed, she hopes to get up next Tuesday, when we resume rehearsals. . . . It has been a bit of tough luck again, but it cannot be helped." Anna did indeed get out of bed in time for the trip to Philadelphia on November 18. She was fitted for her corseted and padded gowns, her figure as sleek and shapely as ever; she may or may not have had an abortion earlier that month. But if she did, it was most likely of her own free will. It's true that her relationship with Ziegfeld was slipping around this time, but there were other reasons for that: Up till then, it was mostly his gambling, financial irresponsibility, and occasional coldness. After the opening of *Miss Innocence*, Anna would have other reasons to doubt Ziegfeld's love for her—but they would not include abortion.

—6—
The Mansion of
Aching Hearts

It has never been safe to judge a show's reception from out-of-town try-outs. Anna had learned that from *Higgledy-Piggledy*, which early reviewers had convinced her was going to be a Held triumph. But it was hard not to get carried away with the advance reception accorded to *Miss Innocence*. The huge company took off from New York to Philadelphia on November 18, complete with three baggage cars, parlor car, and two day coaches. They opened at the venerable Chestnut Street Theater on November 23. It was a visually stunning show, and Ludwig Englander's tunes were so catchy that the gallery was whistling along by the second encore. Anna was a little disappointed that one of the biggest hits was not hers but that of Shirley Kellogg, who sang the jazzy "Yankiana Rag" in a nightclub scene. There was also a "Three Weeks" song—complete with tiger skin—ribbing Elinor Glyn's bestselling and heavy-breathing novel of that name. Anna's own numbers included "A Nicer Little Girl Than You," "I've Lost My Little Brown Bear" (those teddies were still trailing her), and her now-required "eye song," "I Wonder What's the Matter with My Eyes" (one reviewer suggested it was about time she saw an oculist).

Everyone agreed that *Miss Innocence* managed to re-create the best effects from Anna's previous shows, straining out the unwelcome bits and more shocking sexual innuendo. Comparing it to the *Parisian Model*, one Philadelphia critic wrote, "In times past we have felt it to be our duty to criticize some of Mr. Ziegfeld's productions severely for their audacities. On the present occasion it is a real pleasure to be able to commend almost without reservation the entertainment he has presented. It is gay and frivolous, to be sure, but gayety and frivolity are not sins in themselves and in a world that is sometimes a little gray for adults are welcome and enjoyable."

After its successful preview, *Miss Innocence* opened in New York on November 30, 1908, at the New York Theater. Part of Hammerstein's colossal Olympia complex in Times Square, the New York had been called the Music Hall until changing its name in 1899. Since then it had premiered George M. Cohan's smash hits *Little Johnny Jones* and *Forty-Five Minutes from Broadway*, as well as the spectacular drama *Quo Vadis?* The theater's two star dressing rooms were combined into one for Anna, the walls and bench covered with thick red plush; her delicate velvet sofa was improbably publicized as having belonged to Mme de Pompadour. Ziegfeld erected another electric sign out front, despite the disaster with the *Parisian Model* eyes. This time, a huge eight-ton sign, eighty feet long and forty feet high, was placed atop the New York marquee, its light bulbs spelling out the oddly worded come-on, "Ziegfeld's Musical Production, Anna Held, in *Miss Innocence*." The letters were surrounded by moving lightning bolts. Ziegfeld promoted it as the largest sign in America, containing eleven miles of wires and holding twenty-three hundred light bulbs.

Ziegfeld attempted what was to be his last publicity stunt for Anna, though it was somewhat halfhearted. He released a story to the newspapers that the enormous sign had somehow ignited the colorful bunting hanging over the theater's marquee. Anna, rehearsing inside, noticed the smoke, "leaned out the window," and pulled the flaming fabric inside, where it would presumably be safer. This got very little press: It had been a long time since those milk baths and horse rescues.

There was scarcely a discouraging word from the hard-to-please New York critics about *Miss Innocence*; they all but fell over themselves to praise both Anna and her show. "Miss Held has never been in anything that suits her requirements so well as the part of Anna," read a typical review, adding that "Mr. Smith's book is better than can usually be found among the musical offerings of the day, and throughout the two acts and several scenes there is sprinkled any quantity of fun, even if the story is lost in a maze of pretty girls and gorgeous surroundings." The plot began in Vienna and took Anna to Paris, the Rhine, and several mythical lands; as one critic wrote, "To say that this is a magnificent production is putting it mildly. The eye is constantly feasted with a vision of beautiful girls handsomely gowned and scenery that reaches the highest pinnacle of the scene painter's art." As for Anna, she was "as piquant as ever, and as she was in splendid voice all her songs went with a vim. It is worth going miles to see her alone, but thanks to her liberal way of doing things, she allowed others to share in the honors."

"Of all the startling productions which F. Ziegfeld, Jr., has made, this one positively looms up the greatest," read another New York review. "Miss Held is more beautiful and graceful than ever." Amy Leslie, of course, found no fault with the show or its star. "Anna Held and *Miss Innocence* reign the one big noisy triumph over Broadway," she wrote, calling the show "diverting as a frolic of buoyant comedy," and adding of Anna, "never has she been so brilliant in technique, so pretty a dream. . . . Her vivacity and her brilliant rendition stamp her one of the choicest song deliverers in America."

The character of Anna in *Miss Innocence* took the actress right back to the Anna of *Papa's Wife*. Again, she found herself playing a *faux-naif* schoolgirl suddenly plunged into the moral whirlpool of Paris. Anna had learned a few tricks since the show of 1899 and was even better able to portray sweetness edged with irony. Every audience member knew what a sophisticate Anna herself was supposed to be, and this added to the grand joke of her "never having seen a man" and being indoctrinated into the high life by her admiring military escorts. Her performance was a delicate balancing act between wide-eyed credulity and self-knowing sarcasm, with a sly wink to the audience.

After the debacle of *Mam'selle Napoleon*, Anna had done very little to stretch her talent, and *Miss Innocence* provided nothing in the way of a challenge to her— but she also recognized that her performances provided a service. "My work— it has not been so very important," she shrugged toward the end of that season. "Some people . . . they say my work has been bad, which isn't nice of them. But in New York? New York is wise. New York is tired at night. New York wants to laugh and be interested—excited. I have given New York what it wants. For dear New York, no matter what those high-brows say, does not take its theater seriously. Its people go to the theater and see the mimicry of the gay and naughty, and they go home and are just as domestic and church-going as ever."

The critics and audiences didn't know it, but in *Miss Innocence* they were treated to the final Ziegfeld/Held collaboration, their last and greatest show together. While Anna had perfected her art, Ziegfeld had also discovered his true metier. The Ziegfeld touch came to its first peak in *Miss Innocence*. His *Follies* were still spoken of as almost a sideline to his "real" shows, no more than a light summer entertainment. But Ziegfeld's theatrical genius saw its flowering in *Miss Innocence*.

There was, first and foremost, the costuming. Ziegfeld may have learned everything he knew about clothing from Anna, but he took that knowledge and ran with it. The costumes had to be made of the finest silk-satins and chiffons; even the linings and underwear had to be perfect so that the performers would feel as spectacular as they looked. Ziegfeld took the costumes presented to him and turned them inside-out to make sure no cheating had been attempted. As Eddie Cantor recalled, "Clothing was so important to Flo that very often he would call in his staff of writers, composers and lyricists to look over the sketches he had selected and say to them, 'These are the dresses I want the numbers built around.' He would never retain an old set of costumes in a new show even if they had previously been worn only once at a dress rehearsal. He would sell them to burlesque shows or dancing acts in vaudeville, providing the costumes would not be shown on Broadway."

The sets and backdrops, likewise, were so breathtaking that they were frequently applauded as heartily as the musical numbers. Ziegfeld contracted the best painters (in the case of *Miss Innocence*, John Young and Ernest Albert) and worked them furiously, demanding that entire scenes be repainted if they were not up to his standards. "There is one view shown on a darkened stage of Paris by moonlight which brought forth spontaneous applause for the skill with which it had been contrived," noted one *Miss Innocence* review. Ziegfeld also worked closely with his lighting designers, to make sure his favorite pink-and-white combination was seen to best effect in both clothing and scenery (he had a violent dislike, though, for all shades of purple). Ziegfeld did have one blind spot, which infuriated his lighting technicians: Whenever his chorus girls appeared onstage, they had to be set off in blinding white lights. "Bitter arguments always followed this ultimatum," wrote Cantor, "but in the end, whether it was midnight on the ocean or at the bottom of a deep, dark grotto, once the girls came on the stage, a stream of bright white lights flooded the set."

The *Miss Innocence* chorus girls were once again proclaimed the loveliest on the American stage. Thousands of applicants flooded the theater when it was known that a new Anna Held show was auditioning. Not only actresses and singers but also models, society girls on a lark, and factory girls looking for "easy money" tried to knock down the stage door. Ziegfeld himself said that their looks counted for only 35 percent of why he chose them, "cleverness, grace, and vocal ability" accounting for the other 65 percent. "The eyes should be large and expressive," he later said of his selection process. "A regular profile is a decided asset."

First there were the showgirls, who had to be tall and languid and able to carry clothes well. Then there were the dancers and singers, whose talent and spark mattered more than sheer looks. Writer J.P. McEvoy, who later worked with Ziegfeld, mentioned in his book *Show Girl* the scene at a typical Ziegfeld audition: "Tall blondes with complexions like fresh cream and hair like twenty dollar gold pieces and those yellow green eyes like tigers in the zoo have on Sunday when they don't feed 'em. And running all around under them little brunette dancers with legs like acrobats—and perched on a line of chairs against the wall, a lot of those slim, slender-legged young things looking boyish and silky at the same time."

Anna also sat in on the auditions and had a voice in who was chosen. She was often complimented for allowing herself to be seen with—and potentially overshadowed by—such an array of beauties. "I do not understand why a star fears or objects to being seen with pretty girls in her chorus," Anna said at the time of the *Miss Innocence* opening. "No matter what the personal looks of a star may be, if she is a star, her work should be artistic enough to prevent her having any misgivings about being surrounded by beautiful girls."

By 1908 the New York chorus girl was already a well-known folk figure: wisecracking, gold-hearted (and gold-digging), sexy, and delightfully cheap. The same year *Miss Innocence* opened, the *New York Morning Telegraph* printed a series of humor pieces, later collected into the book *The Sorrows of a Show Girl*. An hilarious look into the world of the New York chorine, it detailed the life of its sardonic heroine, Sabrina, who was appearing in *The Mangled Doughnut* company (among the show's forty-two songs were "I'd Rather Be Up in the Air Than Up in the Bronx"). Readers boned up on their slang as Sabrina described a typical 1908 show: "I went over to rehearsal, and of all the frowsy dames I ever piped— far be it from me to knock, but they looked like a bunch of pie-trammers that had just rushed over from Child's." Of the star, she sneered, "It is my personal opinion—of course I wouldn't have you breathe this to a living soul for worlds— but it is my personal opinion that she sniffs the white. She either does that or jabs, though it don't show on her arm." Jaded New Yorkers and rubes alike lapped it up.

One enterprising reporter published a wonderful vignette of Anna's *Miss Innocence* girls, giving his readers a rare glimpse into their dressing room gossip. The girls were discovered in the midst of a poker game, using two hat boxes as a table. "Don't tell 'em when you go out what we're doin'," begged one. "They're all the time scolding us for being late and we told 'em the other day we was learnin' to paint, and they believed it. Ain't they the innocents?" Another girl noted that she was coming down with a sore throat and should have called in sick, but "what would I be doing sitting 'round for a whole week? If I could only swallow I'd be all right, but I can't even take champagne." The light bulbs over the girls' dressing tables were decorated with ribbons, garters, and flowers to brighten the place up. One girl had propped up a photo of Mark Twain, explaining, "I know a girl who knows him and she says he's a perfect dandy." As for the babies in photos scattered about, "they don't belong to anybody. All the girls have babies' pictures and kittens. They go well together." But they weren't

all sweetness and sentiment: The girls threw pamphlets containing Anna's photos into the audience during one number, and some guiltily admitted that they
had bets going as to how many of them could hit people in the eye. The subject
of their nominal boss, Anna, was raised by the reporter. "Ain't Anna Held's
figure simply stunning?" squealed one of the loyal chorines. "I call it just perfect, and her accent, too. Did you ever know anybody who could rolls their r's
the way she can? They sound like a soft rubber ball going down marble stairs
and hittin' each stair. I tried it, but they say it's something you can't acquire, that
you have to have a nurse for it when you're young."

With its happy poker-playing chorus girls, talented supporting players,
and snappy music and dialogue, *Miss Innocence* swept all competition away in its
wake. That season, Elsie Janis was enjoying a huge success in *The Fair Coed*, as
were Marie Cahill in *The Boys and Betty*, and Fritzi Scheff in *The Prima Donna*
(which opened the same night as did *Miss Innocence*). Anna's friend Lillian Russell
was starring in what turned out to be her last hit, *Wildfire*. One of the odder
sights (and sounds) that season was twenty-six-year-old John Barrymore making his ill-conceived musical comedy debut in *A Stubborn Cinderella*.

Tickets to *Miss Innocence* were not easy to come by in those first hectic
months of success. Scalpers bought out the good seats and resold them for a
profit, as noted in *Welcome to Our City*, an astonishingly mean-spirited book of
1912. "As you leave the theater lobby," the author noted, "after being informed
that the house is 'sold out,' a small, foreign-born Jew of the lowest type, will . . .
approach you and try to drag you to the speculator's lair for which he is a
'runner.'" The police force was trying to crack down on such speculators but
was having very little luck.

Despite the show's success, Ziegfeld kept adding and subtracting numbers so second-timers would not be bored. One of the numbers added to *Miss
Innocence* was both spectacular and timely: On December 15 "We Two in an
Aeroplane" had its debut. In the middle of act 2, this elaborate set piece featured Anna and Leo Mars in a full-sized biplane, teetering precariously above
an applause-producing backdrop of Paris by night. As enthusiastic as Anna had
been about bicycles and automobiles, she had not yet become an aeronaut. But
the rest of the world was agog: 1908 was, in the words of aviation historian
C.H. Gibbs-Smith, "the annis mirabilis of world aviation, for the Wright brothers
flew in public for the first time. . . . The crowd could scarcely believe its eyes; the
skeptics were astounded and confounded, and the enthusiasm was uproarious."
Far be it from Ziegfeld to let so spectacular an event pass by without turning it
into a dazzling stage effect.

Ziegfeld even had Anna attend the Mount Morris Park christening of the first airplane to be built in New York; it took her three tries to break the bottle (she managed to drench herself and her bulldog with champagne). But the plane failed to get off the ground—"The machine either had a cold or had been left without oats too long," suggested one reporter. While the plane just sat there making alarming noises, everyone retired to a nearby restaurant for a consolation lunch.

Dazzling as the new musical number may have been, it was also prone to a lot of technical problems. One night the plane's wires jammed as it exited, leaving Anna and Mars hanging thirty feet in the air backstage. The stage manager and some crew members stood below scratching their heads until finally a ladder was found and the two shaken stars climbed gingerly down to safety. This scenario recurred too often for Anna's comfort, and at least once a week the wobbly plane threatened to toss the performers into the audience as they cheerfully sang their little song, hanging on for dear life and trying to look carefree. But the number was a huge hit and was kept in for the duration of *Miss Innocence*'s long run.

The company was a happy, close-knit one, even with Charles Bigelow in residence. For Christmas 1908 a huge tree was erected in the New York Theater lobby, Emma Janvier being put in charge of decorations. Anna raffled off a doll dressed in scraps of her old costumes at the cast's Christmas party. The only rebellion took place on January 14, 1909, when a "Salome Ball" was being given that Anna's chorus girls wanted to attend. They begged Ziegfeld and Julian Mitchell to put the show on fifteen minutes early so they could race to the ball's grand march, but were turned down. The girls petitioned Anna and she somehow sweet-talked Ziegfeld into letting them go.

Anna was smart to treat her chorus girls well and keep them happy; by this time, *Miss Innocence* was taking in twenty thousand dollars a week, with no sign of letup. Some of the biggest drawing points of the show were those chatty, glamorous Anna Held Girls, who in the words of one critic, "display their charms and their lack of voice." Of the lovelies in the *Miss Innocence* cast, two were to make their mark on history, and one of those would change Anna's life. Mae Murray was a twenty-three-year-old dancer when cast as the White Pierrette in *Miss Innocence*; she went on to become a *Follies* star and one of the most glamorous and eccentric movie queens of the 1920s. And then there was Lillian Lorraine.

By her own reckoning, Lillian Lorraine was sixteen when she was cast in *Miss Innocence*, but the "official" birth years of chorus girls must be viewed with vast skepticism. She was born Mary Ann Brennan in San Francisco and by 1908 had already appeared in such shows as *School Boys and Girls*, *The Tourists*, *The Orchid*, and *The Gay White Way*. She had only minimal singing skills, but her looks assured that she would never lack for work. Lillian Lorraine was one of those women who'd have been considered a great beauty no matter what era she'd been born into. She had ivory-white skin and black hair; china-blue eyes and sharp, clear-cut features. While Anna was described as "pert" and "cute," Lorraine was a knockout.

She started in the show as one of seven girls in the Elinor Glyn-inspired "Three Weeks with You" number, but by early March 1909 Lorraine was promoted to a prima donna role, singing the Irving Berlin classic "By the Light of the Silvery Moon" (it was widely proclaimed that Lorraine introduced the number, but it had already been sung in vaudeville by Gus Edwards). She was given six costume changes and her own dressing room—which alienated the other chorus girls—and Ziegfeld's press agent insisted that reporters interview her separately from the other "supporting players."

Lorraine has always been painted as a talent-free, gold-digging opportunist, but it's also important to see the situation from her perspective. Florenz Ziegfeld was the most important producer in New York from a showgirl's viewpoint. Lorraine had been born poor and had struggled for what success she'd gotten in life; if Ziegfeld came on to her, suggesting a tryst or that "accommodating" him would mean more important roles in her future, what was she to do? Slap his face? Sue him for sexual harassment? These were not options in 1909, and it might be argued that Lorraine took the only avenue that was open to her. On May 14, 1909, the *Standard* and *Vanity Fair* reported, no doubt with one eyebrow raised, that Lillian Lorraine had been "taken in hand" by Ziegfeld. Anna was not stupid and she heard the gossip that Ziegfeld was being more than an attentive employer to this lovely new chorus girl. Certainly there had been flirtations before, and Anna, as a modern Frenchwoman, did not expect her husband to be totally immune from hordes of ambitious and beautiful showgirls. But this seemed more than just a passing fancy.

Ziegfeld, who had lived happily with the sane, placid and easygoing Anna Held for twelve years, fell head over heels for the irrational, high-strung Lillian Lorraine. This double love life was to emerge again late in the following decade, when Ziegfeld was married to Billie Burke and had long-term, fiery affairs with Olive Thomas and the mercurial Marilyn Miller. He needed to love several kinds of women, never finding just one to satisfy his needs. It always ended in predictable disaster. Lorraine was a great beauty, true, but she was not the singer or actress Anna was and she could also be temperamental and a heavy drinker. Still, Ziegfeld was hooked and Anna quietly but firmly put her foot down: By the time *Miss Innocence* ended its twenty-three-week run at the New York Theater, Lillian Lorraine was no longer in the cast.

By this time, Anna and Ziegfeld had settled down into a leisurely marital routine when in New York. While Anna was working, she sometimes got up early to fix Ziegfeld's breakfast, then went back to bed for another hour or two. "I go out for a drive," she said, "which means I go to the shops and look over things." At 1:30 she picked up Ziegfeld at his office, and the two lunched together. "Each of us tries to let nothing interfere with that custom," said Anna. "Then, after luncheon, I go for a drive in the park or out in the country, or perhaps I make some calls. But I mustn't do too much before evening or I shall be quite stupid for the performances." Evening was when Anna's workday began. She took a nap from 5 o'clock till 6 o'clock, after which she put on her first-act costume and makeup. Her car picked her up at 7:30, "and I am already humming my songs or going over a few other lines—for sometimes one forgets a little. And the minutes go by faster than ever until the call comes, and almost before I realize it, there I am, again, out in front of those dear people who are clapping and crying out."

Unlike most of Anna's previous shows, *Miss Innocence* did not go out on tour in the winter and spring. It was doing so well in New York that Ziegfeld decided to keep it right where it was: As long as patrons fought for tickets and crowded the New York Theater every night, he was willing to bide his time. It was obvious that *Miss Innocence* would be good for at least one more year of stupendous box office. The show's first season ended in a blaze of glory. On May 1, 1909, Anna was presented with a large gold loving cup by A.L. Erlanger in commemoration of her record run at the New York Theater. It was still doing such huge business on its closing that Ziegfeld had decided to reopen briefly in New York in the fall of 1909, and then take it on an extended tour.

Anna was on top of the world—professionally, at any rate—as the summer of 1909 approached. Her relationships with her husband and her daughter were a bit frayed at the edges, but Anna was the biggest star of the American stage. "Mrs. Florenz Ziegfeld, Jr., is one of the most widely advertised women in the world," it was written at this time. "Her picture is everywhere. You have seen it in hotel lobbies, store windows, on cigar-boxes, billboards, in magazines and on everything in the canned line from cold cream to silver polish." Yet this was the moment she began to talk of giving it all up. It was announced in mid-May that Anna had saved one million dollars and was considering retirement.

As she packed for her summer vacation, Anna told reporters, "No, I am not joking. After next season there will be no Anna Held behind the footlights. I have lasted longer than most women on Broadway. Twelve years I have held my own." As for her million dollars, "I love them. Every single dollar. But every dollar of that money I made because my work was good. I did not speculate much. Very little. If I told how little they would call me a piker. . . . I feel proud of my record and now that I have this large sum of money I intend to take care of it." Only once did she drop an unlikely hint that her husband might have something to do with her plans: "I hate to acknowledge that I am near the end," Anna told one reporter, "but I must obey Mr. Ziegfeld, and he says that next year is the last."

As for her future, Anna spun little fantasies that were just as bucolic as her imaginative memories of her childhood. "I have made arrangements to buy 200 acres of ground around Fort George [Quebec]," she said. "There I shall have a place where nice people can come and enjoy themselves. It will be a restaurant, some shows—all very high class—and gardens. It will not be for the crowd, it will be for the people who pay $2 for their theater seats and sometimes buy a box and who are not afraid to buy champagne. Near that I shall buy a home for myself."

For the first time, she also began to talk about the dark side of show business, warning young girls—such as her daughter—away from the profession. "Young women, unless they are possessed of the very greatest talent, should let the stage alone," she said, "because those without great talent will get along, if they do get along, only at the expense of their innocence and their good name." She told of rich backers who had their pick of chorus girls: "Their object when they prowl about behind the scenes is quite obvious. A girl with a pretty face is soon at their mercy." As for herself, Anna admitted, "The limelight is too strong. . . . I have learned to love the stage. The laughter and the applause are a stimulant that grow on one with a deadly grip."

The news of Anna's million did not go over well with the press, who felt it unbecoming for a bubbly, feminine woman to be talking of bank accounts and investments. Cartoons were printed of her sitting atop moneybags, and rather than congratulating Anna for her hard work and intelligent management, editorialists called her greedy and coldhearted. The fact that a musical comedy actress was able to save that much money from her silliness and "little door-hinge warble" struck some as obscene. "She hasn't much of a voice, and she hasn't much of a figure," complained the *Chicago Record-Herald*, trying to figure out exactly how Anna deserved so huge a bank account. "She's considerably under-size, and her shoulders are too broad for the rest of her slender anatomy. . . . Women have never liked the Held lady. They found her ordinary and a bit common—so they say."

After her wealth was made public, Anna began getting appeals for help from the self-professed needy, most of whom were total strangers to her. "They write with assurance that I am going to give them something," she said, adding that "occasionally I come across an appeal which seems so genuine that I feel as if I should be a monster to refuse. So I send something. But as a rule when I give, I know the people who are going to receive." When it was announced that Anna owned sufficient stock in one railroad to join the board of directors, a group of suffragettes tried to convince her to do just that.

Anna sailed for Europe on the *Krownprinzessin Cecile* on May 18, accompanied by Liane, Beatrice, and her mother- and father-in-law. Anna's former chorus girl Gertrude Hoffmann, now a vaudeville star in her own right, was also on the ship. Ziegfeld himself was already in Europe, having begun his vacation early so he could be back in the United States in time to open his 1909 *Follies* in mid-June.

Anna and Ziegfeld did their best to make up their differences and smooth over the ruffled feathers left by Lillian Lorraine (and, if we are to believe Liane Carrera, by Anna's abortion). The couple motored to Nice, stopping at small towns along the way to repair the car, picnic, and see the sights. More adventurous than her traveling companions, Anna took off on her own for a motoring tour of France and Switzerland. While Ziegfeld returned to Paris to be with his parents and stepdaughter, Anna joined up with twelve other parties and the group took a leisurely tour through Nice, Lucerne, and surrounding villages.

"We had to go miles and miles between and over mountains," Anna later recalled enthusiastically. "We climbed one particularly high mountain, at the top of which we found the monastery. There we met a caretaker, who showed us everything and explained different things to the few visitors who succeeded in reaching the place." Nothing fazed Anna in the way of discomfort, jostling, bad weather, or primitive accommodations. "Traveling this way you see more of the country," she said, "more than can be seen on any wonderful limited or fast train. You stop at some funny marchand de vin and visit the homes and farmyards, and you imagine you get even better meals at these places than you can at Armenonville or the big first-class restaurants in Paris."

Anna and her companions saw untouched countryside that would, in a few years, be blackened by war. "The most beautiful country to motor through is coming from Biarritz to Chamouix," she said. "It is at the foot of Mt. Blanc, and even in August you can see the great mountain with its top covered with ice and snow. They have immense telescopes through which you can look and see the mountain climbers trying to reach the top of the mountain." Anna spent eight weeks with her new friends, "living all day in the automobile and stopping at hotels only long enough to rest and eat."

Back in the luxury and comfort of Paris, Anna gave a Latin Quarter party for Lillian Russell. The Ziegfelds and Liane spent time with Ziegfeld's sister Lulu Buhl and her small son Teddy, who earned Liane's enmity by being always perfectly behaved. "Lili, you should see how nicely Teddy says goodnight to his mother and how he says, 'I hope you have a good time, Mother dear,'" Liane recalled Anna scolding. Liane, then about fifteen, cordially hated Teddy's insides. Anna was still close with the Ziegfelds, having no blood relations of her own. "I love them so much, the dear people," she said of her in-laws, and pronounced herself "desolate" when they went their separate ways at summer's end.

Ziegfeld sailed back to the United States in time to oversee the *Follies* premiere, and Anna spent the rest of her vacation in Paris and Vichy getting acquainted with her teenage daughter. Liane also got to know what it was like being the offspring of a celebrity. She later recalled dining in a Paris restaurant with her mother that summer and being appalled at the fellow diners staring at them. Anna wisely advised her, "As we go out just say to yourself, 'I am the Queen of Sheba. I am the Queen of Sheba.'" They were doing fine until Liane noticed that Anna still had a long white napkin caught in the belt of her dress as they exited—"It was a long time before I recuperated from that public experience," she wrote. On another occasion, mother and daughter went out horse riding in the park. As she cantered energetically along, Anna began to lose the false curls that were popular at the time. "Well, the curls were made especially for mother and cost a lot of money," wrote Liane, "so to my shame I was forced to tell a young gentleman who was riding with us to please ride back and pick up the three little bunches of curls that mother had dropped." Being in the public eye was an excruciating learning experience for the shy teenager.

By this time Ziegfeld was back in New York. He resumed his affair with Lillian Lorraine, who was given several specialties in the *Follies*. She revived "By the Light of the Silvery Moon," sang a bubble-bath song, and even stole a leaf from Anna's airplane number: She sang "Up, Up in My Aeroplane" while flying happily over the heads of the audience, tossing flowers to them. Anna was not amused when this was eagerly reported to her by gossipy friends. Lorraine can hardly be said to have "stolen" the show, though; her competition that year was impressive. The temperamental Nora Bayes was back (to be replaced in July by the equally temperamental Eva Tanguay), and up-and-comer Sophie Tucker belted out "It's Moving Day in Jungle Town."

The mercurial Lorraine was not a good influence on Ziegfeld's personality, and he became involved in a public altercation on the show's out-of-town opening night. On June 10 the *Follies* premiered at Atlantic City's Apollo Theater. When Ziegfeld was informed that the audience included his rival producers Lee Shubert and Lew Fields, he blew up. The thought of Shubert and Fields stealing his jokes or even performers was more than he could take. Ziegfeld stormed down the aisle, pushing through the embarrassed audience, which included Lillian Russell and Diamond Jim Brady. He loudly ejected Shubert and Fields, along with their wives and the delightfully named publicity man A. Toxen Worm. When Shubert took his case to the press, Ziegfeld retorted that he had been thrown out of Shubert's *The Midnight Sons* the year before and was only returning the favor.

This was the kind of public scene Anna never would have countenanced. Her friends Russell, Amy Leslie, and Harry B. Smith's wife, Irene, kept her up to date on the rekindled Lorraine affair, to her chagrin and annoyance. Ziegfeld and Lillian Lorraine were seen at the theater and dining in such high-profile restaurants as Delmonico's, Rector's, and Luchow's. At the same time, Lorraine was rumored to be carrying on with her chauffeur—who was later hauled into court and charged with stealing her jewelry. It was all getting rather sordid. It was also getting into the press. Anna maintained a dignified silence while gossip columnists hinted that her husband had "fallen prey" to this "small, exquisite personage, of expensive ideas, and ambitious aims as to opulence of a material sort."

Ziegfeld made a rather pathetic attempt to reassure Anna of his devotion—not surprisingly, through a planted newspaper story. It was printed that he knocked down one Charles Alexander outside the Apollo Theater for bandying Anna's name about. Alexander, it was claimed, had been showing off a wrist scar and bragging that he'd been shot by Ziegfeld in a duel over Anna's affections. He made sure the stories were sent to Anna—but she, an old hand at such tales, was not impressed. On June 23 Anna wrote to Leslie from France, "I do not hear any more of business and you know what a relief that is to me to be out of it." Referring to her now notorious million-dollar bank account, she mentioned, "I have counted it up a couple of times and I think there are a few cents missing to the million, but with or without it I really think after next season I must have a rest."

One disquieting change Anna noticed in the summer of 1909 was at the dressmakers and on the streets. In the fall of 1908, the couturier Paul Poiret introduced a new longer, leaner look, inspired by designs for the Ballet Russe by Leon Bakst. The wasp-waisted hourglass look that Anna had helped to popularize was outmoded virtually overnight. By summer 1909, it was obvious that this new fashion was no flash in the pan, and Anna had to begin reconsidering her whole appearance. If she was going to take *Miss Innocence* back to America, she would have to discard all her old costumes and appear as a harbinger of the slim, unadorned new "tango girl" look. The very shape of the figure changed with this new silhouette. First of all, the waistline moved upward, creating an

"Empire" effect with a belt right under the bustline. This was not (and is still not) a good look on women with large rib cages. Anna, with her large head and short stature, looked downright top-heavy in these new gowns. To counterbalance, she began wearing her hair closer to her head, slowly discarding the puffy Gibson Girl chignon.

The shape of the corset began changing along with the shape of the dress. Most women did not really begin to go without stays until World War I, but by 1909, the flat-fronted corset replaced the old-fashioned waist-cincher. Rather than reducing the waistline and emphasizing the bust and hips, this new corset flattened the tummy and tried to slim the hips (pelvic bones notwithstanding). Anna's beloved skirts—flared morning glories with sweeping hems of lace and ribbon—also went the way of all last year's clothes. The new skirts were slim and straight, with far less in the way of frills and decoration. All of Anna's old petticoats were discarded, replaced by straight slips. The slim look reached an apex in 1910 with the introduction of the aptly named hobble skirt, in which women could not stride more than six inches at a step. Very few women actually wore hobble skirts; most, like Anna, denounced them as ludicrous and they very quickly vanished from fashion showrooms.

There were other changes in fashion as well: High and rounded necklines gave way to V-shaped and squared ones, daringly exposing the neck and collarbone; huge Gainsborough hats were supplanted by even huger "tea tray" hats and small toques and bandeaux. Pale girlish pastels began to give way to bright, vivid colors. Anna—always proud of her tiny waist—hated this new look, as it emphasized slimness over curves. Until 1908 chubby or matronly women could still be considered attractive, their ample curves envied by their skinny sisters who had to use hip-padding and "gay deceivers" (bust ruffles) to give themselves some substance. But with the introduction of the long lean look, dieting began to raise its head. For a professional fashion plate like Anna, always in the public eye, every extra pound was a cause for emotional trauma. The age of weight-consciousness had been ushered in.

Fashion maven Cecil Beaton reminisced in 1934 that this revolution happened seemingly in an instant. "A fashion world that had been dominated by corsets, lace, feathers, and pastel shades soon found itself in a city that overnight had become a seraglio of vivid colours, harem skirts, beads, fringes, and voluptuousness." Within a few years, he added, there "would be bright futuristic scarves of checkered or harliquinade triangles and squares, all of which could be traced back to Bakst." Paul Poiret, of course, huffily declared that this look was mostly his idea and scoffed at any suggestion that he was simply copying Bakst.

Anna showed her age by complaining about the crazy new fashions the young people were wearing. "It seems to me that the whole tendency of modern fashion is not to make women beautiful, but only to martyr them," she said, sounding dangerously like a crabby old maid. She hated the stiff tea-tray hats: "Big hats are not comfortable," she sighed. "Yet all women wear them. I myself have worse hats than anybody." She hated the new flat-front corsets: "It comes down to the knees and the poor unhappy wearer can never sit down. . . . It is ugly and it has no excuse at all for being." But above all else, Anna missed her elegant, sweeping skirts and hated the new sheaths and hobble skirts. "The poor women are falling and tumbling around because they cannot move in the tight skirts," she said. "They cannot walk. They cannot step up into an automobile." But Anna knew that women came to her shows partly to see her groundbreaking new fashions from Paris. In order to maintain a successful career, Anna would have to dress up-to-the-minute, whether she liked the new styles or not.

In September 1909 Anna enrolled Liane in a "free-thinking, advanced" girls' school in Versailles and sailed with Beatrice for New York. Back in the United States, she prepared for what she still claimed would be her farewell tour. She brought with her some impressive new gowns, including one of pink satin, embroidered with flowers made of real diamonds (three thousand of them). With this was worn pink silk stockings scattered with diamonds; the whole ensemble was rumored to have cost twenty-nine thousand dollars.

The second season of *Miss Innocence* opened September 27 at the New York Theater, to be greeted with throngs of patrons fighting for tickets. Charles Bigelow and Laurance D'Orsay returned as Anna's leading men (Bigelow was so sure of himself that he began interpolating comic bits during the show, to the cast's annoyance). "*Miss Innocence* is still good, rakish, rather improper entertainment," said one New York critic this second time around. The diamond dress garnered astonished applause: "To describe adequately this [dress] would require a pen dipped into the magic ink of the gods," gushed one writer. After a scant two-week run in New York, the company followed the money onto the road, first to Philadelphia. Anna and Ziegfeld took off on the afternoon of their first Philadelphia performance, and, she later recounted, "'way out in the country where there is no one in sight, no house, nothing to eat or drink, we have what you call a busted tire." It took several hours for them to be rescued by a passerby, and Anna arrived at the theater at 7:15, "Dusty, weather-blown and hungry . . . while I dress my maid gets me some chicken. And so no bread, no knife, no fork, with a paper for my serviette I have my evening meal."

Nonetheless, the show was a hit in Philadelphia, and Anna was still game enough to drive to most of her connections that season. Ziegfeld stayed in Philadelphia after Anna left, to oversee tryouts of his new show *The Silver Star* (though by the time that show—which starred Adeline Genée—opened, Ziegfeld had left the project and his name had been taken off the program). Anna's next stop was Boston, where Mayor Hibbard, recalling the scandal of *The Parisian Model*, threatened to close the show down but unexpectedly found it, according to one report, "as proper as a Tuesday afternoon meeting of the Mother's Club in the vestry." Indeed the audience, too, was expecting something much racier, though it seemed happy with what it got. "When it offends," said a Boston critic, "its offenses are against good taste and intelligence, and these in the eyes and the ears of the audience that laughed and applauded at every turn last night were the most venial of short-comings."

In Pittsburgh a large photo of Anna in the theater lobby was confiscated by local police, as her bare feet were offending passersby. No such problems arose in Baltimore, where the show was praised for its "dash and go," and was not too raw for the locals ("*Miss Innocence* decidedly keeps on the safe and sure side"). They moved on to Detroit to see out 1909—that year's Christmas party included an onstage tree with presents beneath for the whole cast (Anna gave her husband a pink pearl scarf pin). Demand for New Year's Eve tickets to *Miss Innocence* was so strong that a ticket auction had to be held.

And so the tour ground on, alternately stultifying and exhilarating for the troupe. They made their biggest hit in Indianapolis, where *Miss Innocence* was compared favorably to *The Merry Widow*. "The entire company, from Miss Held to the lowliest chorus girl, worked last evening as though they thoroughly enjoyed it, and as though it were only the tenth or dozenth time they had played their respective roles instead of the so many hundredth," said the *Indianapolis Star*. "Miss Held keeps her youth remarkably well," added that critic, "and in the schoolgirl scene it was difficult to realize that she is out of her teens."

That same reporter felt that—even at this late date—Anna might leave the musical comedy stage for a try at drama. "She is a better actress than the majority of musical comedy stars," he said, adding, ". . . her light, delicate touches in the acting moments were really more artistic. In flashes she showed the necessary qualifications for a 'straight' star, if there is really any serious intent on her part of abandoning the musical comedy for the legitimate stage." But by 1909 any such thoughts were well in Anna's past. She had chosen her path and was resigned—even content—to be consigned to the world of song and dance.

By the time *Miss Innocence* reached Cincinnati, though, Anna was beginning to wilt. The mayor and a citizen's committee insisted on seeing the show before approving it for public view, then the local papers dismissed it as merely a "New York show." Anna found herself held in low esteem in that city: Critics complained that she "persisted in the high whine and imitation French accent [!] that have made her famous," even scoffing that her chorus girls were of more interest than their star. "They dance on, walk on and off the stage, changing costumes meanwhile in a way that keeps you wondering which is which, and just about the time that you've decided that the one over there at the left in the second row is the one who was in the front row in the scene before they dance away again, and the puzzle has to be worked out once more." Two of these girls managed to get themselves into hot water when the show reached Butte, Montana. Nena Blake and Ursula March met two engaging young stage-door Johnnies and dined so well that they missed their train to the next connection. Happily, their beaus were wealthy enough to charter a special train to get their girls to the next stop in time for their show. March eventually married her Montana man and retired from the stage; Blake stayed in show business and, sadly, died young.

Meanwhile Ziegfeld was enjoying himself in New York with Lillian Lorraine, and the rumors of this rekindled affair were reaching an already over-worked and tired Anna. To keep her occupied and distracted, Ziegfeld asked Julian Mitchell to bring Liane back to the United States with him, "as a surprise" for Anna. Liane later wrote that it was a surprise indeed: When she showed up unannounced in Anna's dressing room, her mother had a fit. "How dare you leave the school without my consent?" Liane claimed Anna screamed at her. "You are a little trollop coming across the ocean alone with a man. Is that what I have tried to raise you to be a decent, sweet girl? Well, not in my house will you stay tonight!" Whether or not Anna's response was actually quite so vitriolic, she was certainly not happy to have her daughter—who she thought was settled in school—back on her hands. She shipped Liane back to the Ansonia in New York, where she was enrolled in a day school.

One reporter had the nerve to ask if Liane herself might not take to the stage. Anna was appalled at the very thought. "No, I want her to write books," she said. "We women find so few ways where we can earn a living. When we find one and win, we know the hardships too well, we know the price too close. We want our daughters to go another road." But the thought had been put into Liane's head—within another few years, the question would come back to haunt Anna.

Anna reached Rochester, New York, in the spring, where one reporter noted that she was "a little stouter than of yore, but otherwise she is much the same as she was in her previous productions. . . . [She] shrugs her shoulders, rolls her eyes and wriggles her body just as she did when she made her first success in *A Parlor Match.*" Some of the less gentlemanly reporters were noting that *A Parlor Match* had been fourteen years ago and that Anna was no longer the dimpled soubrette of yore. Still Anna had the satisfaction that month of turning down an offer of five thousand dollars made by the Arnold Film Company to star in a motion picture. Since her brief flirtation with the Mutoscope Company back in 1899, Anna had not been tempted by that still new and experimental medium.

Hartford was her longest stop in April; that city was still breathless from a recent tour of *The Merry Widow,* so *Miss Innocence* had some big shoes to fill. One critic felt Anna seemed a bit bored and listless the night he saw the show. It was this Hartford stop that saw a final parting of the ways between Anna and Charles Bigelow. He was his usual talented, hilarious and troublesome self on this tour, his frequent "sick leaves" necessitating replacement by his understudies. One night toward the end of the tour, Bigelow failed to show up and his stand-in was, for some reason, unavailable, so director Julian Mitchell had to take over the exhausting part of Ezra Pettingill. Mitchell hadn't acted since he'd lost his hearing, and it was a jittery evening for the cast and crew.

Bigelow was fired and replaced for the duration of this run by William Powers. "Very few people in the audience knew the difference," said the *New Jersey Telegraph.* It was the end of Bigelow's once brilliant career. He appeared briefly in one more show—*The Waltz Kiss*—before his demons overtook him. He was found "running amuck" on Sixth Avenue, waving a gun, and wearing "an eccentric make-up," and his estranged wife, actress Valeria Hyde, had him committed to a sanitarium in Cambridge Springs, Pennsylvania. Bigelow was proclaimed nearly ready to return to his Brooklyn home when he died suddenly on March 12, 1912, at the age of forty-nine.

Miss Innocence hit Boston again on April 11, and Liane, on Easter vacation, joined her mother; the two made a gallant effort to repair their tattered friendship. Anna had gotten back the energy that the Rochester and Hartford critics had missed, and the show went over with a bang. "Anna Held is the same bewitching, vivacious and cuddlesome Anna with the rolling and alluring orbs," said the *Boston Herald.* Still, Anna sighed longingly for her approaching retirement. "I shall retire a week from Saturday night at the end of my season," she said. "I'm tired. I need a little rest and a little fun after all the years of my life I have given to the public; a little retirement where I can enjoy myself and be the companion of my little daughter." Waxing poetic about her hoped-for home in France, she sighed, "I want a little garden where I can raise potatoes and—what do you call it—asparagus; but that takes three years and perhaps I may come back before that, for a little more money to grow it." Reporters did not hesitate to bring up the subject of her marriage, which was now known to be on somewhat rocky grounds. "I want to live in France some of the time," Anna replied carefully, "and Mr. Ziegfeld wants me to live here. We may compromise by living part of the time in France and part of the time in America."

Miss Innocence made a triumphal return to New York on April 18, 1910, for a few last performances, opening the new City Theater way down on Fourteenth Street near Union Square. The *New York World* critic thoroughly enjoyed the show, writing that "Anna Held mounted to glory last night . . . making a real flight in the heart of the White Light District. . . . Miss Held is always frank, and she sheds her illusions as she does her petticoats—with a charming insouciance."

The show closed on April 23. Anna cried prettily into a lace handkerchief about this, purportedly her very last performance, saying, "I have worked very hard and have been very successful. The American public has liked Mr. Ziegfeld's productions and I am glad to be able to say that our business has been such that we hold the records of many of the first-class theaters in America." Anna mulled over a production in London ("I am anxious to play there in a few months before I retire."). She also said, "I have saved my money and I advise all actresses to do the same"—and she reassured her loyal fans that "I have agreed when Mr. Ziegfeld opens his Winter Garden to play for him ten weeks each year, so that I shall not be forgotten."

More than one Broadway sage felt that Ziegfeld's career would take a nosedive with Anna's retirement. Even as late as 1910, he was still best known for his work with her; his *Follies* would remain merely a sideline for another few years. One editorial was quite blunt about this. "Is Ziegfeld going to let his meal ticket get away from him?" asked the writer, mincing no words. "She has been the one excuse for his 'managerial' existence." Getting rather personal, the writer continued, "It was Miss Held's name which has procured him credit. Because of his alliance with her he was permitted to gamble 'in memo,' running up debts at the roulette wheel which he subsequently repudiated by stopping payment on the checks given in settlement. . . . Oh, no! Miss Held will not retire—not if Ziegfeld can help it."

Newspapers commemorated what some felt was the end of Anna's brilliant career. The *New York Telegraph* called her "the most profitable musical comedy star on the American stage," comparing her with David Warfield and Maude Adams. *Miss Innocence*, the paper noted, had made about a hundred thousand dollars in its two years. When Anna and Ziegfeld appeared at the Café des Beaux Arts in late April, the customers stood and cheered her as though she were an abdicating monarch, forcing Anna to sing "I Just Can't Make My Eyes Behave." Others looked cynically upon Anna's retirement, recalling Sarah Bernhardt's dozens of sincere "farewell tours."

There were two fiery explosions in May 1910. One took place on May 18, when Halley's Comet passed over the United States. Nervous types took refuge in churches and cellars, while the heartier partied on rooftops with telescopes. The second explosion took place when Anna Held found out that Ziegfeld had set Lillian Lorraine up in a love nest—one floor above their Ansonia suite.

According to Liane's account, she was the one to tip off her mother about their new upstairs neighbor. Everyone else in the building already knew, even Anna's maid, Beatrice. So it is quite possible that Anna at least suspected as well and was holding her peace. But Liane decided to bring things to a head. One day Ziegfeld and Liane were out walking one of Anna's lapdogs in Central Park, while Anna retired to her apartment. "Suddenly Flo said to me, 'You go on upstairs and tell Mama that I'll be up a little later,'" Liane recalled in the earlier, unpublished, version of her memoirs.

Liane followed Ziegfeld, then went back to Anna and said, "You know, Maman, Flo got rid of me so he could go up to that woman who lives in this building." Liane admitted that Anna tried to brush her off and make light of this news, indicating that she did indeed suspect the truth already. But her daughter—who made no secret of her dislike for her stepfather—insisted that they march right upstairs and see for themselves. "So the two of us walked up, Mother not wanting any gossip among the elevator boys. As we listened outside the door there was no mistaking Flo's voice—and that of a woman giggling. We must have stayed in the hall fully an hour. . . . Though I was terrified I would not leave her alone."

Ziegfeld came to the door, followed by Lillian Lorraine, in a filmy negligee. He kissed her, said, "I'll see you later," and turned, to be greeted by his stone-faced wife and smug stepdaughter. The humiliated Anna marched up to him while Liane scurried back downstairs, her job well done. "I guessed I was not needed then," she wrote. No one knows what went on in that hallway; none of the three principals ever discussed that. Anna was known for avoiding confrontation, for glossing over uncomfortable social situations with her easygoing humor and good manners. Lillian Lorraine, on the other hand, was a scrapper who did not hesitate to get into fistfights. Ziegfeld no doubt had a few nightmarish moments. Whatever happened, it was the last straw for Anna.

As long as she remained officially ignorant of Ziegfeld's affair, she could afford to play it dumb and wait for things to pass. But now she had been publicly humiliated in front of her daughter and her husband's mistress. And she knew that her servants and every employee of the Ansonia would soon be a party to this tête-à-tête, if they weren't already. Anna stormed back to her downstairs apartment and started packing. She, Liane, Beatrice, and a basketful of lapdogs moved back to the Savoy on Fifth Avenue, abandoning her lovely, carefully decorated nest at the Ansonia. She left her Louis XIV furniture, taking with her only the essentials and having some favorite pieces sent over later. Then she made arrangements to return to France immediately. Later Anna would have second thoughts about abandoning the field of battle so quickly, essentially giving Lillian Lorraine the title and deed to her husband. But Anna had had enough; she was tired of acting and she was tired of Ziegfeld.

Anna sailed for Europe on the *La Provence* on May 19. She told dockside reporters that she did not know when she would be returning—not for a year, at least. By the time she left, Ziegfeld and Lorraine were no longer in New York; they'd gone to Atlantic City to rehearse the 1910 *Follies*, set to open in New York on June 20. Ziegfeld knew he had a hit on his hands, and he was right—this edition was to be the first of his classic, hugely successful *Follies* and the first to feature black comic Bert Williams and singing comedienne Fanny Brice (it was to be the first of seven editions for each). Lorraine was well featured in the show this year, too, singing "Swing Me High, Swing Me Low" while tossing flowers to the audience from a huge swing. She was proving to be more unprofessional than ever. She and Brice took a dislike for each other from the first, which did not make for a happy backstage atmosphere.

This was also the only *Follies* in which Anna Held ever appeared—though not in the flesh. As a nod to Halley's Comet, Anna was filmed as the head of an animated comet, projected on a screen. As she streaked through the sky toward the earth, Eleanor St. Clair sang her praises. While audiences applauded this good-natured appearance, the real Anna was furiously unpacking her luggage in Paris. Liane hoped that with Ziegfeld out of the picture—due mostly to her own interference—that "Mother could remain in Paris, move to a newer apartment and let me know what it was like to have a home as other girls did." Things got off to a nice start for the girl when she and her mother took first place at that year's Fête des Fleurs, both gowned in white and riding a carriage bedecked in white orchids. But Anna had had quite enough of her daughter for the time being and shipped her off to Weimar, Germany, to a school run by the Baroness von Prinz.

By the time Anna was settled back into her Paris apartment with Liane sent off to Germany in early June, word about her split with Ziegfeld—and its cause—was already international news. On June 4 she held a miniature press conference, playing the role of the dignified, injured wife quite effectively. "I am not applying for a divorce," she said, "and I have not heard that Mr. Ziegfeld is. Of course, I do not know what the future will bring." She added that since her millionaire status had been made known, she did not lack for marriage offers. When a reporter brought up the subject of Lillian Lorraine, Anna stiffened visibly. "I have heard Miss Lorraine's name mentioned in connection with Mr. Ziegfeld," she said slowly and carefully. "She plays in the Revue for my husband—indeed, I advised him to engage her because she has talent. Mr. Shubert told me that Ziegfeld wanted to marry her, but I think he said so in order to make me jealous. If Ziegfeld wants to marry Miss Lorraine, I will say, 'so sorry,' but he can have his divorce."

But she brushed off any notions of such an occurrence actually coming about. "Mr. Ziegfeld is a fine, splendid fellow," she said loyally to another reporter on June 24. "I know him, and there is no truth in these rumors about another woman. He is not that kind. He wouldn't get in trouble with No. 2 before he was through with No. 1." Now that the subject had been brought up, Anna began to think out loud, trying to come to terms with the subject intellectually. "French novelists . . . say that a man can love two women at the same time—I don't know. Ziegfeld and myself have been practically living apart for a long time. At first he managed only me and we were always together; then he took on other shows and we were apart."

Back in New York, after the successful opening of the *Follies*, Ziegfeld himself settled down to deal with reporters, and with the divorce rumors. "There's nothing to it at all," he scoffed. "I guess my wife was in a pet [bad mood] at the time. She's only a bit vexed because I cannot go over to Paris where she is staying with my father and mother." Anna was infuriated to see her heartbreak and humiliation dismissed so offhandedly. Her friend Amy Leslie confronted Ziegfeld point-blank with the Lillian Lorraine affair, but he wasn't changing his story. "Enemies of mine persist in handing out that Lorraine stuff," he told Leslie on July 8. "I am interested in her enough to believe I can in time make a paying star out of her if she doesn't listen to one of the Goulds and marry him before I can put her before the public ready for starring." Then he told Leslie in a confiding manner, "You know just how Anna feels when she has to go to Paris alone. She is sore because I will not and cannot leave my business and go to Paris. You know that I don't like Paris. I have nothing but misfortune over there and I never want to see it again. But Anna loves every inch of ground in the old false-face bluff, and I am going over there in two weeks to see Anna. And if anybody asks you about a divorce, say 'no' as loud as you can for both of us, will you?"

Anna battened down the hatches in her apartment. She went nowhere, she saw no one except the occasional reporter, and she accepted none of the offers of work that poured in. She had a lot of decisions to make: Was her retirement now as tempting as it had been before she lost her husband? Had she indeed lost him—and did she want him back? As hurt and furious as Anna was, she still loved Ziegfeld and couldn't make up her mind what course to take. In mid-July she received a cable from him which only served to stir up her emotions all the more: He was sailing on the *Kaiser Wilhelm II* and would be in Paris by August 1.

For nearly fifteen years Anna had defined herself as a wife and an actress and had taken great pride in her success in both roles. Now she found herself unsure as to whether she was still a wife or still an actress. She talked airily of "experimental marriages," trying to put a brave face on her situation. "This would be better than having a sudden marriage followed by a hasty divorce," Anna said in early June. "In the United States girls marry for business; by that I mean they marry in order to get a divorce and alimony. It's the alimony they are after; it is a mere matter of business."

Ziegfeld's enemies the Shubert brothers saw this as a golden opportunity to steal his greatest star from under his nose. Their representative—A. Toxen Worm, the same man Ziegfeld had thrown out of the Apollo Theater—approached Anna with an offer of thirty thousand dollars for a thirty-week engagement, as well as a theater named after her. Anna loyally refused this and reported back to Ziegfeld that the aptly named Worm was spreading the Lillian Lorraine story around Paris. Shubert backed off, sputtering that he would never allow someone like Anna Held appear in his clean, family-oriented theaters.

The private battle was aired in the press. The more sympathetic articles had the active participation and encouragement of Ziegfeld, while other reporters hinted that he was washed up without his star attraction. Montgomery Phister of the *Cincinnati Commercial* was saying just the opposite—that if Anna broke with her husband, her career was over. Anna, who kept up with theatrical news in the States, was horrified to read this very personal attack on her. While she lived in luxury in Paris, Ziegfeld was working himself sick for her sake, said Phister, showing great annoyance at Anna's hard-earned million. She was "Little Miss Nobody" before Ziegfeld presented her in the United States. "Florence [*sic*] had shown a decided predilection for the theatrical business long before Anna Held was ever dreamed of," the article continued. Phister dismissed the Lillian Lorraine rumors and said that Anna was just being lazy and spoiled, wanting Ziegfeld to pay her more attention. The *New York Review* stood up for her, citing Ziegfeld's dalliances and saying, "No blame can be attached to Miss Held in this matter. It is not to be wondered that at last she has rebelled and refuses to permit herself to be so used."

An unnamed source claimed that Ziegfeld paid Anna a large salary which she selfishly banked and refused to loan him a cent. "There will come a split someday, and Zeigfeld [sic] will learn that Anna Held cares nothing for him, but only for the money he is enabling her to make," said an unsigned article. Anna's friends told her that Ziegfeld himself had placed the article and not to pay it any mind. But she was so used to relying on her husband's management that she was unsure if she *could* handle her career without him. She recalled other great actresses whose careers declined without the expert management of their Svengalis. Mrs. Leslie Carter was never as successful after leaving the management of David Belsaco, Ada Rehan's career had suffered after the death in 1899 of Augustin Daly, as had Ellen Terry's after Henry Irving's death in 1905. As much as Anna believed in her own talent, she wondered if a post-Ziegfeld career was possible. She knew that even the most enthusiastic Shubert could not give her the kind of handling that a husband would—a husband who'd always needed her as much as she'd needed him.

She saw no one in Paris that spring and early summer, she went nowhere, and she turned away well-meaning friends who tried to match her up with the many available men scratching at her door. "I can't receive attentions from other men, so my life is not happy," Anna said to a reporter later in June, beginning to sound somewhat desperate in her loneliness. "I love Paris; it's my home and I want to live here and enjoy myself. But I can't do this alone. I'm serious. You can tell Mr. Ziegfeld he'd better come to Paris." She read newspaper reports of Ziegfeld and Lillian Lorraine publicly hitting New York nightspots, and friends privately told her that Lorraine was even seen driving one of Anna's cars around the city.

By that time Ziegfeld was steaming his way toward Paris on the *Kaiser Wilhelm II*, determined to win his wife back. But was it for love or business? He had jewelry in his pocket and loving words on his lips—but he also had a contract for a third season of *Miss Innocence* in his baggage. "Everything between us is quite amicable," he told dockside reporters, "and there is no truth in these reports" of divorce. He shot a few darts at the Shuberts, as well. The rumors "have been circulated by my business enemies solely for advertising purposes. Every few days they cause a story to be printed to the effect that they have offered my wife from seventy-five thousand dollars to ninety thousand dollars for an engagement of thirty weeks. I am sure they have not done so, but they succeed in getting considerable free advertising through the newspapers by continuously sending these stories out." He confidently stated that "Miss Held will return here in a month to six weeks, but I do not think she will play the coming season. I have a new piece to read to her, and I may be able to induce her to appear, although she needs a good long rest."

Ziegfeld spent the next three weeks sweet-talking Anna, courting her both romantically and professionally. Fortunately for his case, the meddlesome Liane was safely away at school (she once said of her stepfather, "Like an evil spirit he was able to keep [people] under his influence."). Anna and Ziegfeld went to the races, automobiled around Paris and neighboring towns, dined, and attended the theater. He showered her with gifts, assured her that Lillian Lorraine was no more than a momentary lapse of judgment, and that he was lost without her. He put out a press story that he was about to buy the hit song "Every Little Movement" from the show *Madame Sherry* just for Anna (this never came about).

Anna was very willing to be convinced, and when Ziegfeld returned to the United States in late August, he had a contract for a third season of *Miss Innocence*, beginning in late 1911. "I feel she had earned a long vacation," said Ziegfeld, adding, "I do not believe that the public is in the least interested in my private affairs." Now that she had reconciled with Ziegfeld, Anna spoke of him with a lighter heart. "Why be jealous?" she laughed. "It makes a woman ugly. If there is one who loves you truly he will love you without giving you anxiety; and if he is not of that sort . . . why give yourself trouble about him?" A vindictive Lee Shubert then proclaimed that Anna Held would never play a Shubert theater as long as he had anything to say about it.

—7—

The Unchastened Woman

There was nothing in Anna's new contract with Ziegfeld to keep her from working in Europe over the next year. As she felt more secure in her relationship with her straying husband, her professional pride perked up as well. "Work keeps you young, and I hate to grow old," she told Ormesby Burton of the *Morning Telegraph*. "There is something about the theater which holds me and compels me to make a success." So she accepted an offer to perform in London for the first time in more than a decade.

Anna was paid twenty thousand dollars to appear for a four-week engagement at the Palace Theatre of Varieties in December 1910. She worked up an act of five songs (including "Won't You Come and Play with Me?" but, oddly, not her newer hit, "I Just Can't Make My Eyes Behave"). She rehearsed routines with the Palace Girls, including a number in which they threw brightly colored balls into the audience. Anna's fifteen-minute act came on at 10:15 (right between the Abbaz Ben Zair "Arab Acrobats" and Arthur Prince and his Sailor Boy Jim). Coincidentally, she played on the same bill with the clown bicyclist Ritchie, who had performed with her at the same theater back in 1896. Anna's Palace venture was a modest success, and she had fun reacquainting herself with the town that had introduced her to Ziegfeld. She went riding in Rotten Row and was photographed unaware by an early paparazzo while lifting her skirt to adjust her riding boots.

In all of her London interviews, Anna was asked about the women's rights activists, who were dominating the British headlines early at the time. They had been becoming more militant since 1903, when Sylvia Pankhurst formed the

Women's Social and Political Union. That group moved to London in 1906 and their actions had become less patient and more outrageous year by year. Anna was completely taken aback by the question: She had always been a liberated woman, earning her own living since she was a teenager and looking after herself financially much better than either of her husbands had done. "Equal rights" simply was not an issue that concerned her.

"I love London, but your suffragettes make me nervous!" she told Ormesby Burton. "Why do they go about slapping men? Oh, please tell them not to slap the men, for man was made for woman to lean on, not to slap. . . . A woman cannot appear at her best when she is trying to knock a policeman's helmet off." As for giving women political power, Anna scoffed, "Why, if women had the vote they would give it to the handsomest, the nicest candidate, and that would make a pretty Parliament!" Her other quotes on the subject were equally antisuffragette and amused her theatrical associates, who knew her to be a level-headed businesswoman and smart career manager. "If a woman votes and does all the things a man does," Anna said, "she will be to him only 'my comrade'—never 'my darling, my sweetheart.' . . . It is not that I do not think women are as clever as men," she insisted, "They are. . . . They could interest themselves in votes, if they wanted to, but why do they want to? A chiffon gown is much more interesting than an election," Anna summed up prettily. "I don't care at all who is president, if the lace on my bodice is put on right."

Oddly, it was only on the subject of clothing that Anna sounded curiously modern. "Men understand the art of dressing much better than women," she told another reporter. "They have their hair cut close so that it is easily kept clean. Their clothes do not hamper their movements. They have pockets for their handkerchiefs and money. They have no pins in their hair and no pins in their hats. Do you think a man would ever get anywhere if he went in high heeled shoes, holding onto his hat with one hand and holding up his train with the other—with a hat pin sticking into his head on one side and a hairpin on the other?"

Anna—herself the picture of a curled and corseted fashion plate—suggested that if suffragettes really wanted to do some good for other women, they should campaign for clothing reform. "In these days when women are trying to do so many things that men do, I wonder why they do not follow their example where it would do the most good. Women talk about the disadvantages of being a woman, of the freedom of men, and make no effort to adopt the one thing which would give them nine-tenths of the advantage and the freedom they covet. . . . Women wouldn't have to throw stones and break windows and make talks on street corners to be allowed to dress—not like men, but as wisely.

Left, Roller skating with Earle Reynolds in the finale of *The Parisian Model.* Wisconsin Center for Film & Theatre Research. *Above*, A newspaper sketch of Charles Bigelow and Anna in *The Parisian Model.* Author's collection. *Below*, Sixteen "Anna Held Girls" from Ziegfeld's 1907 *Follies* posing outside New York's Astor Hotel. Harry Ransom Humanities Research Center, The University of Texas at Austin.

Anna lets her hair down. Culver Pictures.

Above, Anna and Liane Carrera in Paris, ca. 1908. Culver Pictures. *Right*, Lillian Lorraine. The Everett Collection.

Above, Anna and Leo Mars "Up in an Aeroplane" in *Miss Innocence* (1908). Wisconsin Center for Film & Theatre Research. *Right, Miss Innocence.* Corbis/Bettman.

Anna, ca. 1910. Culver Pictures.

Above, In her Paris apartment. Wisconsin Center for Film & Theatre Research. *Left,* Ziegfeld and Lillian Lorraine in 1912. Harry Ransom Humanities Research Center, The University of Texas at Austin.

Shortly after 1910. Culver Pictures.

Billie Burke. The Everett Collection.

Anna in 1913, wearing the most hideous gown ever seen on the American stage. Wisconsin Center for Film & Theatre Research

Elevating an Elephant for Kinemacolor, 1913. Wisconsin Center for Film & Theatre Research.

Left, A 1914 caricature of Anna. The caption reads, "The peculiarities of his countrywoman, Anna Held, the Parisian actress of the luminous orbs, are here depicted in the inimitable style of Rabajol, the French caricaturist." *Right,* A 1910 sketch of Anna in performance. Both from the author's collection.

ANNA · HELD

Above, Anna (far left) and her troupe of front-line entertainers, 1914/15. *Left,* A postcard of Anna performing during the early months of the war. Both courtesy of Martensen/ Isola family.

Right, A costume still for a *Photoplay* layout of *Madame La Presidente*, late 1915. Wisconsin Center for Film & Theatre Research. *Below,* Marching through Paris with her troupe of Boy Scouts, 1915. Culver Pictures.

Above, With Liane Carrera on the set of *Madame la Presidente. Below,* With Forrest Stanley and Page Peters in *Madame la Presidente,* 1916. Both from Wisconsin Center for Film & Theatre Research.

Anna in the "peacock gown" designed by Lucile for *Follow Me* (1916). Courtesy of Martensen/Isola family.

Above, Anna recruits for the war effort in Canada, ca. 1917. Courtesy of Martensen/Isola family. *Left,* A tired-looking Anna in her last show, *Follow Me.* Wisconsin Center for Film & Theatre Research.

Anna's rue Faubourg St.-Honoré home, 1999. Photo by Jo Lowrey.

The Savoy, where Anna moved in 1911 and where she died. The Museum of the City of New York. Byron Collection.

Left, Anna's grave, in Mt. Pleasant, New York. 1999 photo by the author. *Below*, Luise Rainer and William Powell as Anna and Ziegfeld in the 1936 film *The Great Ziegfeld*. Photo courtesy of Michael Powazinik.

And it seems to me this is a matter of far more importance than the thing they are making such a hue and cry about. . . . I am sure women can never do men's work in the world nor control the affairs of nations until they learn to dress as sanely as men."

But other aspects of feminism simply did not interest her. As theater historian Philip Lewis noted, "Equality on the job was such an old thing to the ladies working in the theater that the issue had no meaning. Actresses as a matter of course paid their part of the checks, lugged their own luggage without expecting or simpering for male help, negotiated their own contracts, got their own hotel rooms and gave orders like a man." It never occurred to Anna that other women couldn't do the same. Additionally, Anna made her living by portraying—onstage and off—a giggly, flighty girl, bedecked in frills and gauze. It would hardly be in her public image to march for women's rights in a "mannish" suit. She was, in short, a heartache to suffragettes, who never ceased trying to win her over to their cause. It would take a World War for them to succeed.

Anna returned to Paris for New Year's 1911—and a tumultuous New Year it was. Paris suffered the second of two horrendous floods within a year at the beginning of 1911, and shortly thereafter political turmoil resulted in the resignation of Prime Minister Briand (Anna, living right across the street from the president's official residence, was more inconvenienced by this political upheaval than most Parisians).

Back in America, Ziegfeld was enjoying his first hit show that was neither an Anna Held extravaganza nor a *Follies*. *The Pink Lady*, which opened March 13 at the New Amsterdam, was coproduced with Klaw and Erlanger; it played through December 9 before going on tour. It was a show that might have provided a great vehicle for Anna ten years earlier: Newcomer Hazel Dawn starred as a girl who unexpectedly meets her ex-lover's fiancée and has to masquerade as an antiques dealer to protect his new romance. The *Ziegfeld Follies of 1911* (which opened June 26) was also a big hit, starring Fanny Brice, the Dolly Sisters, Leon Errol, Bert Williams—and Lillian Lorraine.

For all his professional success, Ziegfeld still had trouble controlling his feelings for Lorraine. While *The Pink Lady* was enjoying its success and the *Follies* was rehearsing, newspaper headlines announced that Lorraine was mixed up in a fatal shooting in a Denver hotel. Ziegfeld dropped everything to rush out there, only to find her—for once—quite innocent (the altercation was over a blackmail scheme, not her favors). But still, the newspapers heralded it from coast to coast; not the kind of publicity Ziegfeld wanted for one of his stars—or for his mistress.

Anna was spending her summer traveling; she knew *Miss Innocence* backward and forward, so there was no studying to be done. "I have never traveled so much in my life as when I have when I have been 'resting,'" she said of her summer jaunts. "My automobile has worn out six speedometers, and I have covered all Europe." She traveled from Nice up to Norway and the North Sea. "In cold weather I have toured the warm countries and in warm weather the cold countries," she explained. She even managed to scout out an operetta (titled, coincidentally, *Liane*) for her friend Lillian Russell. "The score is in your voice," Anna cabled, "the book is very clean and witty, the costuming must be beautiful and the scenes are laid at Versailles and Newport, so what more could you want?" Something more, evidently, as Russell passed on *Liane*.

But all was not well between Anna and Ziegfeld; rumors (from friends, enemies and gossip columns) told her that Ziegfeld had not put enough distance between himself and Lillian Lorraine. It was reported in the *New York Review* that Anna's contract with Ziegfeld for the fall of 1911 was contingent on his being a good boy—and that he was signally failing to live up to those terms. On June 5 Anna wrote to her husband that Melville Ellis of the Shubert organization had offered her bookings for the 1911–12 season but that she had turned them down, citing her contract with him. The inference being that she would stay clear of Shubert—if Ziegfeld stayed clear of Lillian Lorraine.

Anna sailed back to New York on the *Kronprinzessen Cecilie*, arriving in late September. She didn't recognize her husband, who'd come to meet her at the dock: He'd grown a new mustache, and Beatrice was the one to pick him out of the crowd. Anna was happy and chipper on alighting, telling of a dance contest she'd won on board the ship. She went right away into rehearsals for *Miss Innocence*, which was set to open at the Forrest Theater in Philadelphia on October 16. Ziegfeld put his press agents to work, and Anna's name began appearing in U.S. newspapers full force for the first time in nearly two years. There were no over-the-top stunts this time, just the usual star interviews about fluffy human interest subjects. She spoke of her happy-go lucky demeanor: "I don't have the blues. When I am sad I sing . . . and pretty soon I am feeling so good again that I wonder I have ever been tempted to be unhappy." Brushing off her marital troubles, she smiled, "Nothing ever goes wrong; everything is all right; it is such a good world if you only look for the right things."

Offered a cigarette by a reporter hoping for a horrified reaction, Anna merely shrugged that she'd tried smoking but that "smoking cigarettes is like eating onions—the taste lasts always. Is it not shocking?" She did note, though, that she did not allow anyone to smoke in her newest railroad car, dubbed the Republic. That car, she bragged, was fitted up with all the comforts of a modern hotel. Figuratively girding her loins for her upcoming tour, Anna said: "I just know it's going to be delightful and I'll enjoy every minute of it. I'm so glad to get back to work again." Her vacation had, she said, been a great opportunity to rest, travel, and "be with my daughter . . . yet it didn't cure me of the burning desire to get back to work."

On September 25 she and Ziegfeld got together for a send-off dinner in Atlantic City, where he managed to drop her purse (containing one thousand dollars) while they were riding in a wicker roller chair. It was not the happiest of reunions. *Miss Innocence* opened on schedule, the only disaster being the usual offstage collapse of the prop airplane. This began an exhausting season for Anna. She toured for 210 days, traveling nineteen thousand miles through the South and the Pacific Coast. By the end of October, Anna's grand tour was in full steam. She hit New Orleans, where she hired Albert Krist's orchestra (at her own expense) to entertain the cast. Then it was off to Atlanta for four performances, where wives were seen fighting with their husbands for control of the opera glasses. "Anna's eyes ought to be against the law," said one admiring reviewer. "They are demoralizing. . . . Her perfectly Parisian figure, her bewitching voice and irresistible accent seem to be proof against the ravages of time." As for the show itself, "*Miss Innocence* never drags for an instant, and it hasn't a stupid or vulgar line in it."

Anna came off as thoughtful and honest in one Atlanta interview. Comparing herself with Bernhardt and other great dramatic stars, she said somewhat plaintively, "I am not serious, you know, just a little foolishness." Still coming to terms with the failure of *Mam'selle Napoleon,* Anna continued, "Life is too short for tragedy and it is really very hard to be a comedienne, but I would rather make people laugh than cry. I have only to sing a little, dance a little, and there you are. . . I was glad to get back to the stage, for they seem to like Anna Held."

She spent Thanksgiving in Kansas City, Missouri, where the local hotel would not allow her to bring her new French bulldog, General Marceau, with her: A defiant Anna slept in her railroad car, making sure the newspapers heard of this snub and played it up. She also dropped by the newsboys' dinner at the Elgin Dairy lunch room on Main Street to entertain. It made for good press and earned her a place in the hearts of many a starstruck adolescent. But she undid all her "Lady Bountiful" image by blithely telling another reporter that her yearly living expenses were between forty and fifty thousand dollars. "Traveling to Nice and Monte Carlo and all of that is expensive," she claimed innocently. "I have to stay on the stage to live my life. . . . When I retire I don't mean to count every cent. No, I shall not sit and darn stockings."

She spent quite a few of those cents while in Denver before Christmas, dropping five thousand dollars at one store and flustering a clerk so badly that he stepped on General Marceau. The *Denver Times's* Frances Wayne let loose a salvo against *Miss Innocence,* calling the show "tawdry, stale and vulgar," adding that, "All the perfumes of Arabia will not wash out the spot it leaves on memory." Politicians in San Francisco felt *Miss Innocence* was immoral and tried to have it closed. Anna took her case to the press, telling the *Examiner* her show was "gay, is it not? It amuses, does it not? It is full of lovely girls and fun, is it not? What more do you want? Immoral tendency? Not at all. What is there immoral about the limbs of a woman? Nothing at all. . . . They are all covered, these girls of mine. More covered than the men acrobats you see on the stage and do not consider immoral." Anna needn't have worried; as she no doubt knew (and the politicians never learned), all this publicity was a godsend for the box office. She was thrilled to be the first woman to be feted by the San Francisco Press Club, so the show's immorality seems to have paid off. It was also a boon to her feelings that General Marceau became the first dog admitted to the St. Francis Hotel. "I could not be without my little General," Anna gushed. "He is the cutest doggie you ever saw. We play ball together on the carpets of my private car."

The still tiny, bucolic town of Los Angeles was Anna's next stop; only recently had film companies begun to move there from the East Coast. *Miss Innocence* was booked into the Mason Opera House, where the blue laws were suspended so Anna could play a New Year's Eve performance on Sunday, December 31 (some of the racier lines were cut to allow this waiving of religious rules). While in town, Anna visited a Los Angeles ostrich farm and was photographed jauntily perched sidesaddle atop one of the birds. The Los Angeles press thought the show—the same one that had so offended Denver—was charming and witty, free from vulgarity.

She had an unusual encounter while in Sacramento: A colorful woman calling herself Cherry de St. Maurice called on Anna in her private railway car, telling Anna that she was Maurice Held's sister and therefore Anna's aunt. She was also the proprietress of one of Sacramento's most popular bordellos. "She took a fancy to me," Anna later recalled. "She often told me that when she died I should be the one to succeed her." Anna never did become a house madam, but she nearly inherited the Cherry de St. Maurice fortune. In July 1913 the unfortunate woman was murdered by a prizefighter (who was later hanged for the deed). She left Anna her estate of one hundred thousand dollars—but more legitimate relatives eventually came forward to claim it.

Interviewers followed Anna day and night, into her hotel suites, dressing rooms, and restaurants, but she managed to keep up a cheerful face despite her exhaustion and her worry over Ziegfeld. A *Los Angeles Examiner* reporter quizzed her while she made up for the show one night. The subject of Sarah Bernhardt's affair with a young man came up, and Anna delicately suggested, "Sarah needs the exuberance of a youthful companion as a sort of tonic. . . . It gives her new energies." The reporter watched Anna prepare herself to go onstage, noting with some amazement that she used no "hair rats" or false poufs, simply "a twist and seven hair pins." Anna claimed to detest her stage makeup: "This paint and powder makes me ugly. It keeps me young to be natural."

Anna played mother to her large troupe (which included comic Harry Watson Jr., in Charles Bigelow's old role). She gracefully deflected some of the publicity onto her Anna Held Girls, including Marjorie Bonner (whose family had struck it rich with oil stocks), Evelyn Westbrook (who had been "bred in old Kentucky"), and Esther Olsen (who was stricken with appendicitis while the show was in Philadelphia). Anna did manage to put her foot in her mouth and get in trouble with her chorus when she gave an interview saying what a terrible life the stage was for girls, that they risked being "ruined." It's a testimony to her open relationship with her chorus that they felt free to criticize their boss without fearing for their jobs. And criticize they did, too, as well as praise their situation. "The life is not half as bad as the drudgery of a department store," said Kathleen Florence. "And I have seen more things of a distressing nature going on in a department store than I ever saw on the stage." Westbrook added that for a woman the stage "broadens her mind and sharpens her wits and prepares her for the snares that are laid in her path in life."

On January 8, 1912, Ziegfeld's *Over the River* opened, coproduced with Charles Dillingham and starring Leon Errol and Lillian Lorraine. Ziegfeld was trying to get out from under the managerial thumbs of Klaw and Erlanger and hoped an association with Dillingham—the producer of such varied shows as *Man and Superman, Mlle Modiste* and *The Red Mill*—might be the answer. It was a big risk featuring Lillian Lorraine, even in a supporting role; it was a risk that would not pay off, either professionally or personally, as he found out within a few months.

Anna trouped through Seattle and Spokane in January, hitting February snowstorms in St. Louis and Chicago. In Seattle it was reported that Anna was going to file for divorce. Ziegfeld coldly answered the rumors by saying, "I do not know of any reason why my wife should institute such proceedings if, as reported, she will do so. Our relations have always been amicable. This is a private matter of no interest to the public. That is all I am going to say." Horrified, Anna demanded a retraction from the newspaper, explaining (and cabling to Ziegfeld) that it had all been a misunderstood joke. "I had been riding in an automobile around Seattle," she said. "In all my travels around Europe I had never seen anything like it—the mountains, the water around the pretty spots, the picturesque scenery. I was amazed." The next day a reporter told her other unusual things about Washington state: "And a curious thing, he said, was that one could get a divorce in two minutes. That, of course, amazed me. I said in a joke, 'then a divorce for me!' Then he replied, 'but you have to reside here a year,' to which I said, 'that's too long for me.'"

Another sour note on her Pacific Northwest jaunt came with a review that noted Anna's increasing girth and jabbed her with: "Everybody noticed . . . that Anna was a little stouter (it's nice to be chubby). Yes, she ran to stoutness; she almost galloped to it, but for all that she hadn't lost one grain of the fascination she always had." A train wreck caused cancellation of a Spokane show, and more annoyance surfaced with bad reviews in Minneapolis, where only Harry Watson Jr. scored a hit, being hailed as "a comedy jewel in a tawdry setting." As for Anna, the same reviewer railed at her "inability to act or sing," though saluting her "glittering beauty and her cleverness in displaying it to the best advantage."

Heading east to finish the tour, Anna had a long chat with the more sympathetic Dorothy Dorr of the *Pittsburgh Leader*. Exhausted, Anna fantasized again about retiring and opening a chafing dish restaurant. "I will . . . do the cooking—and charge $10 a plate—and take the things from person to person at the tables," she planned. Anna also pondered writing a beauty book, as "there are so many women who do not know how to fold their clothing, put their clothes on or even go to bed." But she was not quite willing to abandon her career yet, and also spoke of her pride in her craft and the difficulty of staying on top of the heap. "Why, right now if I could discover a new song suited to me and my personality, I would give $1000 or more," Anna told Dorr.

The third and final season of *Miss Innocence* closed in Washington, D.C., in March 1912. Reunited with Ziegfeld in New York, Anna delicately felt her way back into her marriage, afraid to glance up at the Ansonia ceiling for fear of hearing Lillian Lorraine's footsteps. She and her husband hit the social scene, investigating the newer clubs and retiring to their usual restaurants and theater openings. In early 1912 a trip to the theater provided a bit of talent-scouting. She and Ziegfeld spotted the nineteen-year-old Mae West performing at the Columbia Theater and stopped backstage to congratulate the singer. West later claimed in her memoirs that Ziegfeld offered her a leading spot in the *Follies*, which she turned down; this is hardly likely. But Ziegfeld did cast her in a small role, as Le Petit Daffy, in *A Winsome Widow*. Based on the old hit *A Trip to Chinatown*, that show opened in April 1912, though it failed to do much for West's career.

In March, Lillian Lorraine shocked Ziegfeld (and probably delighted Anna) by abandoning her part in *Over the River* and eloping with Frederick Gersheimer, a young Chicago man she'd met during the summer of 1911 while at Atlantic City. "He was in his bathing suit and looked perfectly grand," Lorraine told reporters. "He said he could teach me to swim. . . . I jumped into the surf with him and in five minutes he had me paddling around like a little tadpole." Lorraine, while still living at Ziegfeld's expense at the Ansonia, had entertained Gersheimer on the side. Within two weeks, she was back, hat in hand: Gertrude McCauley, to whom Gersheimer was still married, had shown up to put a crimp in Lorraine's honeymoon. Her marriage annulled, Lorraine continued to see Gersheimer while he legally divorced McCauley. On April 25 the two remarried, this time legally. They honeymooned at the Savoy Hotel, which was still Anna's legal residence while she tentatively stayed at the Ansonia with her husband.

A new romance entered Anna's life at this time, in the form of a man whom she'd known for some time merely as her husband's lawyer. Charles Hanlon was a colorful San Francisco character, a dashing and handsome widower in his fifties. A yachtsman, horseman, and auto enthusiast, Hanlon also flitted around the theatrical scene (he had previously been Lillian Russell's lawyer as well). Hugely successful in his law practice, Hanlon had the reputation of being somewhat fast and loose in his business dealings. "Hey, haven't they put you in jail yet?" Ziegfeld wrote to him in 1908, during a political shake-up. "You are a sly old fox and don't think that I ain't on [to you]."

Hanlon had long been smitten with Anna, even signing his business telegrams to her "J'taime." Ziegfeld kidded him about his "bum French," pretending to mistake his sign-off as "Tabor" ("You probably had so many cocktails aboard that you could not write your own name," Ziegfeld pointedly teased him in a 1908 letter). Ziegfeld never took Hanlon's crush on Anna seriously; neither, in fact, did Anna, according to her daughter, who later added that "though Mother liked him she never seriously considered him for a husband."

But Hanlon spent more time with Anna and less with Ziegfeld in the early months of 1912, pouring doubt and suspicion into her ears. It wasn't difficult to convince Anna that her husband was still being untrue to her; he probably was. Though his romance with Lillian Lorraine had cooled off, Ziegfeld was still in touch with her and gifts of money, flowers, and jewelry followed her through her vaudeville tours. And there were other showgirls more than willing to take her place. Besides, at this point he considered himself Anna's husband in name only, a business partner as much as a lover. Anna, for all her modern European talk of trial marriages, was still very much in love with Ziegfeld and each of his meaningless affairs cut her to the quick. Hanlon was happy to play on her insecurity for his own advantage. As a lawyer with much experience in affairs of the heart, he managed to convince Anna that all Ziegfeld really needed was a good scare: Look how he had dropped everything to rush across the ocean in 1910 when all she had done was drop a few hints about divorce. If she actually filed papers, he would no doubt come crawling to her in a frenzy of remorse.

So on April 14 Anna served Ziegfeld with divorce papers. She accused him of misconduct with Lillian Lorraine on a train in Nevada on April 2, 1909, and at the Ansonia Hotel on April 1, 1910. Lorraine was referred to in the papers as Mary Ann Brennan and D.E. Jacques (the latter had been an early stage name). Ziegfeld forwarded the papers to his own lawyer, Leon Laski, and told reporters that he did not wish to discuss his private affairs, saying of Anna, "I believe she plans to retire from the stage—at least so far as America is concerned—and if she does the American stage loses one of its greatest drawing cards and an artist who has been consistently a credit to her profession. Anna Held is one woman in a million."

Anna had done the right thing, Hanlon assured her; now the best move would be to let Ziegfeld stew in his own juices. She sailed for France on the *La Savoie* on April 25, shakily telling dockside reporters, "Please do not ask me to talk about my divorce. Because Mr. Ziegfeld and I are such very good friends, it is only a little matter quite between ourselves." She even hinted that she and Ziegfeld might remarry after the divorce. "He looked so forlorn, I might give him another chance," she said, adding that she would remain under his management when she returned to the United States next year.

Anna had more than her marriage to depress her; she had also lost the companionship of General Marceau, who had been such a comfort on her recent tour. The dog had eaten a stuffed British lion "and the glass eye of the lion and the pins that are stuck in him and the sawdust it all make him very sick—and then he is dead," Anna relayed sadly. "Poor General Marceau. . . . I can get a new husband, but not a new dog."

Anna had been making ocean crossings nearly every summer for the past sixteen years. But this trip was a little different for everyone on board the *La Savoie:* Only two weeks earlier, the *Titanic* had gone down in the North Atlantic, taking with her more than fifteen hundred passengers and crew. Up till then, few passengers had given much thought to lifeboats or "unsinkable" ships; they'd just crossed their fingers and put their faith in the hands of the captain. Anna, after her first few crossings, was a good sailor and not nervous. It took a week, more or less, to cross the Atlantic in Anna's day. Since the 1890s, ocean cruises had become more elaborate, as ships got bigger and more elegant. "Barring a bridle path for the equestrian, a smooth road for the automobilist, and a forest for lovers to walk in, everything else seems to have been provided," noted one nautical expert. Anna and Ziegfeld favored German ships, which were the largest and most well appointed in the early years of the twentieth century.

Ships were social gathering places for first-class passengers, and Anna was expected to be entertaining and glamorous for her fellow voyagers; she was also expected to take part in ship's shows, concerts, and dance contests. Not everyone appreciated this. One New York society matron noted in her diary, "Our table neighbors were of a queer sort, a harmless quiet man in company with two impossible 'ladies,' and a woman who must have been Altman's 'sales lady.' Miss Anna Held was our 'star;' she did not give us her great 'undressing act,' but she did give us two songs at the concert that were beyond the limit." One can almost see her glaring daggers at Anna through her lorgnette.

When Anna settled back into her Paris abode, she was finally a free agent and producers besieged her with offers for musical comedies and vaudeville tours. She was offered a one-act sketch called *In the Wee Small Hours* by the author of *Madame X* but turned it down. Manager M.S. Bentham offered Anna one hundred thousand dollars for a twenty-five-week tour, but she opted instead to return to London's Palace in June. She also played a smash hit engagement at the Folies-Bergère, happily telling a reporter: "I really did intend to retire, but I have come to the conclusion that I am not nearly so old as I thought I was. I have been taking very good care of myself, and I am very careful of what I eat and drink, and I feel sure that I made a mistake when I thought I should like to leave the stage." Her reviews, she said, had changed her mind. "I was delighted to find how kind they were to me. Reading what they said, I wondered whether it was really of me they were talking."

Anna had made another liberating change in her life by 1912: She had given up wearing the corsets that she had helped to popularize and with which she is still associated. Anna now wore a wide elastic girdle rather than the new-fangled (and much hated) straight-fronted corset; this certainly gives lie to later stories that she squeezed herself to death.

She was even able to joke about marriage, as the date for her interlocutory decree approached in August 1912. "Yes, yes, I am seeking a husband," she laughed to reporter John L. Eddy. "As soon as the right man asks me, I shall say, 'it is not good for a woman to live alone.'" When Eddy commented on the prevalence of divorce among the theatrical set, Anna objected. "I do not think theatrical people are different from any others," she said. "If there are more divorces among them than among other classes, it is simply because wives and husbands are separated so much, not because they are stage folk. Some actors may make temperament an excuse for immorality, but so do painters, musicians, and other artists." She also added that there are "quite a few businessmen who go in for temperament" as well.

With an ocean between herself and her husband, Anna felt like philoso-phizing on marriage and divorce, and a *New York Evening World* reporter found her views to be quite modern. "I cannot understand these society people who will not get a divorce because of this scandal," Anna told him. "Scandal, what is that? Pouf! And also they forget—if a man and woman are unhappy together, they cannot conceal it. The world will see, the world will talk—the divorce will not make more talk. To me [divorce] seems so much better, so much more dignified, than the continual quarrels and fights. . . . Oh, I think it is wicked for a marriage to be a chain!"

Anna found her own marriage to be a chain not as easily broken as she'd thought: Later in August the news broke that Anna's interlocutory decree had been turned down by Judge Edward G. Whitaker. Part of the problem was the news that Anna and Ziegfeld had never married; Anna had to file testimony from Paris about their informal "wedding" of 1897, and that they'd been living together in New York long enough to qualify as legal man and wife. There was amazingly little public outcry about this arrangement; common-law marriages were not as unusual in the early twentieth century as they would be within just a few decades. Anna also resubmitted testimony about Ziegfeld's misconduct with Lillian Lorraine. Judge Whitaker told Anna that her divorce would be finalized sometime early in 1913, but Charles Hanlon assured her that Ziegfeld would never really let her go.

In October Ziegfeld's 1912 *Follies* opened, featuring Lillian Lorraine sing-ing "Row, Row, Row." The song proved to be a great hit—but not in the *Follies*. Ziegfeld willingly put up with Lorraine's drinking, her backstage temper tan-trums, and her lateness. But his coproducer A.L. Erlanger was not having an affair with her and was not so forgiving. When she failed to show up for a rehearsal in early November, he fired her—some felt Ziegfeld was secretly re-lieved. Lorraine took "Row, Row, Row" off to Hammerstein's Victoria and scored a hit in vaudeville. "Miss Lorraine . . . instantly wins her audience," wrote one reviewer, ". . . by her grace, the sweetness of her voice, and an inter-esting repertoire."

As his affair with Lillian Lorraine cooled off, Ziegfeld began making romantic overtures to Anna via cables and letters; Anna reponded in kind. As 1912 ended, there was some talk of reconciliation. Anna gratefully felt that Charles Hanlon's "scare tactic" had worked after all—and Hanlon was terrified that she was right. "I have decided to be a good boy," a chastened Ziegfeld said on December 20, "and she has promised to take me at my word and come home and begin all over again." Their plans, though, seemed somewhat eccentric: "We will allow the divorce proceedings to continue and Miss Held will secure a final decree. . . . Then we are going to remarry and begin all over again. And we're going to begin right, too."

The couple sent each other affectionate Christmas greetings, and Anna did not forget her in-laws. "I have learned to appreciate her now; there is no one like her," Ziegfeld said. Anna, however, was playing it cool to the press. "I have the friendliest feeling in the world for Mr. Ziegfeld," she said. "But as to remarrying him, I had not thought of it. I like him, but I do not love him, I am sorry to say." Still hurting from the unforgivable Lorraine episode and suspicious of Ziegfeld's sudden about-face, she added nastily, "If he does not wish to make me his wife again for love, perhaps he is actuated by business motives."

Every producer with enough money to meet Anna's price was begging for her services. For the first time she was without Ziegfeld's enthusiastic backing and did not know where to turn. Anna had met theatrical manager Michael B. Leavitt on an ocean cruise, and he'd offered to introduce her to his friend John Cort. Cort was nearly as picturesque a figure in show business as Ziegfeld. An ex-vaudevillian, he formed the Northwest Theatrical Association, and within a few years owned nearly a hundred theaters, the majority of them in the western United States. Like Ziegfeld, Cort was torn between the dueling powers of Klaw and Erlanger's Syndicate and the Shubert brothers, his affiliations changing with the wind. In May 1913 Anna signed an agreement with Cort for a five thousand dollars-a-week tour through America—but within a year she was to bitterly regret meeting both Cort and Michael Leavitt.

As her career as a freelance variety artist beckoned, the expected finally happened, nonetheless taking Anna by surprise: After sixteen years of marriage, her divorce from Florenz Ziegfeld became final on January 9, 1913.

Anna's life nearly ended shortly after her marriage did. On February 26 her chauffeur was driving Anna and a gentleman friend, H. Keene Hargreaves, along a cliffside road in Monaco. In a foreshadowing of Princess Grace's death nearly seventy years later, the driver lost control of the car and it tumbled off the road and toward the sea. Fortunately all the occupants were thrown from the car and suffered only bumps and bruises. A passerby (according to one account, he was the local chief of police) gave the shaken trio a ride back to Monte Carlo. One newspaper claimed that Anna's famed sable coat fell into the sea and was lost, but that would have been quite a flying leap for such a heavy garment.

Anna laughed off this brush with death, but it confirmed for her that she was indeed starting over, beginning a new life. Friends in Paris said that the newly single Anna seemed as happy as a lark, shopping for groceries and even inviting Liane home for holidays. She darted through the crowds in front of newly appointed president Raymond Poincaré's palace, satisfied to be just another anonymous pedestrian in the throngs.

She returned to the stage in April 1913 with a one-act, two-character playlet called *La Chic Américaine*, at the Théâtre Marigny. She sang several songs (including "I Just Can't Make My Eyes Behave," and a comic "Votes for Women" number poking fun at the movement). Anna played an American sparring verbally with a flirtatious Frenchman. More philosophical than comic, the play had Anna insisting that American women "have grown up in a new country where space is greater, traditions less numerous, masculine domination less fixed than in Europe. They have been able to develop an independent character. They were born free and have remained so voluntarily, resolutely, obstinantly." *La Chic Américaine* was not a milestone in Anna's career, but it did keep her busy while hammering out her agreement for her upcoming American vaudeville tour.

That agreement with John Cort was finally signed in March, through the offices of theatrical agent H.B. Marinelli. Meanwhile, back in the United States, Ziegfeld's 1913 *Follies* were about to open, in a new home, the New Amsterdam Theater on Forty-second Street (the show would stay at that venue through 1927). That edition showcased the talents of Leon Errol, Rosie Dolly, Ann Pennington, and "tramp comic" Nat Wills. After her debacle in 1912, Lillian Lorraine was no longer in the show.

Ziegfeld was having other troubles with his tempestuous mistress as well. Her marriage to Fred Gersheimer ran into rough seas immediately—perhaps because she maintained her suite at the Ansonia in addition to the Gersheimer suite at the Sherman Square Hotel. In late June Ziegfeld and Lorraine were dining at Louis Martin's restaurant in Times Square when they noticed Gersheimer loitering menacingly outside the front windows. The couple hastily exited through the back door, with Gersheimer hot on their heels. "Say! You know that woman is my wife!" a witness heard him yell. Gersheimer brought his walking stick down on Ziegfeld's head as Lorraine screamed, "Oh, Freddie! Don't! Don't!" Gersheimer then felled Ziegfeld with a right to the jaw and fled in a taxi.

Ziegfeld went home in his own car and called his doctor. The next day, nursing a black eye and bruised jaw, he tried to play down the fight to reporters. He claimed he'd gone with a male friend to Louis Martin's after the theater, "and as we were about to enter the restaurant I caught sight of Miss Lorraine. She was in a cab in front of Martin's. We are old friends, you know, and in a most natural and proper way she nodded and beckoned to me. Of course I joined her at once, and stood chatting with the lady through the open window of her cab. Then 'bif, bim,' something struck me on the head and down I went." Needless to say, no one bought this version for a minute—there were too many witnesses eager to talk to the press. Lorraine filed for divorce shortly thereafter. "My husband's only occupation was betting on the races," she complained to the court. Gershheimer could not be found for comment: After the fight with Ziegfeld, he'd fled to Europe and was not heard from again thereafter.

This squalid and embarrassing incident did not put an end to Ziegfeld's relationship with Lillian Lorraine, but it certainly dampened it. She did not work with him again professionally for another five years. While he stayed in touch with her, and supported her financially when she was in need, their affair flickered and sputtered and she went off on her own as an actress. Lorraine continued in vaudeville with mixed success, and in 1915 moved to Los Angeles, where she starred in a serial called *Neal of the Navy* and a drama called, ironically, *Should a Woman Forgive?*

Anna could not forgive such public goings-on. Fisticuffs on Broadway not only made Ziegfeld look cheap and foolish, they made her feel dragged down into his tawdry affairs. She spent the rest of the summer filling music hall engagements in France and England, with mixed success. In June she made a hit at the Folies-Bergère, but her July appearance in the revue *Come Over Here* at the London Opera House was, as the expression went, "a frost." She refused to make changes in her act and walked out on the show in early August. She retired to the beach at Shoreham, England, for a holiday, wearing a shocking, formfitting one-piece bathing suit. Another car accident spelled the end of her stay in England—she and Beatrice were thrown from her car after skidding into a ditch outside London. All in all, Anna was glad to see the last of that country. Later that month she returned to the more welcoming arms of Paris via a stint at the Olympia Théâtre. She sang "La Griserie" and "Everybody Loves a Chicken," performing on the same bill as the wildly popular dance team Vernon and Irene Castle.

Anna also saw a great deal of Charles Hanlon, who, according to Liane, put evil thoughts about Ziegfeld into her head and tried to further his own case as a suitor; but she continued to turn down his offers of marriage. She met socially with producers Charles Frohman and Charles Dillingham, bringing Liane along. Dillingham had with him a trunkful of tricks and gadgets, and the ladies amused themselves with Chinese finger traps and various puzzles. "'It takes someone real clever to do this,'" Liane recalled Anna sighing prettily. "She could not manage to make a single one of them work," the daughter gloated. Liane solved them all—but Anna later took her aside and told her in a motherly way, "I have seen these little tricks many times before. But you'll never catch a man if you let him think you are too smart."

Preparing for her return to the United States, Anna gave a hurried interview to her old champion, Alan Dale. He caught up with her at an actor's fund benefit, where Anna touched him for twenty francs. She lightly brushed off any talk of reconciliation with the man who had become her recent ex-husband. "It is quite lovely being single," Anna defiantly laughed, "and I much prefer it. I can have just as good a time, and no trouble. That's the way I feel about it. Why should I remarry? I don't want any more marriage—yet. I'm sorry to disturb that pretty picture of a remarriage, but I must do it."

She went on to taunt "poor Ziegfeld," telling Dale that "I am sorry for him. He is so used to managing me." She then discussed her proposed tour for John Cort, peppering Dale with questions about the current Broadway scene: "Now, tell me all the news in New York. How was the season? How were the new plays? Who has appeared there of late? Has any big artist been over there?" Actually, the only big news had been the 1912 premiere of the Shubert *Passing Show*, a yearly variety review put on for the sole purpose of competing with the *Follies* and annoying Ziegfeld.

Anna left for New York at the end of August, but with no Ziegfeld to arrange her passage, things did not go smoothly. Her entourage managed to get to the ship in time: Liane, Beatrice, another secretary, a maid and a valet, a brace of Pomeranian dogs, a Manx cat, twenty-one wardrobe trunks, a jewel chest, and a new Graflex Kodak. But Anna herself missed the boat train. She was on an outing with a new beau, aeronaut Cort St. Croix de la Roncière. The two were watching a safari film being shot outside Paris and lost track of time. (Anna later fancifully claimed to have shot a tiger that attacked them, but no one took her very seriously.) When the couple finally realized how late they were running, the count flew Anna to her La Havre connection in his biplane—he wanted to fly her to the ship from the dock, but authorities insisted she take a boat with the other late passengers.

Anna and Liane arrived back in the United States on September 5, 1913, on the *La France*, a brand-new ship known for both its lovely Empire decor and for "rolling like a sick headache," being set rather low in the water. John Cort met Anna at the pier with a huge floral horseshoe, but Liane dimmed the effect somewhat by trilling (in full hearing of several reporters), "Isn't it beautiful? Mama spent over $50 to have that brought down here!" Process servers from the Hexter Stable Company added to the joyous occasion by handing Anna a bill for $288; she smiled thinly and handed them each a rose.

After more than a year away, Anna found a new America. Show business had changed, and *Miss Innocence* suddenly seemed rather quaint. The kind of big, floral-bedecked, waltz-filled show Anna starred in was about to receive a death-blow. In 1913 Jerome Kern's *Oh, I Say!* opened; it was to be the harbinger of the smaller, plot-driven musicals of the rest of the teens and throughout the twenties. But the biggest change in show business—indeed, in society at large—was the ragtime dance craze. This had been slowly building up steam since 1899, when Scott Joplin's first "rags" were published. These were polite, almost classical, tunes; over the next decade, popular music was infused by the cakewalk, minstrel songs, and finally the earthshaking syncopations of songwriters like Irving Berlin, whose "Grizzly Bear" (1910), "Alexander's Ragtime Band," and "Everybody's Doin' It Now" (both 1911) changed the sound of popular music.

Only the rock 'n' roll revolution two generations later can be remotely compared with what happened soon after 1910. Of course, the waltz, the polka and the quadrille had all been cursed as evil influences in their day, but when the one-step and two-step became popular with the young set, alarms went off all over the nation. These new dances involved touching: not just holding hands or clasping a waist, but couples clinging to each other as they jounced up and down, legs intertwined, leaning into each other's faces while executing such suggestively named steps as the Bunny Hug and the Grizzly Bear.

The older generation—the generation that by now included Anna and Ziegfeld—was taken by surprise, and many hated this new music and its unnerving influence upon youth. According to the historian Mark Sullivan, ragtime gleefully smacked of "overthrow, of revolution. It consciously jeered at the older music, always in spirit, often in words." Churches and newspapers inveighed against it. In words that would be repeated almost verbatim in the 1950s about rock (and again, later, about rap), one paper thundered that modern music was "responsible for deterioration of manners, taste, and right thinking. . . . The real danger to the community is the songs that give young folks a false and perverted impression of love and romance, and which hold a pure and romantic sentiment up to slangy ridicule." In January 1914 the Vatican issued a condemnation of ragtime songs and dances.

Anna had seen it all coming: The biggest hit in *Miss Innocence* was not her own lilting tunes but the jazzy "Yankiana Rag." She saw it in New York in 1913, the first big year for cabarets and tango teas. Office workers headed for these establishments at lunchtime to dance and socialize. They even mixed class—the younger social elite attended (to their parents' horror) along with shopgirls and clerks.

Writer Julian Street, who hated everything newfangled, not surprisingly hated ragtime and those cabarets springing up in its wake. "From Little Italy in Houston Street, to Pabst's vast armory-like restaurant in 125th, you will find them everywhere," he complained. "Rag-time, turkey-trotting spots upon the city map; gay cabarets, jay cabarets; cabarets with stages and spot-lights, cabarets on ground floors, in cellars, and on roofs; cabarets where 'folks act gen'l'mumly,' cabarets where the wild time grows. . . . You can't escape the cabaret. As you drive up to the apartment house which you call home, you discover that the janitor has started up a basement cabaret while you've been gone." As one song accurately put it, "Everybody's Doin' It Now," while Irving Berlin's 1913 "International Rag" triumphantly elaborated:

> What did you do, America?
> They're after you, America!
> You got excited and you started somethin',
> Nations jumpin' all around.
> You've got a lot to answer for,
> They lay the blame right at your door—
> The world is ragtime crazy from shore to shore!

With this new emphasis on complicated dance steps, the Anna Held Girls of old looked somewhat clomping. Most were competent but not professional dancers, and they were now being pushed aside—literally—by the new ballroom dance teams. New standards for theatrical dance were being set by Vernon Castle and his slim young wife, Irene; Anna's former employee Mae Murray and Clifton Webb; Maurice and Florence Walton; and a lithe teenage immigrant from Italy, Rudolph Valentino. When the third season of *Miss Innocence* was cast, more emphasis had to be placed on dancing.

The New York of 1913 didn't only sound new, it looked new. Since Anna had first arrived in 1896, the city had taken a great leap from the nineteenth century into the twentieth. Many of the low, elaborately decorated buildings had been replaced by the creeping of skyscrapers into the Manhattan outline. It seemed to happen overnight, rather than in one decade. Since 1903, there appeared the still famous Fuller ("Flatiron") Building, the beautiful Times Building, the Singer Tower, the City Investing Building, the Metropolitan Life Tower, and finally the literal pinnacle of New York architecture, the fifty-eight-story Woolworth Building, completed in 1913.

There were other new landmarks, too, not as tall but just as important in changing the look of New York: Pennsylvania Station was acclaimed the nation's most beautiful train depot when completed in 1910, and the third (still extant and recently refurbished) version of Grand Central Station was unveiled in

1913. The eerie Croton Reservoir at Fifth Avenue and Forty-first Street was replaced in 1911 by the main branch of the New York Public Library. Right outside Anna's windows at the Savoy on Fifty-ninth Street was the Grand Army Plaza, which in 1913 unveiled its huge National Maine Memorial.

Between 1909 and 1911 Fifth Avenue was widened to accommodate automobile traffic. This necessitated chopping back sidewalk space and eliminating the decorative steps, entrances, and gardens of many Fifth Avenue mansions, shops, and churches. The cars Anna loved had, sadly, made Fifth Avenue a little less beautiful. But there was another change, which she found more amenable than did many Fifth Avenue residents: The carriage trade shopping district was edging eastward and uptown. In 1896 most of the better stores had been along Ladies' Mile, a stretch of Broadway and Sixth Avenue from 23rd to 34th Streets. But now Anna found herself within just a short stroll of some of her favorite shops, which were creeping up Fifth Avenue toward the Savoy—the huge, gaudy Windsor Arcade, Gorham's, B. Altman's, Tiffany's, Cartier's, and Lord and Taylor's. The Vanderbilts and Morgans may have been horrified, but Anna found this development delightful.

In September Anna finally gave in to years of pressure and appeared in a motion picture. She'd filmed short clips before but had always refused further offers. But the Long Island-based Kinemacolor Company, which held U.S. patents for color film, was signing such celebrities as Lillian Russell, Blanche Ring, Eddie Foy, and Raymond Hitchcock for a series of short home movies, marketed as "Popular Players off the Stage." For an undisclosed sum, Anna agreed to accompany a Kinemacolor camera crew to the Central Park Zoo on September 9, where she fed a baby calf from a milk bottle, cuddled a lion cub (which scratched her arm), and—with the help of zookeeper Bill Snyder—danced with a trick elephant named Hattie. This last maneuver gave the title to her segment: *Elevating an Elephant.* The "Famous Players" series was a hit for Kinemacolor, but not a big enough hit. They sold out to the World Film Corporation in 1915, and Anna had to sue to keep World from reshowing her little film without her permission. Anna herself did not take the film very seriously. "It does not seem like myself, but a stranger," she said. "She did some things I never thought I would do. Have you hurried past a shop and caught a reflection of yourself in the shop window and not recognized it? That is like seeing yourself in moving pictures."

Anna now found herself, for the first time in years, putting herself into the hands of an unfamiliar manager. John Cort seemed to know what he was doing. Eva Tanguay and Weber and Fields were making up to six thousand dollars a week in vaudeville tours, and Cort's handling of Lillian Russell was going smoothly. But there were incipient signs of trouble. For one thing, he bypassed the United Booking Office, which arranged for the majority of vaudeville tours through the United States: The UBO was very unhappy and threatened to make trouble (Cort had also made enemies of the Shuberts and managers A.E. Albee and Martin Beck). And Anna was used to the huge Ziegfeld backing: Cort simply could not muster the strength of publicity and advance men, newspaper mileage, and local goodwill that Ziegfeld could. This would be a scaled-down version of her previous tours, and an overworked Anna would find herself doing much of her own publicity.

Cort placed silly Anna Held-bylined articles in papers nationwide to get her name back before the public. They were typical beauty tips, fashion, random thoughts on love and life. Anna (or her ghostwriter) told of a skin lotion made from boiled cucumbers, alcohol, rose water, and glycerin, "which will keep your skin free from roughness all during the winter, and in the summer will provide a foe to sunburn." There were tips on how Anna cared for her misbehaving eyes: brushing her brows with warm oil, dashing cold water on her eyes thirty times daily, using cold cream compresses for swelling, and avoiding eye makeup.

And all through the fall of 1913, Anna was spotted out on the town with Ziegfeld, as gossip columnists were quick to note. They dined at Louis Martin's (the scene of his earlier altercation with Gersheimer), so deep in conversation that they hardly noticed patrons ogling them. Ziegfeld attended rehearsals of Anna's new show at the 44th Street Theater, no doubt to the alarm of John Cort. Less romantically, Anna won a judgment against Ziegfeld for an unpaid debt of $3393 that same month. Still, Anna played it cool when asked about a reconciliation. "One does not re-light a dead cigarette," she laughed. "Why should I marry my former husband? It is true we are good friends and—yes—it is true he wishes me to marry him. He pursues me with attentions, with letters and telegrams and flowers." She would marry any man who could present her with pearls as big as her eyes, Anna joked. She thought she was playing Ziegfeld as if he were a large trout and was enjoying every minute of the game.

Anna was not starring in a book show for Cort; rather, she was the head of a self-contained vaudeville troupe. She starred in the short musical comedy sketch Mlle Baby, in which she played a French girl who tries to discredit her boyfriend's guardian by putting him in a compromising position; that tiny plot took the manpower of Anna, fifteen costars and twenty-four chorus girls. Mlle Baby and George Beban's dramatic playlet The Sign of the Rose were the two longest pieces of the evening. The rest of the time was filled with acts such as the

Imperial Pekinese Troupe, pianist Herschel Hendler, comic bicyclist Charles Ahearn, and the dance team of Francis and Florette.

Anne got a rousing send-off with a party at the Hotel Marseilles, where her theatrical friends wished her luck, and she sang some of her *Mlle Baby* songs, accompanied by their composer, Henry Marshall. On September 24 *Anna Held's All-Star Variety Jubilee* took off on what was to be an exhausting five-month tour of the United States. She was accompanied by Liane, Beatrice, and her British-born secretary and publicist, Vincent Wray. Without Ziegfeld's management and with the United Booking Office throwing obstacles in her path, Anna could not play many of the bigger and better theaters. She did not have the advance men she was used to and had to call in her own contacts at every town to get the kind of publicity needed to pull in audiences.

She also did not have Ziegfeld's costume designers and wore in *Mlle Baby* what had to have been the ugliest dress ever seen on the American stage. It was a knee-length creation apparently composed of wilted lettuce leaves, a long black neckerchief, and a billowing top-heavy bodice. This was topped by a flat hairdo and a hat as wilted as the skirt. The overall effect was ghastly. Anna sounded nervous and a little depressed in October as she gave a long interview to the *New York Review*. She had spoken to the same reporter fifteen years earlier and was happy to reminisce. Maintaining stardom was much harder in 1913 than it was in the 1890s, Anna asserted wearily: "You must know everything, singing, acting, dancing. . . . It has become very difficult. Even I must work to keep up with the times. The art of singing even simple little songs has advanced," she elaborated. "It is not the songs, or merely the singing, but what you can do with it in suggestion."

When the subject of her private life was brought up, Anna lamented the false flattery actresses were subject to. "No one ever tells us the truth, even those we love," she sighed. "We get lonely—oh, so lonely—and we come to suspect everybody of having some design on us or our purse." Happiness, the ordinarily cheerful Anna said, was "an imaginary condition, an ideal state, which we never attain. . . . I have given up trying to be happy. It is no use and leads to nothing. I try to be right, to do what is right—and let my personal feelings take care of themselves. I find that works better." As for love, she added rather bitterly, "men easily recover from the disease, but it seems to last with a woman until it wrecks her life."

On that cheerful note, *Anna Held's All-Star Variety Jubilee* took to the road. One of their first stops was at Wesleyan College in Macon, Georgia, where Anna's song "Roll Those Dreamy Eyes" was a big hit with the students—though not with the shocked administration, who'd booked "Anna Held, the singer" without the slightest idea who she was. Anna's entrance in *Mlle Baby* particularly disturbed the college staff: Anna was glimpsed "nude" in silhouette behind a curtained window, then leaped through some French doors to the accompaniment of a calcium flash: fully dressed, of course.

The troupe played a week in San Antonio, Texas, and Anna arranged for a tour of the local missions, dating from the eighteenth century. As Vincent Wray nervously looked on, Anna clambered happily up ladders to peer in windows, joking what a good publicity stunt it would be to "fall down and break my neck." The only bad moment came when Anna spotted an innocent green snake and let out a genuine shriek of horror: "Ooh! The beast! The reptile! The horrible thing! Oh, how my heart beats—I cannot stand the snakes. I cannot stand them." As she retired to her car, Wray explained that Anna had a phobia about snakes and that once "a horrid snake charmer, a crazy woman, quite, threw a great rattlesnake at Madame Held one day when she went to a circus, and frightened Madame Held almost to death. Awful experience."

Snakes aside, Anna's show went over well in Texas, where one paper called it a "fast and furious kaleidoscope. . . . Nothing quite so elaborate had ever before been attempted in a local theater. . . . The two and a half hours seemed but a few short minutes." From Texas they moved to Colorado, where Anna visited a Denver jail to give her best wishes to the incarcerated, chatting up bank robber James Nelson and telling murderers Harold Henwood and Oscar Cook that she hoped they would evade the hangman's noose. She also gave the warden money to buy sweets for the prisoners.

By this time she herself felt rather imprisoned in her slow-moving and overheated railroad car, which traveled at an average of eleven miles per hour through Texas. "I became so restless one time," Anna recalled, "that I got off and walked around the train a few times, and do you know, it came near catching up with me, once." They next headed to Spokane (which loved the show) and Victoria, British Columbia, where Anna attended her first hockey match and caught her first salmon on a fishing trip. Early in November she marveled at her first sight of bucolic San Jose: "What a country to live in! Apricots, prunes, grapes—a veritable Garden of Eden, if it were not for the flies! Why don't you kill them off?" she inquired innocently.

Later in November, she toured California, and worked out a lot of frustrations by driving hell-for-leather from one stop to the next, while the rest of her troupe took the train. She drove from San Diego to Tijuana in the pouring rain just for the ride, and while racing through the desert found what she was sure was a mastodon skull. She displayed it proudly in her various dressing rooms, even after several reporters assured her it actually belonged to a cow. The

All-Star Variety Jubilee made two major stops in California, San Francisco and Los Angeles, both in November. Receipts were falling off by then, as was the morale of the All-Stars. In San Francisco she played John Cort's own Cort Theater; she also visited a children's hospital, putting on a show for the patients and staff. Arriving in Los Angeles, she made a rare public faux pas by telling reporters, "I hope Los Angeles women are more beautiful than those in San Francisco. The women there—most of them—are too big, too fat and too coarse." Needless to say, Anna did not return to San Francisco anytime soon.

But she had bigger problems: John Cort had finally thrown up his hands and decided to pull the plug on Anna's show. Rather than touring for another few months, she would play a handful of December dates in the West and Midwest, then hop straight to New York on December 29, and close on January 10. Anna tried to put on a cheerful face, telling reporters, "What's the use of worrying? One must take things as they are. I remember not long ago a gentleman sitting next to me at a supper spilled glass of Champagne over my new $800 costume. The costume was ruined. He was sorry, so was I; but we had to laugh. That is the way to kill regret and rob misfortune of its sting."

As if Anna didn't have enough on her mind, Liane chose this moment leave Anna's tour and announce her plans to go on the stage. She'd already made a tentative debut in 1912, accompanied (according to one review) by "six large ladies who moved in bovine measures—Anna's child danced a little and squealed a little and smiled a great deal." But in late 1913, Liane signed a contract to open at Hammerstein's Victoria in a two-act with Bobby Watson (who later became better-known as a Hitler impersonator in a number of films and as the harried vocal coach in *Singin' in the Rain*). "I was shocked," Anna said when Liane moved back to New York. "I never wish to see my daughter become an actress. There is no reason why she should work: she will have all the money that she can desire; she will be rich, with an enviable position in the world—why should she wish to act?" For a woman still playing the sexy soubrette, having a nineteen-year-old daughter onstage was not a good advertisement.

Liane herself later admitted that her stage career had more than a little to do with spite. "I asked to be given five dollars a week pocket money without strings to it," Liane wrote in her unpublished 1930s memoirs. "I knew mother was getting $3500 a week and all expenses. She refused, saying that the day had not come when she'd pay her own daughter to travel in a private car and on the fat of the land." Money was a constant sore spot between the two and the subject of frequent quarrels, and Liane saw a way to earn her own salary and annoy her mother at the same time. "I don't want to be in musical comedy," Liane sniffed haughtily to a reporter. "I want to say, 'I love you.' I want to say, 'I hate you.' It is real acting I want—real drama." And she would get real drama when next she saw her mother. Ziegfeld attended Liane's opening as Anna's spy. The girl—billed as "Anna Held's Daughter"—danced out with some grace, singing a ditty guaranteed to horrify her mother:

> I got my mother's big brown eyes
> I've got my mother's teeth like pearls
> I hear my manager say that I resemble her
> From my toes to my nose to my curls.
> The way I roll my brown eyes shows
> I know just what my mother knows.
> And when I grow to be a great big star
> Just like my mother thinks I'll be
> If I make half the money that my mother made
> She'll be mighty proud of me!

Ziegfeld's wire to Anna informed her that Liane had a "nice act; well-staged; has very little voice; but made success. Audience pleased with her . . . but she will never be an Anna Held." When Liane's career did not take off like a shot, she blamed her mother and Ziegfeld. "He would do nothing for me," Liane wrote. "I wondered why I could not get any job and he informed me, 'Everyone in show business adores your mother, Lili, and she's made it known that she doesn't want you on the stage. You haven't a Chinaman's chance to get anything.'"

Ziegfeld may not have had much to do with Liane's lack of success. The vaudeville field was a crowded one, and it took more than a little graceful dancing and a famous mother to win a seat at the table. As Liane's act was booked on the Orpheum Circuit in late 1913 and early 1914, her reviews were not star-quality. She flopped in Brooklyn, and a rather unkind Chicago reviewer called her "a rather heavy, dull, clumsy young person with little talent," as well as "an ungrateful little monkey."

Meanwhile, Anna's *All-Star Variety Jubilee* was grinding its unhappy way through the rest of its truncated tour. In Seattle (John Cort's hometown), a reviewer from the *Sun* wrote, "The show is a sad disappointment. Leaving the theater we heard various persons calling it 'punk.' It's the word you are likely to use yourself if you invest $2 in a seat and see the show." Anna's hardy troupe worked their way eastward through Montana: Missoula, Helena, and Butte. More good reviews greeted the company in Duluth, where they spent Christmas. Their last outpost was Youngstown, Ohio, on December 27.

Anna also spent much time getting good press for her charity work, and she made sure that her chorus girls joined her in the effort. She sold Red Cross seals in Portland and auctioned off a baby doll for twenty-five dollars. In Seattle she and some chorines sold newspapers on the street to benefit a children's charity. In Spokane she sold apples for the Good Fellowship Fund. It was a better way to get into the newspapers than milk baths.

December 29 saw Anna's train pull into Grand Central Station in New York, where she would finish out her tour. They opened at the Casino Theater, where she had appeared in *The Little Duchess* back in 1902. By the time *Mlle Baby* reached New York, *Variety* noted that the costumes were somewhat in need of cleaning. The *Dramatic Mirror* felt that "too much dependence was placed on Miss Held's inability to make her eyes behave. Anything can be overdone." Nonetheless, Anna bravely invited Elsie Janis, the comedic duo Montgomery and Stone, and other professionals to be her guests for a matinee. Anna also finally saw Liane onstage for the first time in New York, succinctly telling her daughter, "Lili, you have the biggest mouth of anyone I have ever seen on the stage before."

As 1913 drew to a close, Anna had a lot of hope and aggravation in her life. Aggravation in the form of her rebellious (and now competitive) daughter and her unraveling tour for John Cort. But she was also rekindling her relationship with Florenz Ziegfeld. Both on a professional and personal basis, the two were communicating on a friendlier level than they had in months. As her tour came to an end, Ziegfeld offered to help her with a smaller act to be booked through the more legitimate vaudeville services of the United Booking Office. A few songs, a fifteen-minute act—much easier than heading her own troupe, and she would be paid three thousand dollars a week.

Then came the night of December 31, 1913, when Anna, Ziegfeld, and Billie Burke all attended the New Year's party at the Astor Hotel. Writer May MacKenzie saw Anna and noted, "She looks very well—better than she did down at Weber's, for instance, and gone are the tiny waist and big chest. She has returned with the straight little smooth body of the times." But Ziegfeld had eyes for no one but Billie Burke.

Mary William Ethelbert Appleton Burke had been a star for nearly ten years by the time her path first crossed with that of Ziegfeld. She was born on August 7, 1885, in Washington, D.C., but schooled in London. Her career began there with West End comedies like *Blue Moon* (1905), *The Belle of Mayfair* (1906), and *Mrs. Ponderbury's Past* (1907). Charles Frohman brought Burke to the United States in 1907 to costar with John Drew in *My Wife*—and she swiftly became the era's most popular ingenue, bouncing amiably from one light comedy to the next. "I was a contented little thing," she recalled. "I had my work, which was easy, pretty clothes, security and applause." She looked like a fluffy little bunny, with her pipsqueak voice, big blue eyes, and baby face. But she was no dumb redhead: Burke numbered among her friends and admirers Mark Twain, Somerset Maugham, James Barrie, Booth Tarkington, and Enrico Caruso. With a quick mind and a spine of sheer steel, Billie Burke was a force to be reckoned with in the theatrical world.

There was an instant electricity between Burke and Ziegfeld that night; both felt it. "I knew Flo Ziegfeld was a dangerous man," Burke recalled in her memoirs. "I had known that before I met him, and I felt the impact of his threat and his charm at once. But even if I had known then precisely what tortures and frustrations were in store for me . . . because of this man, I should have kept right on falling in love." As the two danced, Burke saw Anna from the corner of her eye: "She was utterly beautiful," wrote Burke, "this Empress, strange and dark, with enormous jealous eyes, which followed us around the floor." By early January, Anna began to realize just what a threat Billie Burke was. Ziegfeld remained friendly and interested in Anna's new vaudeville idea, but his manner grew somewhat distant as he pursued this new acquisition with growing ardor. Flowers and gifts overwhelmed Burke; invitations to dine, theater tickets, and telegrams bombarded her. Ziegfeld also cleverly courted Burke's mother.

Anna wasn't the only person disconcerted by this new romance: Burke's manager Charles Frohman was furious. He did everything he could to get Burke to give up her burgeoning romance, which probably just threw the couple closer together. Burke and Ziegfeld met at Grant's Tomb at odd hours; they dined (with Mrs. Burke in attendance) at the Ansonia, while Anna fumed across town at the Savoy. Ziegfeld had a private telephone line installed from his offices to Burke's home, Burkeley Crest, in Hastings-on-Hudson, New York.

Anna Held's All-Star Variety Jubilee wheezed to a finale at the Casino Theater on January 10, 1914, admist a flurry of lawsuits. Michael Leavitt sued Anna for five thousand dollars, claiming that he had set up the contract with John Cort (Anna contested that the introduction has been a strictly social one). One M. Collis Marsh also sued Anna for the cost of some ceiling paintings he had done for her at the Savoy. Leavitt's suit was eventually found to be baseless, but Anna did have to pay Marsh $2432 for those paintings.

With Ziegfeld's help, Anna set to work on her new streamlined vaudeville act, which consisted of sixteen minutes of songs: She opened with "You Were Made for Me" (not to be confused with the 1929 song of the same title), then a Kewpie doll number during which she flung the newly popular dolls into the audience, closing with a medley of popular tunes. Her Kinemacolor short was projected while Anna quickly changed costumes backstage. It was all so much simpler than managing *Anna Held's All-Star Variety Jubilee*.

Ziegfeld arranged for Anna's act to open at the Palace Theater in New York in mid-January. The Palace, on Broadway at Forty-seventh Street, was only a year old when Anna made her debut there, but it was already acquiring its reputation as the premiere vaudeville house in the country. It was built by Martin Beck, who ran the huge Orpheum Vaudeville Circuit. But—typical of the cutthroat feuds in theater management—it was soon taken over by Beck's archenemy E.F. Albee, who ran the Keith Circuit. Sime Silverman, editor of the trade paper *Variety*, also hated Albee, so acts booked at the Palace rarely got reviewed in *Variety* (and anyone caught reading that paper was promptly fired by Albee). The Palace was not a happy house in its first few years. But, nonetheless, by February 1914 the Palace was the place to be seen. That month the theater featured Fanny Brice, Eddie Foy, the Avon Comedy Four, Mae Murray and Clifton Webb, and George White (soon to produce his *Scandals*, another competitor for Ziegfeld's *Follies*).

As the Ziegfeld-Burke courtship steadily heated up, Anna packed for her tour, which was to last through early April. The *New York Review* noted snidely that Anna would need "a rattling good show" to make money, adding that "Ziegfeld and Miss Held both are quite likely to find out that the good old days are gone." She opened in Chicago, Anna enthusiastically told the press, in order to "play and sing once more to my America under the management of Mr. Flo. And when I see him again I feel that, after all, nothing has passed that cannot be forgotten!" Indeed, rumors of their remarriage were gaining ground in the press.

The show went over well, one Chicago paper calling Anna "the comet that out-twinkles them all." She "astonished and delighted" the Cincinnati reviewers, where she shared the bill with the sketch *A Bowery Camille* and Yankee and Dixie, trained fox terriers. In Cleveland she drew large crowds, though the critics were divided on her charms: The *Plain Dealer* was mystified by her success, complaining that "she lisps a few songs in English words with a decided French accent." The *Leader*, however, thought her a delight. "It is impossible to take her performance other than good-humoredly," the critic wrote. "Her assumption of ingenue airs and graces is so transparent, she is so obviously conscious that it is a mere bluff, that she shares the joke with her audience."

Her three thousand dollars a week had to be stretched to meet Anna's standard of living. Items on the budget included her staff's salaries, her car's upkeep, costumes to be mended and cleaned. "I stop only at a good hotel, where the lights are softly shaded," Anna told a reporter while on tour. "Where the atmosphere is agreeable, where the people are chic." She also gave parties on the road, "with a nice petit menu et champagne, liqueurs, etc. . . . And forget not the flowers and the parfum. Always I must have flowers. Always I must have parfum. The tips! they come to quite a little . . . [so that] the waiters et maids do not look like a hungry tiger when you come around."

Anna also had the competition of Liane, who was traveling the vaudeville circuit herself, still billed defiantly as "Anna Held's Daughter" (when Ziegfeld offered to bill Anna as "Liane Carrera's Mother," she failed to see the humor). Liane also gave out some rather mean-spirited interviews in which she chided her "old fashioned" mother. A photo of Liane—looking every inch the modern tango girl—accompanied an article (the title of which, "What I Think of Mamma," must have given Anna a shudder).

Liane made fun of Anna's corsets (which Anna no longer wore), her kissing marathon, and her fabled milk baths ("horrid, sticky things!"). "What a way to become famous," Liane scolded, "letting the public peek into your bath, even if you are covered with milk." She unwisely continued, "in the old days . . . you didn't have to do much on stage to please the audience. All mamma did was sing a few songs and use her eyes. . . . Oh, it was easy money in those days. Just sing a naughty song to the men, and zing! you were a headliner." Anna was greatly loved and admired in her profession and by her audiences, and interviews such as that did much to kill Liane's budding career.

Anna herself tried to be kinder when speaking of her daughter. She talked of what hard work and disappointment awaited an actress. "Perhaps she thinks that everything comes suddenly," said Anna, "but little girl, she'll find out differently." Of her own career, Anna said candidly that "it seems that I am not pleasing people as well as I did once," an amazing admission for a working actress. "One of these days I may find a musical comedy again that suits me and appeals to me. . . . But then again, I may quit very soon forever. I can't trust myself to say anymore what I shall do, for the first thing I know, I break promises I have made to myself."

She played another week in New York in late February, and the *Telegraph* encouragingly called her "Glitteringly glorious, as she was in *The Little Duchess*, bewilderingly beautiful, as in *Papa's Wife*, and just as fascinatingly feminine as in *Miss Innocence.*" From New York she traveled to Brooklyn, Philadelphia, and Pittsburgh, playing to generally appreciative audiences and critics. By early April Anna was in Baltimore, playing the Maryland Theater. The *Baltimore American* wrote that "she has the old-time vim and looks young and bewitching," winning "storms of applause." She had only two weeks left of her tour: It was on to Washington, D.C., next, then back to New York at the end of April. That summer she planned to spend in Paris, of course; but who knew what opportunities fall 1914 would have to offer?

On April 13, Anna picked up the newspapers and read that Florenz Ziegfeld had married Billie Burke two days earlier.

—8—

Under Two Flags

The news of Ziegfeld's marriage came like a thunderbolt to Anna. Just as she had tried to ignore and deny his relationship with Lillian Lorraine (until Liane had forced the issue), Anna had managed to convince herself that his interest in Billie Burke was nothing more than a flirtation—perhaps just a way to win her professionally from Frohman. She read on April 13 what had transpired: After a matinee of Burke's show *Jerry*, she and Ziegfeld had taken a boat to Hoboken, New Jersey, accompanied by Mrs. Burke and Ziegfeld's parents (this last bit of news particularly hurt Anna). Burke later recalled that they were married in a crowded back room at the parsonage: "It was what was known in those days as a rummage room," she wrote, "crammed and disorderly with baby carriages and cribs, old paint buckets and stepladders." The understandably confused parson kept calling the groom "Billie" and the bride "Flo." The couple returned to Ziegfeld's suite at the Ansonia, where Burke promptly began getting rid of Anna's furniture, which she dismissed as "too opulent . . . with all its gilt."

A stunned Anna had to face the reporters who crowded around her dressing room that night, and she couldn't help but sound hurt and bitter. "I don't know Miss Burke," she told the assembled mob, "but I understand that she is a nice little girl, but as for me, I do not think that I shall ever marry again—but if I do the man must be a big man. . . . To be happy a woman must look up to her husband." Asked about Ziegfeld, she said that he "is a good manager, but as a husband—oh, he can think of nothing but business, business, business!" Anna had been very young when she married, she said, "and for fifteen years he kept me in captivity. I knew nobody else, but since I have been around I have seen so many men whom I like better."

Two days later, a somewhat calmer but no less pained Anna told *Variety:* "I have not sent my congratulations to Mr. Ziegfeld, but I wish them both much happiness. He may have learned by this time how to hold a woman. He may even have discovered that a man possesses a soul. But for me henceforth it is the single life." Privately she told Liane: "It is too bad for her. Billie Burke is a great star. He will make her very unhappy. She is throwing herself away. . . . He never, never can produce a successful play for her—she is not at all his genre. I wonder why she did it." Burke, for her part, always tried to be ladylike about her former rival, saying years later that "Miss Held, unlike certain other beautiful women with whom my husband was associated, was never my enemy and never, so far as I know, attempted in any way to do me disservice." But Burke also insisted somewhat ingenuously, "Flo was attracted by Anna but never wholeheartedly in love with her."

The show had to go on: Anna still had her vaudeville act to worry about. She opened in Washington, D.C., on April 20, "with such gowns as never were seen on land or sea and the same bits of mannerism, accent and personality which have made her one of the most impersonated personages in her world," according to the *Post.* The *Star* added knowingly that "her smile has lost none of its charm . . . even with her nose out of joint." Her tour ended in late April, and Anna lost no time packing for Europe. New York had too many bad memories, and she was taking no chances on running into the happy newlywed Ziegfelds. She gave herself a going-away dinner at Rector's on May 3, entertaining Lillian Russell, Russell's husband Alexander Moore, and a number of professional and "civilian" friends. Once again, the Kinemacolor short was hauled out and shown for her guests' amusement. Anna was heard laughing at her own image, "That's silly, Anna—how foolish of you!"

There was one last bit of unpleasantness before she left: Anna sued Ziegfeld for an unpaid debt of three thousand dollars. He released an ungentlemanly and threatening statement to the press: "There are many things I can say, and if I am to be bothered all the time I will certainly say them. There is much that the public would be interested in concerning Anna Held, and it will not do her any good if I make those things public." The suit was dropped, and on that bitter note Anna parted from her former husband. She sailed in early May, telling reporters in a rare flash of clairvoyance, "I never know exactly what will happen in France." That spring of 1914 she was looking to get away from her hurt, to travel to Deauville, to see friends in Paris—and perhaps to do a little work, if convenient offers came up.

Paris was in the midst of a scandal when she arrived. On March 16 Henriette Caillaux, the wife of a former liberal prime minister, had shot and killed Gaston Calmette, editor of the right-wing newspaper *Le Figaro.* The paper had been carrying on an anti-Caillaux campaign, even printing a letter from his mistress and suggesting that he had supplied inside financial information to Kaiser Wilhelm. All Paris was abuzz with this latest "crime of the century" and the subsequent trial, which was scheduled to open on July 20. (By the time Madame Caillaux was found not guilty on July 28, France had other dawning worries.)

For a woman who professed to be uninterested in politics, Anna had some incisive comments on the case (being an acquaintance of both the victim and the former prime minister). "Monsieur Calmette was a man of the highest probity, with a fine sense of honor and a journalist of great talent," Anna said. She dashed fears that the murder might result in the overthrow of the republic and the reestablishment of the Bourbon pretenders. "This conjecture is utter folly," she scoffed. "The Royalists in France are a noisy and motley group, but their day has passed and they are now only a picturesque and oftentimes laughable element in that great city where the political pot ever boils over. That the ministry might be overthrown is quite another proposition, for the men who are tainted by this scandal must get out of public life, but that the republic is in any danger is the veriest folly."

It was not often that Anna revealed to the public her steel-trap mind and intelligent political views; her image was still that of a fluffy and carefree entertainer. As if to backtrack, she also talked lightly of a short-lived Parisian fad that has somehow escaped the notice of fashion historians: Inspired by the futurist movement in art, some avant-garde women were tinting their skin to match their hair. "Can you imagine that dancing, clasped by cerise arms, will be a new thrill, and that a delicate shiver will pass through you beholding a blue shoulder rise from a white foam of chiffon?" Anna asked. "The new dyes for the skin are quite harmless and wash off at the slightest touch of a special preparation which accompanies them." She told of the "wonderful symphonies I have been able to create with my tinted hair, my colored complexion and the harmonizing tones of my gown." Skin dyeing, however, proved the most ephemeral of fashion crazes.

Ziegfeld was not forgotten as Anna settled back into her Paris life. Still rankled and hurt, she came up with her own fiancé, one to put Billie Burke in her place. Prince Paul Naklianoff began to appear in stories about Anna. This tall mustachioed bodyguard of Czar Nicholas ("a fellow student of the Grand Duke Cyril") was said to have given Anna a $180,000 pearl necklace and a touring car. She brushed off marriage: "I don't believe in hasty marriages," she said coyly. "The prince's attentions to me are quite true, but I had rather no notice were taken of them just now because nothing is really settled. . . . Of course the prince, manlike, is for a hurried wedding." Naklianoff swiftly vanished from Anna's press once his purpose was served; whether or not he even actually existed is unclear at this point. It was typical of Anna to pick a prince for her new fiancé; Liane later said that "she was always vulnerable when it came to titles. Many a hard-earned dollar she spent on an impoverished marquis, duke, or baron."

By early July Anna was bored and began looking about for work; Felix Isman booked her to play a week in Bucharest. Isman, described in his obituary as "one of the most colorful realty and theatrical figures of years gone by," had made his fortune in Philadelphia real estate before turning to his true love, show business. He had dealt more successfully with booking vaudeville performers in lengthy tours than had John Cort, so Anna put her trust in him and let him shop her around for further European theater dates.

She was still in Paris on June 28, 1914, when Austrian Archduke Franz Ferdinand and his wife were assassinated in Sarajevo by a Serbian nationalist, Gavrilo Princip. The killings made the front pages around the world, of course, but were forgotten within a few days. For the next month the world at large was mostly unaware of the danger as the military leaders of Germany pressed Austria to use this as an excuse for all-out war. Poor Franz Ferdinand and Sophie were simply red herrings; the main reason for war was Germany's long-standing desire to extend its land into French and Russian territories. The month of July 1914 passed in a kind of dream for most of the world: While politicians and military leaders fought, made deals, and advanced their private hatreds and ambitions, people blithely went about their business, oblivious to the abyss that was opening beneath their feet. Anna certainly saw nothing amiss, even as politically aware as she was. She signed her contract to play a few weeks of vaudeville in Bucharest and headed to Vichy and Auteuil to enjoy some socializing before taking the long eastward train ride to Romania.

As August began, Anna was at a racetrack in Auteuil with Evelyn Nesbit Thaw, the notorious "girl in the red velvet swing" whose deranged husband had killed her former lover, architect Stanford White, in 1906. On August 1 Germany declared war on Russia, and the unease began to grow. Two days later Germany declared war on France, and the following day the Germans invaded Belgium: The panic was starting in earnest now. By August 12 Anna was in Vichy. On that day, France and England—following long-standing political agreements to protect and defend their allies—declared war on Austria and thereby its partner, Germany. The first word of war came to Anna in a casino: The dealer turned pale when a friend whispered in his ear, and before long the news was being passed from patron to patron. The casino emptied out as everyone—Anna included—packed and made a desperate rush for trains and autos. Within a day or two, Anna was back in her Paris home, nervously eyeing the president's mansion across the street, as if she could divine news from the hurried comings and goings. A friend who worked in her bank told Anna to take out all her cash and convert it into gold—but the next day when she arrived to attempt this, Anna found her bank closed.

As August ended, the new war was going into high gear. Only two months earlier, Anna had been jabbering happily about cerise shoulders and her royal fiancé. Now she grabbed the newspapers off the street and read the latest horrors: On August 20 the French suffered their first major defeat, at Charleroi, then another two days later at Rossignol—the beginning of what was to be the long and bloody Battle of Mons. She wrote to Amy Leslie in late August of her grief at the war and her fears for France; Leslie described the letter as "only a blurred incoherent shriek." That spring Anna had faced what she'd thought was her worst tragedy, the loss of the only man she'd ever really loved. Now she faced the loss of her country, and Ziegfeld faded into the background as her life and priorities quickly shifted gears. The old Anna Held was left behind as she fashioned herself into *Liberty Leading the People*, just as Sarah Bernhardt had done during the Franco-Prussian War of 1870. Anna recognized the theatricality of her position, but her patriotism was genuine. A converted Frenchwoman, she was more French than those born in Paris. She was quite willing to give up her career or even her life for her adopted country, and there was nothing false about her determination.

Show business personalities plunged right into the war effort, and immediately Anna began to lose old friends and acquaintances. The first casualties began showing up in the trade paper *Variety* on September 26, 1914, with the death of British comedian Lionel Walsh. Soon, "War Casualties" mounted in the show business news, and entire columns were devoted to those in the profession who died on and off the battlefield. The most well known was dancer Vernon Castle (killed in a training flight). But hundreds of others, now long forgotten, had lives and careers cut short in the war: movie director C. Ryse Pryce, contortionist Charles Woodson, actor and playwright Harold Chapin, ventriloquist The Great Lorraine, "Hebrew comedian" Steele Cohen, comic whistler Hugh Allen, authoress of the hit song "Keep the Home Fires Burning" Lena Guilbert Ford (killed in an air raid), "Merry Demon" Arthur Bertella, actress Bradda Athleta (shot by German troops in Belgium), female impersonator Teddie

Woodhouse, and such varied actors as Charles Lambert, Basil Hallam (who popularized the song "I'm Gilbert the Filbert, King of the Knuts"), Alan Mudie, Scott Craven, Charles Biddy, Fraser Tarbutt, and the startlingly named Cash Slippery. All are just names on war memorials now, but once Anna's coworkers and fellow players.

Anna fired off a 150–word telegram to President Woodrow Wilson, urging him to enter the war immediately—"I never received a reply," she shrugged later. Determined to get into the fray, she gathered together a few nurses and a small theatrical troupe, including revue artists Eugenie Buffet, Renée Devannes, Paul Ardot and Fursy. She equipped several cars as tiny sleeping coaches—her own car was a huge Renault town car, with an ice-box and a fold-down table that acted as a perfect makeup tray. The interior was in mahogany upholstered with ivory broadcloth, and the windows had screens. And so Anna and her little band set off—with no governmental approval—to entertain the troops and help out at field hospitals. She loaded up with gum, candy, and nuts for the soldiers; she also brought with her cartons of cigarettes, difficult to obtain at the front. It was during this war that so many thousands of men switched from unwieldy pipes and cigars to cigarettes. Lung cancer—almost unheard of in the nineteenth century—began to claim its toll after World War I.

Anna was turned back from the Belgian border on August 28, her car requisitioned by Chief of Staff Joseph Jaques Joffre. A tourist on the spot took photos of Anna willingly surrendering her car, which Joffre found very useful (her fold-down makeup shelf was perfect for maps). "I would gladly give a dozen automobiles to the service of my France," she said nobly. Around the same time, Germany started dropping both bombs and leaflets over Paris, the latter announcing the defeat of the French troops. A panicked retreat from the city began: Along with Belgian refugees streaming through Paris, some one million citizens (one-third of Paris's population) packed up and fled south and west. Even the government decamped for Bordeaux; it seemed Anna, Beatrice, and Anna's cook, Louise Chauvin, were the only people left on the rue Faubourg Saint-Honoré. By September 3 the German army was only eight miles from Paris.

Throughout the autumn of 1914 Anna and her volunteer nurses and entertainers continued making sorties to the fighting lines, wherever those might be from day to day. It was not easy—or even strictly legal—for Anna to volunteer her services. The government passed an ordinance against women being on the road anywhere near the front, so she was subject to arrest for her good deeds. In these early days of the war, the efforts of most women to aid were scoffed at and dismissed. In his 1928 book, *The Cause*, Ray Strachey noted: "Even the women doctors, when Dr. Elsie Inglis approached the War Office with their offer of fully staffed medical units, were told, 'To go home and keep quiet,' and that the commanding officers 'did not want to be troubled with hysterical women.'" It was another year or two before the services of female factory workers, street-car conductors, clerks, farmers, and the like gained any respect from the military and the public at large. Four years of war inadvertently did more than ten years of militant suffragettes to gain enfranchisement of women.

The winter of 1914–15 was a rainy one. Vehicles, trenches, and horses were all mired deep in endless mud. A popular song parody among the soldiers went,

> I've a wet little home in a trench,
> Where the rainstorms continually drench,
> There's a dead cow close by
> With her feet towards the sky
> And she gives off a terrible stench.

But Anna and her troupe slogged through the mud and the rain and tried to bring a little glamour (and some much-needed medical supplies) to her boys. Anna wasn't the only star to tour the battlefields: American Elsie Janis later became famous for her work at the front. Bernhardt herself—now seventy—got into the war effort with most of her old energy intact. And even Anna's old enemy Yvette Guilbert, by then in something of a career slump, hit the same hospitals and camps that Anna visited. Guilbert, married to a German Jew, was harassed about her loyalty and fled for the United States in late 1914 for the remainder of the war years.

A lot of what Anna saw and heard in those field hospitals was not the stuff of noble patriotism being put out by the official press. By the time the war was a few months old, soldiers were becoming disgusted by the outmoded and senseless way it was being run. The French and British troops had little personal animosity against the Germans, and many—unfamiliar with the years of behind-the-scenes statesmanship—had no idea what they were fighting for. In his 1922 book, *England after the War*, Charles Masterman recalled the soldiers' "complete disillusion and disgust; the hatred of the old men who have sent the young men to die; of hatred and contempt for the army command and staff; which has not even the sense to make itself intelligent enough to give a chance of living to the common solider; of hatred and contempt for the politician and diplomat, whose actions have resulted in the young men of one nation slaughtering in all methods of torture and hideous mutilation the young men of another with whom they had no quarrel."

The hospitals themselves were often improvisational affairs, understaffed and woefully ill equipped. They were set up in tents, churches, schools, homes—anything that could be requisitioned (sometimes from unwilling owners). The staff not only had to deal with wounded soldiers from both sides but with civilians. Ordinary death did not take a holiday during the war, and villagers came in with battle wounds, starvation, pneumonia, as well as run-of-the-mill illnesses. "The wounded pour in day and night," one nurse wrote home. "We discharge our patients as fast as we can, and bury dozens a week. It is all like a weird dream, laughter (for they laugh well, the soldiers) and blood and death and funny episodes, and sublime, also, all under the autumn stars."

Anna had equipped herself with as many medical supplies as she could carry, and these were more appreciated than her entertaining. That same nurse wrote, "When I tell you that I have one large needle for my whole Pavilion, and that I am obliged to give on an average of fifteen injections a day with it and as if that were not enough, the doctor frequently asks to borrow it for another hospital, you may guess how it all goes. But when the doctor brings it back he knows I hate to lend it; he always says with his most winning smile, 'I am bringing back the baby to its mother.'"

Surprisingly, both staff and patients were happy to interrupt their daily chores when a theatrical troupe like Anna's hove into view. When battles were on, no one had time for frivolity—but between rushes, frivolity was much needed. "You can't imagine, I suppose, that we laugh and jest all day long?" asked one frontline nurse. "If you can't do that, you might as well get out, for all the good you will ever do a French wounded soldier. Why, I believe his very wounds wouldn't heal if he were not allowed to make merry over them, and he will jest with you up to the hour before he dies, a mixture of wit and pathos too poignant ever to reproduce."

Anna stood in awe of these nurses, and her long-held view of the perfect woman as cute and clinging began to change during the early months of the war. "Nobody who has not seen the thing can imagine the horrors of a base hospital," she wrote. "It is there that you realize what a frightful thing, a wicked thing, a basely inhuman thing, is war. I am no suffragette, but let me say here and now that the women are facing the ordeal magnificently." When she heard gossip that many nurses had joined up simply to flirt with soldiers, Anna reacted with as much grief as rage: "I have seen; I know that is not the truth. I have seen these lovely women, most sweet and kind, taking care of these poor men in the trenches. You know these wounded lie sometimes many days in the trenches before they can be moved, and when they are brought out their wounds are all of the gangrene, their feet sometimes frozen that the toes fall off, and I have seen these women wash and cleanse these poor men, so full of dirt and vermin, they are like angels after the battlefield."

Anna also got into a public feud with social reformer Jane Addams, who was quoted as saying that soldiers fought mainly under the influence of drugs and liquor. "The men who are giving their lives for principle and love of homeland in the Great War need no other stimuli than patriotism and honor," Anna retorted hotly. "Miss Addams knows the gospel of the weak, but she and her kind cannot comprehend the hot and heavenly joy that comes to the fighting male when national honor is at stake and the existence of his country as a proud and fearless nation."

Anna brought as much laughter and gaiety to the hospitals and trenches as she could muster. It was not easy: By the end of 1914 the French casualty figures stood at three hundred thousand dead; six hundred thousand missing or wounded. But Anna was smart enough not to let her feelings show to the injured or to the exhausted doctors and nurses. "All of us artistes agree to using only the liveliest, merriest numbers of the music halls," she reported back from the front lines. "Give them the glad, bright, zippy, zestful things that put joy into their hearts and the ambition to be back on the boulevards with a pretty girl on the arm and the lights of the theaters just ahead." The "Laughing Song" she'd used in her vaudeville tour was just the trick; gazing out over the sick and dying, Anna laughed and laughed and quite often got them to laugh along. The thought that hers was the last voice some of them heard was never far from her mind.

Her friends asked her eagerly what her impressions were of the front lines. "It is the extreme, unbelievable contrast between the carnage and gaiety in the trenches," Anna told them. "Both the Germans and the Allies have turned their trenches into veritable vaudeville halls, and often the troops spend the evening singing, dancing and reciting. . . . It only shows that men can make the best of fighting, just as they can of everything."

She handed out sheet music so her audience could sing along with her, though this was of course not needed for the ever popular "Laughing Song." "No fortune, no necklace of pearls could give me the deep pleasure I felt as I saw the laughter in the faces of those pathetic figures," Anna later said, "and they would continue laughing for five minutes." But she also recalled "one man just from the operating room, broken to pieces and dying, [who] insisted that he be carried in where he could hear the singing. And I had to keep on with the 'Laughing Song.'"

The drives to the hospitals themselves were appalling. Anna had a chauffeur for her excursions, and she gazed out the window at the ruins of what had been the same quaint, friendly towns she and Ziegfeld had visited year after year. The French countryside was largely farmland, and as fields were destroyed, the farm families fled, their livelihoods gone along with their food supply. Ruth Gaines of the Red Cross described the village of Combles, once "so alive and so fertile before the war, but now so desolate, nothing is to be seen but a vast chalky plain, quite white and everywhere reduced to powder. . . . This soil, which is now mixed with all sorts of rubbish and scraps of shells, will take more than fifty years to recover its fertility." The centuries-old churches, homes, monuments, and squares of Combles—and hundreds of towns like it—were reduced by shelling to "a mass of ruins."

Later in the war Lillian Gish covered the same ground while filming *Hearts of the World* with D.W. Griffith. She remembered later how stunned the soldiers were to see women on the battlefields and recalled as well the burned and shattered territory. "We passed ruined towns and abandoned trenches, bleak markers of the former battle lines," she wrote in her autobiography. "I remember the odd feeling I had seeing a coffee pot perched on top of a pile of rubble, the sole evidence that a house had once stood on the spot. Closer to the front, we saw acres of woodland and orchard scorched by shellfire." An American nurse told of similar scenes: "We passed through three ruined villages, the very abomination of desolation, only an occasional wall or chimney left standing . . . small, intimate things stand out almost intact where heavy masonry has completely vanished, now a sewing machine, now a tiny stove, now a baby's cradle quite recognizable."

Even the roads Anna traveled on were all but destroyed: bridges blown up, streets blocked by felled trees, craters, barbed wire—much of it put there on purpose to foil enemy troops. It was hard to know from day to day even where the "front line" was, as territory changed hands acre by acre, back and forth. Anna had a harsh lesson in this in early 1915, when she drove unawares across French lines into German-held territory. She suddenly found herself surrounded by enemy soldiers and was marched, at gunpoint, to an ominous-looking tent. "I explained to the lieutenant who I was and my mission, pointing to the heap of tobacco and cigarettes in the car," she recalled. "But he replied in perfect English, 'Oh, that's an old trick. You are not the first woman spy we have caught. You must come and see the major.'"

Women—even famous ones—were not safe in this war. British nurse Edith Cavell was later executed for helping prisoners of war escape, and the Dutch-born dancer Mata Hari (a contemporary of Anna in 1890s Paris) was duped and set up by both sides and executed by the French in 1917. Anna was transported from Albert, where she had been captured, to an outpost near Peronne. "Terribly frightened I was, too," she candidly admitted. "The major turned out to be a short, stout man with a grizzled gray moustache. I showed him my passport, but he didn't seem to understand and summoned a junior officer."

Anna Held was completely unknown to this major—perhaps she should have played more dates in Berlin. Just as she had given herself up for lost, her hero arrived in the form of a German soldier, a "tall, slender young man with an ideal tango figure," who not only spoke perfect English ("with a slight Yankee twang") but also was an Anna Held fan. He examined her papers and said, "Why yes, Herr Major, it's all right. This is Miss Held. Don't you know her? She is of the theatrical world." Anna found her heartbeat starting up again. "After that all went well. I was treated with great courtesy and was cheered enthusiastically when I distributed my tobacco and cigarettes in one of the trenches and in return I received several spiked helmets as souvenirs and was escorted safely out of the lines." She tried to make light of this experience, sending Amy Leslie a photo of herself brandishing her "captured" German helmets and guns.

That spring saw a stalemate on the western front. On May 9, though, the French and British mounted a huge offensive, pushing the Germans back three miles but suffering heavy casualties. Later in May the French lost more troops in particularly bloody battles at Artois and the Meuse-Argonne front. Anna read all of this in the papers, gathered what other information she could on her travels and from military friends, and took all of it very much to heart. "I cannot tell you how my poor France is suffering," she wrote, sounding more every month like an avenging goddess of war. "All the golden youth that are at the front. Thousands have given their lives for La Patrie and thousands more will die. . . . My beautiful France will fight until her last citizen is dead before she will consent to an inglorious peace. We are resolute in this. We did not seek the war. It was forced upon us, and now that it is here, every man, woman and child is firmly resolved that death is preferable to defeat."

Of course Anna did not spend all of her time at the front lines: She had to take a break from sleeping in her car and on cots, from the blood and the mud and the horrors. She drove back to Paris to rest—but there was little rest to be had, especially not on the rue Faubourg Saint-Honoré. Anna took in what Belgian refugees were willing to live across the street from the president's house. By the beginning of 1915, air raids became a constant horror to unnerve the populace of Paris. "When the first Zeppelin came to Paris I was at my home there," Anna wrote to her friends back in the United States. "We had been told that at the approach of a Zeppelin a bugle would be blown and everyone in the city was to put out any lights and take refuge in the cellars. It came at 2 o'clock in the morning. We heard the bugle call, and instantly every light in Paris was extinguished. We could only hear the swift automobiles rushing through the streets sounding the bugle call."

Anna later told her daughter the true horror of those air raids. "At night you are asleep and the wild shrieks of sirens wake you and you run helter-skelter down to the cave," Liane recalled her mother saying. "It's dark and the steps are old and broken; you fall as you run. You don't know if this time you'll reach it before the bombs fall. You dare not light a match for fear it might be seen and tip off the enemy." She took a joke photo of Beatrice and herself huddling in the cellar, but the air raids began to unhinge Anna. She got little rest, making her trips to the front lines all the more exhausting.

One aspect of the war that Anna noticed in Paris, and that few others commented on, was the lack of unthinking anti-German sentiments. Despite the government propaganda, Anna found, "The French are not bitter against the German people. There is no sign of hate between man and man. The French soldier and the men who direct him from Paris dislike the thought that they are striking blows at the simple, fine German people, but they know that as matters stand now, they can strike at the evil government which has been saddled upon Germany, only through the people." Anna had never been a fan of Germany—it was one country she had generally avoided during her halcyon summer trips. But even during the worst of the war, she was able to separate the people from their government.

While in Paris, Anna helped to organize charity bazaars and even tried to socialize and see what theater there was to see. "The stage is outwardly dead in Paris," she sighed. But private performances did go on, "in ballrooms, in cha-teaux, in places where only invitations will admit." Wartime censorship banned many darker plays, shows that might injure public morale. But Anna and her comrades put them on anyway, if only for themselves. The price of the tickets went to war relief, and playwrights and performers kept themselves in practice. "When the war is over," said Anna, "there will be an abundance of great mate-rial for the theater. The arts will not die in France—far from it. They will arise glorious like a sundawn, and my beloved theater will be the first of the arts in the new era."

She also held open house for any Americans in Paris, as one guest later recalled: "It was quite enough to hear they were in the city and a pneumatique was speeded on its way with the reminder that Miss Held was always at home at

No. 86 Faubourg, St. Honoré." Indeed, Anna relished the company: Her house was ghostly in its emptiness, and she willingly put up anyone brave enough to stay in such a dangerous neighborhood. The Paris Anna knew and loved became a different, quieter place in wartime. By eight P.M. the streets were empty. "Even on the boulevards you get the mysterious and creepy feeling as if you were inside a sombre cathedral. . . . A healthy man with both arms, both legs or both eyes is almost never seen in the streets of Paris anymore," she lamented. "If he is, women walk right up to him and ask, 'what are you doing here?'"

In April 1915 Anna recruited a troupe of boy scouts to travel with her, though she was sure to keep them far away from the more dangerous areas. Areas were indeed getting more dangerous in the spring of 1915: That same month, Germany used poison gas for the first time, against two French divisions at Langemarck. On May 1 a notice was put into newspapers that all Allied ships were fair game for Germany. A week later the *Lusitania* was sunk, taking with her (among the nearly twelve hundred casualties) Charles Frohman, who had never forgiven Billie Burke for marrying Florenz Ziegfeld.

All this time, amazingly enough, Michael Leavitt was still trying to sue Anna from the United States for her John Cort contract (Cort himself still owed Anna four thousand dollars in unpaid salary). By this time her deeds had been thoroughly publicized throughout the land (thanks largely to Amy Leslie), and Anna was known as a war heroine. Leavitt unwisely bad-mouthed her, calling Anna "more temperamental than Eva Tanguay." When Leavitt complained that Anna had not appeared in court to answer the charges, her lawyer, Harry Steinfeld, drew himself up with great dignity and replied, "She is sewing shirts for soldiers in Paris." When some laughter broke out at this reference to the popular novelty song "Sister Susie's Sewing Shirts for Soldiers" he insisted, "She is, really. In addition she is caring for some of the Belgian refugees. She has about 25 families on her hands. It would be necessary for me to get her testimony before I could proceed." The judge ruled in Anna's favor on June 11.

Friends noticed Anna's nerves beginning to fray and her energy wearing down. In the summer of 1915 she was invited to dine with friends at Le Havre, and Anna's new, more serious, personality startled them. They were expecting the bon vivant of old, but a drawn and high-strung woman sat down with them. "The dinner was served on gold plates," Anna later explained. "Think of it! The idea of such luxury in the midst of starving war refugees, and want, misery, filled me with repugnance. . . . After a little deliberation I pushed my plate away and rose from the table and left the room." That summer the German army entered Anna's hometown of Warsaw, "liberating" it from Russia. Anna had to have known about this—her reading of the newspapers was obsessive by now—but she never made any comment on the matter.

Anna was driving herself to the edge of collapse. Now in her mid-forties, she was no longer as strong as she once was, and she was not eating or sleeping as much as she should have. It all came to a head in September 1915, while she was entertaining in a hospital for the blind. "They were all seated in a great room with a stage at one end," she later recalled. Anna strode jauntily onto the stage ready to sing her happiest number and took a look at her audience.

> They sat erect, but their faces were mostly turned toward the floor. These faces were like masks, quite impassive, with no sign of emotion upon them. Some of these men were very handsome fellows. There were boys there, and there were great officers. Some were terribly mutilated. Some were quite well, and only the black glasses told what had happened to them. . . . I tried very hard to be gay, but it was impossible. I started to sing but I could not go on. I wept instead. And yet the expressions on the faces of these brave blind soldiers did not change. I shall never forget their exit from that room. They stood up and went out in file, each soldier's hand upon the shoulder of the man before him. They groped a little and did not walk with ease, for you see they are not yet accustomed to blindness. It was my saddest experience.

After thirteen months of constant entertaining, helping out at hospitals, bazaars, charities, Anna had reached the end of her rope. Beatrice and her other friends and acquaintances put their respective feet down: Anna had to return to the United States or she herself would become a casualty of the war. To make her feel better, they convinced her that she could raise more money in the United States, and do more good by campaigning for America to enter the war. It took a lot of conniving to get Anna to abandon her post—she felt like a shirker. But her work and high spirits had already made her a genuine heroine throughout France. "She was the idol of the wounded soldiers and of the Belgian refugees because she was good to them," writer Edward O'Day said later in 1915. "Paris will not soon forget what Anna Held did for its war sufferers. And along the Normandy coast the peasants speak of Anna Held rapturously as the singing angel of mercy."

As she booked passage for the United States, Anna was also "outed" as Polish, though no one made very much of this—her true heritage had been admitted by everyone but Anna herself for two decades. She went to Rome from France, and tried to book passage from there to the United States. But she had no French passport, only a Russian one, issued to its Polish-born owner. The American Consulate in Rome had to OK her passage, and the press got wind of this transaction. Even then Anna tried to bluff her way out of it, claiming she had no idea why she—as a Parisienne born and bred—had mistakenly been issued a Russian passport.

She set sail on October 5 on the *St. Louis*. This ocean voyage—which would prove to be Anna's final one—was perhaps her least glamorous. Aside from the terror of submarine attacks, the *St. Louis* was hardly a luxury liner. It had been launched in 1894 as one of the first American-built high-class ships, but by 1915 was somewhat the worse for wear. It was acknowledged to be fairly hideous, and its use as a military ship during the Spanish-American War had not improved its appearance.

Anna arrived back in New York, to be greeted by no family, no producers, only a few friends. She took a cab uptown to the Savoy, which was to remain her permanent New York residence. Even though Anna had no welcoming party, she was besieged by offers once she had settled back in. "I've been seeing managers ever since I arrived," she confirmed, "and each offers a million more than the last." Looking them over, she chose the two most promising from a financial standpoint: a vaudeville tour and a movie. Anna signed with H.B. Marinelli to book her for a brief vaudeville stint in late October, to open at the Palace in New York. Marinelli was one of the most successful vaudeville agents of his day, and one of the few who booked and searched for acts internationally. A superb businessman, he somehow managed to keep bookings in several different countries sorted out. But the war was playing havoc with his carefully arranged booking system, and by this time his business was about to spiral into disaster (Marinelli died after a nervous collapse in 1924). She also signed with producer Oliver Morosco to make her first feature-length film, to be shot in Los Angeles in the late autumn.

New York seemed strange to Anna after more than a year at war. She could hardly reacclimate herself: "I really am dazzled and bewildered by this riot of pleasure. . . . A whole city at peace and people going about their business just in the usual way!" she marveled. "And then at night—the lights on Broadway and everywhere. It seemed as though I was seeing them for the first time. I found it hard work to keep from crying, 'Put out the lights! The Zeppelins will get you!'" Her other complaint about New York was the same one still heard today: "When will you finish tearing up the streets?" But she managed to get back in the swim and was soon spotted dining at the Ritz with "a painter, two brokers, a diplomat, a world famous iron master and Diamond Jim Brady," according to a gossip columnist. "You Americans are so wonderful," Anna said enthusiastically. "I'm coming back to America every year until I am an old lady and my teeth fall out."

She also caught up on the latest gossip, and friends were more than happy to fill her in. Ziegfeld and Billie Burke were still married, but the honeymoon was over. Soon after their wedding, Frohman had vindictively sent Burke out on a cross-country tour in her show, *Jerry*. Ziegfeld, who was still not quite over Lillian Lorraine, began a serious affair with Olive Thomas, who appeared in his *Follies* and rooftop *Frolics* in 1915. Thomas, like Lorraine, was a breathtaking brunette, but unlike her predecessor, she was also a hardworking professional and a real potential star. "I was pretty dramatic about it," Burke said of this affair. "I played the scene big, with gestures, and a covered a lot of territory. . . . He was a dreadful man to quarrel with." But unlike Anna, Burke did quarrel, and the affair with Thomas faded away (Thomas did indeed go on to become a film star but died mysteriously in 1920 while vacationing in France with husband Jack Pickford). Anna made no public comments about Ziegfeld, but she avidly followed his career.

Reporters, who had been taking note of Anna's wartime escapades, came calling at the Savoy. They found a totally different Anna Held than they'd known a few years earlier. She even looked different: She was now an obviously middle-aged woman, still chic and lovely but no longer the ingenue. Her strong bone structure held her in good stead, but the bags under Anna's eyes had grown to steamer-trunk proportions, and the lines around her mouth could not be denied. She had also lost an alarming amount of weight.

But perhaps the biggest change in her was emotional. She could no longer chatter happily about fashions and cars and playing ball with her dog (the late, lamented General Marceau had been replaced by Ting-Ting, a two thousand dollar miniature Pekingese). Anna was now possessed by the war, and reporters' efforts to change the subject were to no avail. She recounted her experiences, she sang the praises of the French, and she admitted sadly, "I am not the Anna Held of old. I am another woman—a woman with a mission and serious motives."

Her main motive was to get the United States into the war. Anna's emotions and opinions were mixed—she wanted the war, the slaughter, to end immediately—and she recognized sadly that the only way that would happen was if more men—the Americans—were to throw themselves into the hellish fray. Anna had a hard job ahead of her: America was happily isolationist in 1915 and saw no reason to sacrifice lives for what it saw as a meaningless, bloody, and endless European quarrel. Films like D.W. Griffith's *Intolerance*, Thomas Ince's *Civilization*, and Alla Nazimova's film debut, *War Brides*, (all 1916) effectively preached the stupidity and horror of warfare. A hit song of the day summed up the general view:

> I didn't raise my boy to be a soldier,
> I brought him up to be my pride and joy.
> Who dares to place a musket on his shoulder
> To shoot some other mother's darling boy?
> Let nations arbitrate their future troubles,
> It's time to lay the sword and gun away—
> There'd be no war today if mothers all would say
> I didn't raise my boy to be a soldier!

She spent October and November playing vaudeville dates in the New York area, including a return engagement at the Palace Theater. She managed to revive her "Laughing Song" despite its now-tragic associations, and also sang a new number called "Oh, Oh, Oh!" The *Brooklyn Daily Eagle* wrote that Anna looked "almost as youthful as ever," and that upon her entrance she received such a round of applause that several minutes passed before she could begin her act. More than a beloved actress, she had returned a symbol of the war, a conquering heroine.

Her brief stage comeback accomplished, Anna prepared for her first feature film, *Madame la Presidente,* to be shot in Los Angeles. She was contracted to work for three weeks at ten thousand dollars a week (plus a thousand dollars a day for each additional day's work). Her entire salary, she stressed, would go to the Allied Relief Fund. Producer Oliver Morosco had signed Anna nearly as soon as she'd gotten off the boat, and the *New York Telegraph* noted that "nearly every moving picture concern in town had planned to make her an offer." On November 2 Anna embarked on her cross-country train trip, after posing in New York for the *Photoplay* photographers in her extravagant *Madame la Presidente* costumes. *Evening Mail* reporter Pete Schmid was present at that photo session and wrote that Anna's lack of egotism and democratic nature "will be a great assistance to her at the studio. . . . Her director need not fear that he will offend the star by suggesting this or that, as in the case of many of our prominent stage folk when they enter the studio for the first time."

Indeed, Anna sounded like a girl on her first day of school as she left from Grand Central Station with Liane, Beatrice, and Ting-Ting. "I can hardly wait to get to the studios," she said, displaying a less-than-delighted Ting-Ting for the reporters. "I have heard so much about these wonderful motion pictures and have seen such marvelous things on the screen that now it really surprises me when I think that I have kept away from this new field so long." She had been going to as many movies as she could to do her homework, and she bubbled happily about the recent improvements in the "silent drama." "I have seen several wonderful American photoplays and feel that I will be able to work as effectively on the screen as I have on the stage," she said. "In fact, I have become so enthusiastic over it all that I can hardly wait to begin work before the camera."

As usual, Anna managed to bring up the subject of the war, explaining that in France, "the picture theaters are the only places where the people rush, as they are the only establishments in an amusement way where money can be made. The stage is handicapped because everyone is in a serious mood—you can't show joy. Everyone is in mourning, money is not circulating, there is no employment for good actors. The players who are working are paid very little."

Anna's amiable producer, Oliver Morosco, had begun his professional life as an acrobat. By 1908 he'd become a successful theater manager, eventually producing such huge hits as *Abie's Irish Rose, Peg o' My Heart, Bird of Paradise,* and *So Long, Letty.* In 1913 he and two partners formed the Oliver Morosco Photoplay Company, setting up shop in the old Hobart Bosworth Studio at Council and First Streets in Los Angeles. This had been one of the first to be built from the ground up as a film studio, and not refashioned from an old barn or factory. The impressive lot consisted of a two-story office building, theater, carpenter's shop, prop room, and a shooting stage with a retractable roof. "With surprising rapidity the cameras began grinding out money," wrote Morosco in his memoirs. "Play after play of mine went into pictures." One of these plays was *Madame la Presidente,* which had begun life as an 1898 French play and had been translated into a Broadway hit in 1913 for Fannie Ward.

On her layover in Chicago, Anna was presented with some freshly shot partridges, which she feasted on for the rest of the journey (poor Liane managed to break a tooth on a bone). Anna got a grand reception when she arrived in Los Angeles, but clearly Morosco's heart (and mind) were not on picture making. He later admitted sheepishly, "I refused to take my illegitimate child, the picture company, seriously. To me the profits derived from it were but the revenue with which to open greater fields in theatrical production." This attitude did not bode well for *Madame la Presidente.*

Anna, Liane, and Beatrice were greeting upon their arrival by a contingent of Morosco's associates. They were put up at the Hotel Alexandria, though Anna announced her plans to rent a "little bungalow" for her stay. The movie magazines sent reporters, including one from *Screen Book* who jotted down Anna's makeup tips: grenadine for sensuous lips, rouge for too-large ears, and no eye shadow under the eyes ("this gives the impression of age and infirmity"). Anna went to movie after movie and was feted by the Los Angeles film community as her own project got ready to begin shooting.

Los Angeles in late 1915 was not the industry capitol it would become in just a few years, when wartime coal shortages sent companies fleeing to the warmth and sunshine of California. True, many film producers had already happily set up shop in Los Angeles, but there were many equally successful communities turning out movies in Fort Lee (New Jersey), Philadelphia, Chicago, and other cities. The year 1915 had been a watershed for the film industry, which was one reason Anna had agreed to take the plunge (that thirty thousand dollars was the other). Feature-length films were gaining in popularity, and such brilliantly directed examples as D.W. Griffith's controversial *The Birth of a Nation* and Cecil B. De Mille's *The Cheat* gained success with both critics and audiences.

More and more theatrical stars were lining up in front of the camera, as well. In 1915 Lillian Russell, John and Ethel Barrymore, Geraldine Farrar, Fannie Ward, Mrs. Leslie Carter, Richard Bennett, Weber and Fields, Mrs. Fiske, Sarah Bernhardt, Anna Pavlova, and Marie Dressler all had films in release—as did Lillian Lorraine. But these performers had to compete with the younger crowd of movie-bred stars, who did not have to unlearn stage technique for the movie camera. Fresh and vital performers like Lillian and Dorothy Gish, Charlie Chaplin, Theda Bara, Mary Pickford, Pearl White, and Wallace Reid were attracting bigger crowds than the aging "has-beens" of the theater.

Shooting began on *Madame la Presidente* in early November. Anna portrayed Mlle Gobette, a "vivacious" French actress who is thrown out of her hotel by a moralistic judge after being caught partying with three prominent officials. To get revenge, she goes about town passing herself off as the wife of her persecutor (while his real wife is somehow mistaken for a washerwoman). Mlle Gobette also vamps the local minister of justice but finally drops her charade when he falls in love with her. Anna managed to wangle Liane a small role as a nightclub patron.

Director Frank Lloyd did his best to put Anna at ease, but she found the filming a far cry from her lackadaisical short subjects. She was in bed by ten o'clock so she could be on the set and ready to work by nine the next morning, made up and costumed. There was much about filming that the stage actress found strange and difficult, such as staying within the camera's narrow range. "Such a little space in which to move, to stand, to act!" Anna complained. "When I walked in that picture, there was just room for my two feet on the side of the curb and I must take such little steps and so fast!" Like so many others new to the medium, "I had to unlearn all I knew when I faced the camera,"

Anna told Louella Parsons. "When I stopped to think that every move I made was being photographed I got so conscious. I 'acted' all over the studio; the director said, 'stop.' I stopped and started all over again." Slowly, Anna learned to tone down her technique for the big screen.

The film terminology also threw her—especially when she heard the director yell, "Shoot!" She had a flashback to the battlefield and had to sit down for a moment. "Oh! it is terrible!" she laughed shakily. "No one had said there was to be any 'shooting' in my photoplay, and when I cautiously peeped in at the door to see who was going to be shot, I learnt that the only 'shooting' would be done by the camera." On a lighter note, Anna had just noticed a fly at her feet when the cameraman shouted, "Kill it!" "Thinking he meant the fly, I stamped upon it, and later saw my action reproduced on the film," Anna told a reporter.

All the time she was filming, Anna kept up with the war news—and there was very little good news as 1916 dawned. Things were not going well for the Allies, and the next few months held one tragedy after another. The French suffered appalling casualties in Verdun at the end of February 1916; by the end of March some eighty-nine thousand French had been killed or wounded on that one battlefield. Anna wrote scores of postcards to the soldiers she had befriended in France, also sending them cartons of gum that she got by posing for Adams's Black Jack chewing gum ("good for coughs and colds"). While in California, Anna drove in her new touring car to the San Fransico World's Fair, with the still hopeful Charles Hanlon. He continued courting her, but Anna was no more interested than she'd been back in 1913.

Madame la Presidente was released on January 15, 1916, through Paramount Pictures Corporation, Morosco's distributor. At five reels, it ran about an hour and got nearly unanimous rave reviews. *Motion Picture* called it "diverting" and "praiseworthy," and the *San Francisco Post* added, "That adorable, never-crack-a-smile drollery of Miss Held is continually in evidence." Louella Parsons, in the *Chicago Herald*, also approved: "Miss Held looks young and slender, and her expressive French manner of conveying pantomimic emotion is absolutely original." And the *Buffalo Enquirer's* critic felt that *Madame la Presidente* "is a picture which keeps one amused all the time. There is no waiting for things to happen. . . . Anna Held uses her well-known eyes to good advantage on the screen."

But Anna herself had some reservations, agreeing reluctantly with the columnist who sniped that "crow's dancing pumps are inapropos about eyes which one cannot make behave." The harsh lighting and film stock required in movies of the day made Anna look every day of her age (officially forty-two but actually about forty-five). "The close-up, it is terrible," Anna lamented. "I see wrinkles around my eyes that I never dreamed were there. My eyes, they look old and tired." Despite the success of *Madame la Presidente*, Anna never filmed again, and let her contract with Morosco lapse.

As had so many of her stage shows, *Madame la Presidente* ran into censorship troubles. A Boston lawyer, Samuel Bailen, complained that the film libeled the morals of Frenchwomen. Anna somewhat unfairly threw her war record in his face: "Perhaps Mr. Bailen does not know that I have visited the French hospitals, gave my talents, time, and money to make lighter the burdens of wounded soldiers, that I have sent sums of money from this country in only the last few days to aid the afflicted; that some of the greatest businessmen of this country have declared that I am doing more than any other one person to show the horrors of war and so stir up action for peace. . . . I shall not allow the criticism of Mr. Bailen to disturb my thought that I have been, and am, of service to my country, and here this matter rests." That effectively settled Mr. Bailen's hash, but the Reverend Festus Foster also complained that *Madame la Presidente* "would make most any married woman suspicious of her husband. . . . Miss Held displays her lingerie and a little too much of her personal charms . . . with the intention of stirring masculine passions." Anna retorted somewhat oddly that the Reverend Foster was "the kind of a man who would live in a narrow little chicken coop," which no doubt silenced him.

Anna was back at liberty by the early spring of 1916, but Corneil Miles had plenty of plans for her. Miles ("Connie" to his friends) was Anna's new manager, and immediately romantic rumors about the couple were bandied about. "Just because Mr. Miles goes about the city with me some folks hint that we will be married," Anna laughed. "Oh, no! no! We have no such plan." Citing Miles's background as a reporter, Anna did muse that "if I would get married . . . I think I'd pick out a newspaperman rather than a millionaire. A newspaperman is a regular fellow." For his part, Miles gallantly said, "I doubt if there is a man on earth I would call good enough to marry her."

A four-month vaudeville tour was arranged, taking Anna through much of the country's midsection, playing in the B.F. Keith chain of theaters. She arranged that during her journeys she would be able to speak at town meetings, at clubs, and at war bazaars across the country. In early 1916 she helped raise seven hundred thousand dollars for blinded soldiers in a New York war bazaar, where she told of her breakdown in the hospital for the blind. Her sense of humor had returned, however, and Anna was able to joke about the shortages in the United States, threatening to eat her pearls if the price of eggs continued to skyrocket. And she admitted sadly how silly her old life seemed to her. "Before the war I had worries," she said in a veiled reference to Ziegfeld, "and they were telling on me. For example, I used to worry about love affairs. . . . It seems utterly absurd now. . . . But the war, the suffering of France, the agony of the wounded, the cries of the widows and the little children in want—those things I have seen and heard and passed through, as one passes through a fiery furnace, and that has purged my heart and soul of all the petty worries that used to bother me and make life miserable." Shaking herself out of her dark mood, Anna laughed, "And it is not easy to show that in a musical comedy, is it?"

Her tour opened in New Orleans, with a disquieting notice that called her "a great artist" but also reminded readers that she was "the same Anna Held that father used to rave over." It had now been twenty years since her American debut, Anna realized. She spoke at the New Orleans Press Club, sold newspapers on the street for the Belgian Relief Fund, and was escorted through town by a brass band. At her next stop—Milwaukee—she addressed the Rotary Club and worked herself up into a burst of tears. She appeared in *The Champus Mouser* at a benefit for Kansas City's Mercy Hospital and performed at Fort Dix, serving refreshments in a tent afterward. In Omaha she took some time out to romp in a playground with some local children and Ting-Ting. Realizing she was late for her show, she cried, "It takes me an hour to make up my eyes! I will have to go on with only one eye made up!"

Anna's war message was a somewhat contradictory one. She spent some time telling about the horrors of this needless war, describing in vivid detail the death and mutilation she had seen in the trenches and field hospitals—then she told the audience that the United States must enter the war, that they must send their own sons and brothers into the same horror. Anna noted with concern in June that the Germans used a new, deadlier gas in Verdun, wiping out a whole division. "It is too late now to even think of the cause of this most awful disaster," she told the St. Louis Ad Club in early 1916. "Only action will count and all must act together. Only a few men will mean nothing. You must go—go together carrying the same determination with which you have built up the great city of St. Louis." But after hearing her chilling tales of frontline agonies, few leaped up to enlist.

Her tour ground on into spring: In Buffalo she had a friendly reunion with Joe Weber, the *Higgledy-Piggledy* disaster of a dozen years ago forgotten (a few months later, she and Marie Dressler also put aside their old enmities at a war-benefit clambake). She sold papers in St. Paul, addressed the Detroit Chamber of Commerce, and played to enthusiastic capacity crowds in Buffalo. The tour ended in Broadway's Palace Theater in July. The obviously hungry reviewer Walter Kingsley enjoyed her act but concentrated on her costumes: "There is one gorgeous affair that's just the color of cream of tomato soup, and there's another that looks exactly like a salad, a nice shrimp salad, trimmed with mayonnaise and green stuff, and there's another frock with pantelettes, just like they decorate lamb chops with."

The timing may be a coincidence, but just when Ziegfeld unintentionally hurt her again, Anna intentionally did something she knew would infuriate him. In the summer of 1916 it became known that Billie Burke was expecting a child (Patricia, who would be born in the Ansonia on October 23). And Anna did the one thing Ziegfeld could never forgive: She signed a contract with the Shuberts. The show was to be called *Follow Me*, and Anna herself was a major investor in it, incorporating herself as the Anna Held Production Company, Inc. She spent the late summer and early fall of 1916 in rehearsal. She shuttled between her Savoy suite and the rehearsal space in the 44th Street Theater, going over costumes, scripts, casting and sets with director Wilmer Bentley, musical director Frank Tours, and whichever Shubert brother could spare her a few moments. She also bowed to the Shuberts' demand that she take voice lessons from Madame Else Kutscherra; Anna admitted that her singing was no great shakes and willingly accepted the tutoring. Keeping up her war work, she also donated a fifteen thousand dollar diamond-and-emerald ring to a refugee relief bazaar.

And on October 21, Anna took a decisive step to show her faith in the war's outcome: She laid out one hundred fifty thousand dollars to buy a chateau in Compiègne, to live in after France had emerged victorious. Anna had fallen in love with Compiègne on her frequent trips to the region, which lies about sixty kilometers north of Paris. Set near a forest of oak and beech trees, it was—and is—a lovely area, heavily laden with French history. Charles V had a castle there, Joan of Arc was captured outside Compiègne in 1430, and the town boasts a fifteenth-century chateau (actually reconstructed in the nineteenth century) as well as churches and abbeys dating back to the 1100s. Compiègne would be Anna's home after peace returned, she confidently decided.

November approached, along with the planned midmonth tryout of *Follow Me* in Boston. The show was scripted by Felix Dormann and Leo Ascher, with music by the popular Sigmund Romberg (as usual, a number of other songs were interpolated as well, to be changed throughout the run). Anna, of course, had her "eye song," "I Want to Be Good, But My Eyes Won't Let Me." She was to portray Claire La Tour, a naughty French actress pursued by the Marquis de Lunay (William Carlton); meanwhile, his wife (Letty Yorke) innocently asks Claire to break up his affair with his new mistress. The bulk of the show consists of mistaken identities as Claire attempts to reunite the couple.

Anna had a chorus of nine Anna Held Girls, as well as another thirty-four dancers and showgirls. Character names had not progressed very far since *A Parlor Match:* They included A. Knutt, Miss Watchcharm, and Worth Muchmore.

As the opening approached, Anna was heavily distracted by the war news, which came in fast and furious that month: In November the Battle of the Somme drew to an end; more than fifty thousand French soldiers had been lost there. On the November 7 Woodrow Wilson was reelected; Emperor Franz Joseph of Austria-Hungary died on November 21; the British liner *Britannic* (now a hospital ship) was sunk that same day; and London was heavily bombed at the end of the month. It was all Anna could do to traipse about singing "It's a Cute Little Way of My Own" or "Stop Tickling Me."

It had been four years since *Miss Innocence* had closed, and Broadway had changed since then. Shows were smaller, more intimate, and peppier. Among the competition *Follow Me* was to face in the 1916–17 season was *Oh Boy!*, the hugely influential hit by Jerome Kern, Guy Bolton, and P.G. Wodehouse. Long-legged comedienne Charlotte Greenwood had a star-making showcase in *So Long, Letty.* Reviews included the *Follies*, of course (featuring Fanny Brice, W.C. Fields, Marion Davies, Will Rogers, Bert Williams, and Ann Pennington). Ziegfeld himself had stiff competition that year, with *The Passing Show.* To make matters tougher for Anna, Al Jolson and Sarah Bernhardt were both playing Boston the same week that *Follow Me* was due to open. Even so, the show went well and packed up for Broadway.

All preparations were put to the test. Anna's final show, *Follow Me*, advertised somewhat oddly as "A Bewildering Entertainment," opened on November 29, 1916, at the Casino—the same theater where she had triumphed in *The Little Duchess* fifteen years earlier.

—9—

The Last Rose of Summer

When *Follow Me* opened on November 29, 1916, people lined up around the block for the event. Not only was Anna celebrating her twentieth anniversary on Broadway and her comeback after a four-year absence, but she was no longer "just" a beloved actress—she was a genuine war heroine and people were anxious to see her in the flesh. Everyone was delighted with the show and with Anna: *Follow Me* became one of the season's biggest financial successes. Even the critics were willing to forgive its lighter-than-air script and the fact that Anna was at least fifteen years too old for the role of Claire La Tour. Time, said the *New York Journal*, had "wrought little change in Miss Held, either in appearance or in her methods of playing. Her voice is as peculiar as ever, and her eyes still misbehave, as she complains in her new song." The critic then noted, "The first-night audience seemed to be immensely pleased." They must have been especially pleased by the anonymous chorus girl who managed to lose the top of her costume not once but five times.

The hard-nosed *New York Times* called *Follow Me* "one of those ornately staged entertainments with all the girls and ginger you could ask ... clean, lively, melodious and thoroughly amusing." The *Toledo Times* summed up audience appreciation of both the show and its star. "There is no one today and there never has been anyone who can do the sort of thing Anna Held does with half the snap, a third the 'chic' or a tenth the interest she manages to crowd into the moments that are hers onstage." Burns Mantle in the *Evening Mail* felt that Anna's singing voice had actually improved with the years, "except when the strain of a high note trips her," and complimented her for being one of the least naked actresses in New York that season. The *Philadelphia Star* felt that *Follow Me* "is the best thing Anna Held has done in years. . . . Here there is taste, wit, humor, grace, and charm." Heywood Broun in the *New York Journal* thrilled Anna more than he could have known by calling her "the Sarah Bernhardt of musical comedy." The only off-key note came from Ashton Stevens, who said that Anna looked "not sixty seconds older than Lillian Russell," who was in fact some ten years her senior.

Anna made sure that the war was written into *Follow Me:* Act 1 took place at a charity bazaar for wounded soldiers and act 2 backstage at a benefit performance. But she made it more personal than that—to the Shuberts' dismay, she insisted on bringing her obsession with the war virtually into the audiences' laps. Midway through act 2, Anna walked downstage and recited an antiwar poem by Alfred Bryan that included such lines as,

> What matters it who caused the trouble?
> What matters now who is to blame?
> If kings should light the fires of battle
> Shall common people feed the flame?

"It is a daring innovation in musical comedy," Anna admitted, "for it makes people sad, but nevertheless I feel it is my duty to express the sentiment contained in the poem." Knowing what Anna had been through, even those critics who felt it a bit much held their tongues and lauded the star for what they recognized as a sincere plea.

The costumes in *Follow Me* were not quite up to Anna's old Ziegfeld-produced standard. Indeed, one number featured her chorus wearing what appeared to be crumpled-up cellophane. One dress, however, created as big a sensation as had her panne velvet number in *The Little Duchess*. Anna hired the designer Lucile to make her a "peacock gown" that never failed to elicit gasps from the audience (the dress was strutted out as part of the fashion parade in act 3, to the tune of "My Bohemian Fashion Girl"). Lucile—a colorful character who was also well known as Lady Duff-Gordon, the sister of authoress Elinor Glyn, and a survivor of the *Titanic*—designed a short spangled gown for Anna, with a fifty-two-inch train. The train was stiffened by thin wooden stakes, and when Anna lifted it over her head by silver-cord pulleys, it formed a jeweled and embroidered peacock plume. The gown was such a success that Ziegfeld later hired Lucile to redesign it for his *Follies*. Also appreciated was Anna's "fire-fly dress" of heliotrope taffeta covered by orchid-colored chiffon and finished with a flaring hem of flame-colored tulle and silver roses.

Anna's costars were also lauded by the press: Henry Lewis, as poet A.

Knutt, and "singing and whistling comedienne" Helen Trix, who had a speciality during the act I title song, never failed to make a hit. Also appearing in act I were "dancers to the Spanish Court" Eduardo and Elisa Cansino, a brother and sister act; two years later, Eduardo became the father of future actress Rita Hayworth. Edith Day, who played the small role of a fortune-teller, went on to star in the hit musical *Irene* (1919).

The chorus girls of *Follow Me* were a far cry from the ones who had supported Anna way back in her earliest shows. With more and more musicals being produced, the level of singing and dancing had been raised. Mere beauty would not suffice anymore; now real talent came into play. British theater historian W. MacQueen-Pope lamented the decline of the old-fashioned chorine in the post-Edwardian period. "In their place were clever efficient chorus girls, who worked harder maybe than their sisters of old; but who lacked alike the distinction, allure, the individuality of their predecessors." Anna bragged of her *Follow Me* girls: "Of the sixty young women, forty of them have had high school educations and can play the piano or some other musical instrument. Now, that was not the rule in other days. The girls associated with me in *The Little Duchess* and *Mam'selle Napoleon* were comely enough, but as for culture and refinement—that is another story."

MacQueen-Pope also noticed the slow disappearance of the classic stage-door Johnnie, with his bouquet of roses, perhaps a diamond bracelet tucked inside. "Such people as did haunt the stage door were other girls," he said, "stage-struck young ladies who commented audibly on their favourites as they emerged, and even called them familiarly by their Christian names." A little of the magic had gone out of the theater, and Anna felt more and more like the mother of her chorus girls rather than their contemporary. Anna's only bitter moment came in December, with a replay of the Michael Leavitt lawsuit. In this case Anna had to pay one Eugene Kaufmann $1528 for having been introduced to the Shuberts by him. "I was shocked when I got a bill from him," Anna huffed—quite correctly, as the Shuberts had been after her for well over ten years. Nonetheless, she paid up.

Follow Me played to packed houses through the beginning of 1917, after which the Shuberts began making noises about a short tour and then folding up. In January 1917, Anna struck a deal with the Shuberts. She wanted to take *Follow Me* out on tour for an indefinite period, stopping off from town to town to do her war work. This did not fit in with their plans, so Anna purchased the rights to the show, becoming her own producer. The Anna Held Production Company, Inc., prepared to take the show on the road, while the Shuberts—to show there were no hard feelings—announced plans to build an Anna Held Theater on West Forty-fourth Street (this, sadly, never came about).

Becoming her own manager seemed easy; after all, she had lived with her manager for years and had been paying close attention. But as soon as Anna had taken the reins of *Follow Me*, both she and the show were caught in a January snowstorm in the Midwest. Determined to make her next date in Milwaukee, Anna was forced to hire a private train with enough cars to shuttle her company and scenery to the next town: This cost ten thousand dollars from her own pocket.

Early in 1917 Anna heard that her beloved Renault town car, requisitioned by Chief of Staff Joffre, had been shelled and abandoned somewhere in France. By that time she had more than replaced it: At a New York auto show, she had purchased twenty-four ambulances and shipped them off to France. Anna also arranged for a manufacturing firm to send one thousand cartons of chewing gum to her soldiers, and in Denver she and her chorus girls set up a barrel and collected cigars and cigarettes to send overseas. She kept in constant touch with her boys, who by now included forty-nine soldiers she "adopted."

Anna kept up with the war news while on tour, grabbing local newspapers as soon as her train pulled in. When Czar Nicholas abdicated in March 1917 Anna told reporters that the kaiser would no doubt follow suit. "The Russian royal family has not had much happiness in life," she said sympathetically. "America's poorest workingman knows more of the real joy of living—and I believe that as long as no violence is done them, they will be glad to be taken away from all the horrors which the imperial state has compelled them to endure, along with its magnificence and power." The fate of the Romanoffs and the "violence done them" in July 1918 was not made public until after Anna's own death.

It was also in March 1917 that Anna began admitting a feeling of achiness and exhaustion—due, she felt, to the exertions of starring in and producing her own show. Just fresh from Cincinnati and giving an interview in Baltimore, she complained lightly: "I have had a cold or something for a week, and it gives me pains." Getting ready to head to a soldier's home down in New Orleans, where she would entertain Civil War veterans, Anna spoke of the need to "keep face." "The public expects to see me wear handsome clothes," she said, "and I try to give them what they want. They would not come to see Anna Held looking drab—or tired, or sick. My public likes to hear of me gay and dashing." But Anna was not feeling particularly gay or dashing as the spring of 1917 wore into summer.

She had always taken good care of her health and had been relatively athletic for her day. In an era of eight-course dinners, Anna ate sensibly and healthily. She kept active and had not worn corsets for nearly ten years. In the fall of 1913 she had bragged, "I have not had to have medical aid for ten years. When I first came to America . . . I saw a chorus girl in my company who looked well always. I asked her what she did and she told me about her gymnasium. I went and received instructions. It did me much good." She added that "I take a cold shower every morning and after every performance. When I get up and before retiring I spend two minutes with breathing exercises. If I did not do these things," she said, "how would I look so young?"

In April 1917, one of Anna's hopes came true as the United States finally entered the nearly three-year-old war. There had been several "last straws:" Germany had offered Texas, New Mexico, and Arizona to Mexico if it turned against America; there was also the announcement in February of unlimited ocean warfare. In early April the House of Representatives and the Senate voted in favor of war, and on April 6 President Wilson announced America's entry. The first U.S. troops would reach Britain on May 18; and on June 5, the first draft since the Civil War was enacted.

"There is no glory in war," Anna said in Minneapolis when U.S. engagement was announced. "The present conflict is horrible in its fierceness." Agreeing with ex-president Roosevelt on military training, Anna said that "you should be so prepared that war will never be necessary; that it will never be necessary to send your young men forth to pour out their life's blood in a useless conflict." Despite her longtime irritation with President Wilson, Anna loyally stated of the president that "none other has ever been placed in such a position as he is in, and none other could have dealt with the situation more fairly."

As Anna tired more and more easily, the company pitched in to help. Connie Miles was on hand to take business worries off her shoulders, and the rest of the troupe was eager to help, as well. "Everybody is so kind to me that I am allowed to do nothing," Anna said. Her role was not quite so exhuasting as the typical star vehicle. "Any one of several principal has as much to do as the star and some of them were given hands that might make some stars jealous," the *Pittsburgh Gazette* noted in April 1917. April was a busy month: Anna also played in Detroit (where she eagerly sampled creole spaghetti, quite foreign to her French tastes) and headed north to play a benefit at a convalescent hospital in Toronto. At this latter stop wounded soldiers serenaded the company with the Canadian national anthem, and Anna had to gently chasten some of her girls for crying.

As Anna traveled through the United States, she noted something that had been absent in France: strong anti-German bigotry. As late as it was to enter the war, the United States jumped in with an enthusiasm that sometimes bordered on the maniacal. The Committee of Public Information did as much as it could to sell the war to Americans after years of isolationist propaganda. Hundreds of speakers (including authors Booth Tarkington and Rex Beach) were hired to make prowar speeches throughout the country. The motion picture industry was also urged to make "appropriate" films.

In October 1917, President Wilson signed a bill limiting the freedom of the German-language press, and such newspapers across the country went out of business. The following month alien enemy regulations were enacted, and many Germans in America were forced out of work. German books were banned and burned in town after town, and American citizens of German heritage (or even with German-sounding names) were harassed or lynched, even arrested "for their own protection." People who voiced skepticism about the war or the draft were run out of town or forced to kiss the flag; the same fate awaited those who did not buy Liberty Bonds. Lynch mobs, dubbed "Neutrality Squads" and "Knights of Liberty," ran wild throughout small towns, terrorizing innocent citizens.

Anna's long-held nineteenth-century notions of a woman's place in the world had finally begun to change by this third year of war; by this time Anna sounded like a veritable feminist, as she spoke of the need for American women to pitch in during wartime. American women, she said, "are of great mental strength as well as physical power, and they will be prepared to act at once. They are far the superiors of their sisters in Europe. The European woman is more like the petted darling, a doll whose slight acquaintance with the problems of the world made her unfit to do her part at first, though she must be credited with being a greater creature now."

The U.S. entry into the war did not make Anna's day-to-day job any easier. Many theaters closed because of coal shortages; train service was curtailed and prices went up. The draft, instituted in May, assured that actors and stagehands would be harder to find. Theater tickets were taxed, and people were spending more on essentials than on shows. As delighted as Anna was that the war's end was now in sight, her show began to struggle financially. She still owed the Shuberts a good deal of money after having bought out her contract, so *Follow Me* had to stay on the road.

Throughout the summer and fall of 1917, Anna and her loyal troupe crisscrossed the United States, playing in St. Louis; Washington, D.C.; Newark, New Jersey (with a stop at Fort Dix); Portland, Oregon; and Santa Barbara, California. While not performing, Anna continued to speak at Press Clubs, Rotary Clubs, and town meetings; she appeared at war bazaars, she sold newspapers on the street to aid war charities. The tour's musical director, Whitney

Bennington, told a reporter that Held "worked early and late, giving concerts in camps throughout the country." It was in Santa Barbara that Anna missed her first performance, suffering from what seemed to be a slight case of flu or possibly just overwork. In early December the tour continued to Red Bluff, California.

It was a busy company but a happy one: One showgirl's scrapbook is stuffed with photos of the cast and crew posing happily by railroad cars or in front of local landmarks and monuments as the company moved from town to town. A chorus member was quoted in a newspaper interview as saying that their boss "doesn't know how to be peevish, and say, she won't stand for anybody else being cross around a theater where she's playing. She wants the members of her company treated like human beings, and that's more than I can say for some stars!" Perhaps Anna remembered her own first experience as a chorus girl all those years ago, when a jealous cast member blackened her eyes. But she managed somehow to be not only star and producer but conciliator and peacemaker as well.

As the fall of 1917 turned into winter, Anna was visibly fading. Her appetite gone, she was losing an alarming amount of weight and looked haggard. Like most actresses, she became energized when onstage; the love of the audience acted like a shot of adrenaline. But she could barely drag herself from stop to stop and was relying on mysterious white pills to keep her going (Liane later said that Anna was taking one "every fifteen minutes," which sounds rather unlikely). What the pills might have been—amphetamines, aspirins, mere placebos—is a mystery at this late date.

It was obvious to the company, to Beatrice, and to Connie Miles that Anna needed help. "No one else but a French woman, and no other French woman but Anna Held, would have sung and danced in such a condition," Miles told the press. Anna herself, determined not to disband her show, agreed to wire Liane to join the troupe and help out with the moves and the day-to-day paperwork and trauma-soothing that goes with running a show. Neither Anna nor Liane was enthusiastic about this reunion. But Liane was glad for the excuse to temporarily abandon her own career. She'd been appearing in vaudeville and briefly in a show called *Too Near Paris*, as well as doing much charity and war bazaar work, like her mother. But the brilliant career she'd hoped for had not yet come about.

In December 1917, *Follow Me* hit Portland, Oregon. On December 19, Anna was diagnosed with pleurisy—an inflammation of the membrane surrounding the lungs—and had to cancel a tour of Fort Stevens, though she managed to carry on with the show. As 1918 dawned, Anna was hopeful about the progress of the war. But the progress of *Follow Me* and her mysterious health problems continued to plague her.

The company moved on to Milwaukee in mid-January 1918, where they played the Davidson Theater. Exhausted and painfully thin, Anna was nonetheless lauded by critics. "Miss Held has a grateful role that affords her abundant opportunity for her talents and she displays, incidentally, some of the most wonderful gowns and jewels ever seen on the Milwaukee stage," said one critic. But Anna was coming to the end of her strength. By her January 19 performance, she was too weak to lift her peacock train in the fashion parade, and had to be assisted by two chorus girls. Still, she stubbornly refused to let Liane take over her role, or to cancel a single show. "Do you realize that an entire company of fifty people depend on me for their bread and butter?" Liane recalled her saying. "Do you realize that the Shuberts expect another $30,000 out of this show? . . . I'll finish out this show in a wheelchair if I have to."

It was obvious that Anna could not long continue with her role, and Liane began watching her carefully from backstage, memorizing every movement, every gesture. On January 20 Anna collapsed and was rushed to St. Mary's Hospital, where she was once again diagnosed with pleurisy. Liane took over the role of Claire La Tour and was, by her own account, a huge success. "Before I knew it I was doing Anna Held's songs and dances as though I had been doing them all my life," she later wrote. Surviving newspaper clippings suggest otherwise: One Milwaukee reviewer said that she "works valiantly in a part not suited to her. . . . She has a certain monkeylike fascination" (Liane cannot have appreciated this, the second simian reference to her in several years).

Liane was well liked among the *Follow Me* company; although Anna and her daughter could not get along with each other, both managed to have friendly relations with the company. But everyone knew that Liane was simply not cut out for the role of Claire and that it would only be a matter of time before the show folded. In addition, of course, everyone was worried about Anna. As her condition failed to improve, a visibly upset Whitney Bennington stressed that "those who work with Anna Held love her. To us she is not simply a famous stage character; she is a charming human being who treasures a flower given her; a woman who always has a kindly greeting for her co-workers." The music director then went on to add rather darkly, "We who know her best know there are others who could be spared more easily." It was February before Anna was well enough to be transferred to a hospital in Asheville, North Carolina, where her condition remained both serious and baffling. She ached all over, was exhausted, had no appetite and was losing weight rapidly. It sounded like the flu but was lasting much too long. The company was worried about its jobs—but they were also genuinely worried about Anna, who had been a kind boss and a friend to them.

As Anna languished in Asheville, *Follow Me* continued its rather depressed and worried tour through Alliance and Sandusky, Ohio, in February; up to Ottawa in early March; and to Bennington, Vermont, later that month. Liane did her best and was steadily improving in her role, but people wanted to see Anna Held—box office fell off severely. The Shuberts sent out a press release stating, "Consultations of physicians yesterday report Anna Held out of danger, and showing encouraging improvement. Their judgement now is that she will be able before long to join her company." But by March this was appearing less and less likely. As the show got closer to New York, it was agreed to disband the company in early spring.

In April Anna was put on a train to New York, so weak she had to be carried on and off. Rather than going into one of New York's many hospitals, she was transferred back to her suite at the Savoy on Fifth Avenue and Fifty-ninth Street. Few wealthy people went into hospitals at that time, no matter how sick they were; they were looked upon as one step up from alms-houses, fit only for people who could not afford home care.

It was in New York that Anna's condition was finally diagnosed: After lengthy tests, she sat with Corneil Miles while Dr. Donald McCaskey told her that she had multiple myeloma and that in all likelihood she would be dead within a few months. According to Miles, Anna broke down in tears and had to be led back to bed. A brave press release was given to reporters shortly thereafter, with Anna declaiming, "It is the last curtain. I have lived and I will hold out to the last—it is the spirit of Joan of Arc and the spirit of my parentage—the unconquerable French." But much more believable is the friend who heard Anna whisper sadly, "No use for my friends to hope that I get well. The doctor says no. I should have liked to die in France. But it won't greatly matter—afterward."

Multiple myeloma had only been discovered in 1889 and was still considered a rare disease; today, it attacks about thirteen thousand people a year, most of them over seventy. A cancer of the white blood cells, it spreads through the bone marrow and breaks down both the immune system and the bones, eventually the entire body. As oxygen-carrying red blood cells are replaced, anemia results. The bones themselves thin, fracture, and dissolve into the blood, creating high blood-calcium levels. Eventually, the kidneys also are affected by the diseased blood. Ironically, Anna's insistence on keeping *Follow Me* open probably extended her life. Her active lifestyle strengthened her bones and delayed the absorption of their calcium into her bloodstream.

Today multiple myeloma can often be treated (though not cured) with bone marrow transplants or chemotherapy. But in 1918 it was a virtual death sentence. No one knows what causes multiple myeloma, but Anna was frequently blamed for her own illness: overdieting, corsets (which she had actually given up nearly a decade earlier), "rib removal," overwork. One of the most popular theories was, of course, a broken heart caused by her loss of Ziegfeld. Dr. McCaskey became Anna's chief physician, and he clashed with Liane from the first. In her memoirs, Liane refers to him as a quack "who had hypnotized her into thinking he could cure her just by the magic of his hand. He demanded day by day his fee of $100 a day." Liane also charged that McCaskey refused Anna pain medications, so "at least she would not be a dope fiend when she got better."

Liane was not popular with McCaskey, either, so her accusations must be viewed with some skepticism. She claimed to be at her mother's bedside twenty-four hours a day, protecting her, soothing her, making sure the wicked doctors did not abuse her. But Anna's financial manager, Samuel Kingston, later told a different story. He tried to reconcile the mother and daughter in this trying time but to no avail. Liane, he said, "kept away from her mother on purpose, for whenever she saw her mother there was a row." Anna told Kingston that Liane came by only when she "wanted money" or she "had trouble," and Kingston said she left Anna "crying and prostrated." Liane, who was working on a new vaudeville act, tried to get money through Kingston, as well. Anna refused.

Lillian Russell, who visited Anna at her sickbed, backed up Kingston's account. "The daughter was seldom at the mother's bedside, although she lived in the same hotel," Russell later told the press. Anna went so far as to put Russell in charge of funeral arrangements. Kingston stated that Anna wanted Liane to have nothing to do with buying a gravestone, as she "would not get it or would get a cheap one that would not be appropriate." Anna considered leaving the bulk of her estate to the Lambs Club rather than to Liane, but Kingston—foreseeing a messy legal battle—talked her out of it.

As sick as she was, Anna tried to keep up with the war news, and when she was too weak to read the papers herself, she insisted on having them read to her. Thus Anna learned of the Allied victories in Passchendaele in mid-April, of the German bombing raids on Paris in late March and June (killing hundreds of Parisians), and of the Allied army pushing the Germans back more than five miles in July. (Among the young solders in that battle was Corporal Adolph Hitler, who was awarded the Iron Cross that summer.) In June Anna would also hear of the earliest cases of the Spanish influenza that was to kill millions worldwide over the next year. In those early months it was feared that the flu was actually another form of nerve-gas warfare invented by the Germans.

In early May, McCaskey had Anna transported to the West Ninety-sixth Street offices of Dr. John Kantor, where she was x-rayed. She was down to eight-four pounds, and the films showed serious bone deterioration. Grasping at straws, McCaskey recommended a blood transfusion. On May 5 truck driver Ernest Lane donated twenty-five ounces, after which Anna was put under ultra-violet rays "to nourish the blood." McCaskey professed himself happy with the results: "Her blood condition continues good," he said, "her food is well as-similated, and she is handling all her system will stand." A press release from Anna—probably composed by Connie Miles—read, "You can tell the Ameri-can people that I appreciate their many good wishes and that I am going to fight on. I know I am going to win out because they are praying for me."

On May 13 Anna was well enough to sit up at her window and watch the Red Cross parade as it passed down Fifth Avenue. But the very next day her ever frailer skeleton failed her: While walking across her bedroom, she fractured her eighth dorsal vertebra and became partially paralyzed. "This greatly increases the pains of which she is unfortunately a constant sufferer," said Dr. McCaskey, adding ominously, "Just how much more crumbling or fracturing of the bone tissue is going to occur is impossible to state, as her disease is of steady malig-nant advance." Anna's pelvis, shoulderblades, and several ribs also had hairline fractures by this time, and McCaskey finally agreed to give her opiates for the pain.

It was generally known that her days were numbered, and steps were taken to make her as happy and comfortable as possible. Anna's last hurrah came on May 23, when she was visited by the Serbian delegate to the United States, Alexander V. Georgevitch, who presented her with a bronze medal for her war work. By this time Anna's condition had been thoroughly publicized in the same newspapers that had first brought her to fame via milk baths and kissing contests. Locals and tourists alike pointed out her window from Fifth Avenue as the place where the great star was slowly and bravely dying. The question on everyone's lips was of Ziegfeld: Had he visited? Would he? Ziegfeld—or at least Billie Burke—had sent fresh food from upstate New York, and Victrola records. Most importantly, Burke sent her own doctor, Edward Overton, who began slowly taking over McCaskey's duties.

At Lillian Russell's suggestion, Ziegfeld staged a show for Anna in the Savoy ballroom. He arranged for *Maid of Honor*, a play about Joan of Arc, to be put on. Anna was wheeled in to the tune of "La Marseillaise," and after the show had flowers sent to the leading lady, Josephine Victor. Ina Claire, who had been in Ziegfeld's 1915 and 1916 *Follies*, later recalled him saying tearfully at this time, "Why does that poor, good woman have to suffer so?" But did he actually visit Anna's deathbed? Most sources say no, and the only one to say otherwise is—oddly—Liane Carrera. In her unpublished memoirs of the 1930s, Liane recalled a Dr. Schoen cornering Ziegfeld and telling him that Anna wished to see him. "Flo did call on mother," Liane wrote, "and I remained in the bathroom during their visit which lasted about an hour. I heard their conversation but it is too sacred for me to reveal. Poor mother was pouring out her whole soul to that man. If he was sincere, even for a moment, I doubt it." Liane's story has the ring of truth—why would she shine even a partially flattering light on the man she hated so? It would have been easier to simply say that Ziegfeld had ignored Anna's pleas.

McCaskey told reporters that "her pain is agonizing and she sleeps but little," but Anna still telephoned friends and received callers, trying to look her best and act her most cheerful. New York Star reporter Ada Patterson assured fans that Anna "will die game." Newspaper writer O.O. McIntyre visited and told his readers that she was "the most courageous little woman ever I saw . . . who looks upon death, as did Charles Frohman, as the great adventure." Anna was not much enjoying her great adventure by late May, when an attack of bronchial pneumonia had Dr. McCaskey giving her up as near death. "Mentally, her condition is as clear as a bell," he said. "Her philosophy and courage are wonderful. But Miss Held's bone tissue still disintegrates. . . . She is slipping backward slowly, steadily, surely, to the end."

Not so steadily at that: By early June she'd made an amazing comeback both in strength and spirit and took her last outing. Connie Miles and Dr. McCaskey carried her out to one of her cars, and she enjoyed a brisk ride through Central Park, reveling in the cool early summer breeze and her last view of the outdoors. When Miles complimented Anna on her pink cheeks, she smiled, "Ah, that's a trick the doctor and I have." But the disease continued to torture and ravage her as summer wore on: When the temporal bone in her left ear collapsed, she went partially deaf. "Even my poor little head," she sighed. June and early July were cool in New York that summer of 1918, but there was a heat wave in late July and early August, with record-breaking temperatures as high as 102 degrees. The heat wave did not break until August 8. In an era before air-conditioning, Anna's Savoy suite must have been stifling.

By the beginning of August, Anna began slipping quickly away, and there were to be no more remissions. She asked again for Ziegfeld, and Liane called the Lake Placid hotel where he and Burke were vacationing. "Billie Burke answered and said she'd give him the message," Liane wrote. "He never called back." On August 2 Anna developed another case of bronchial pneumonia, and slipped in and out of consciousness over the next two weeks as friends gathered in her suite and fans kept watch below. "I never thought to go like this," she whispered during one of her last lucid moments.

"The end might come in a few days," said Dr. Overton, "and then again the patient might live two or three weeks." She could still hear and understand when spoken to, he added, but was too weak to respond. Just before four o'clock in the afternoon of Monday, August 12, Anna's breathing stopped. Dr. Overton placed the blanket over her head and called for the undertaker, and newspapers were notified. Then, as Connie Miles later related, "We were sitting around her grieving when suddenly we noticed the blanket moving. Dr. Overton reached out, threw off the covering, and there Miss Held was, again, breathing! It startled us for a moment, it was so unreal." The papers were hurriedly called back, the undertaker cancelled, and the small crowd gathered again around Anna's bed: Liane, Miles, Dr. Overton, Beatrice, and Lillian Russell's sister, Susanne Westford.

More than an hour passed. At 5:22, Anna stopped breathing again. This time she did not return.

Epilogue
The Melody Lingers On

Anna's death was hardly unexpected, so her funeral was a well-planned and celebrity-studded event, thanks to Lillian Russell's expert arrangements. Anna's coffin, draped in the French and American flags, was on view at Campbell's Funeral Church, at Broadway and Sixty-sixth Street. On August 13 crowds lined up by the hundreds to view the celebrities arriving for the 11:30 services, read by the Reverend John Murphy of Baltimore. Russell, Eva Davenport, Gertrude Hoffmann, Bert Williams, Lew Fields, Lee Shubert, and Charles Evans of *A Parlor Match* were among the famed attendees—Florenz Ziegfeld, with his horror of death and funerals, merely sent a huge floral arrangement of orchids, lillies of the valley, and roses, with a note reading "Flo." The Witmark Quartette serenaded the crowd with "Nearer, My God, To Thee" and "Lead Kindly, Light." That night, Campbell's stayed open till 2 A.M. to accommodate the thousands of fans who filed by to pay their respects.

On Wednesday, August 14, Anna was taken to Greenmount Cemetery in White Plains, New York, where a temporary plot was acquired. Lillian Russell later bought a site in Gate of Heaven Cemetery in Mt. Pleasant, New York, where Anna was eventually interred. She was one of the first people to be buried in the just-dedicated cemetery, which was owned by St. Patrick's Cathedral. She was later joined there by such famous neighbors as James Cagney, Babe Ruth, Dorothy Kilgallen, Sal Mineo, and Dutch Schultz. Lillian Russell did right by Anna: Her attractive, Empire-style grave boasts a stone arch and two benches.

Anna's forlorn suitor, Charles Hanlon, was her executor. At the time of her death, she owned 86 rue Faubourg Saint-Honoré, the chateau in Compiègne, shares in several Parisian grocery stores, nearly $290,000 in liquid assets, and a huge amount of jewels (many of which were left specifically to friends). After her bills had been settled, her estate was auctioned off in September 1919: The jewelry brought in $71,000. The estate auction was a sad and shabby affair, held in suite 117 of the Waldorf-Astoria. One newspaper described "a row of trailing, bedraggled gowns, a worn hat or two on a chair, a little pile of soiled satin shoes in the centre of the room. . . . Those tiny . . . shoes lying there in the centre of the room struck me as being unusually pathetic. They seemed so little, so helpless, with their high French heels." A.J. Adelson, who was conducting the sale, told the reporter, "It is funny how many come here just as souvenir seekers. Yesterday a woman came in and bought some shoes. She must have worn size eight herself, and Miss Held's are threes, but the woman explained that she had always heard that Miss Held was lucky, and that she wanted some of her things." The reporter overheard another shopper say enthusiastically, "My little girl is going to be married, and this is the most wonderful place for bargains!" Anna's evening gowns and stage costumes sold from $25 to $300. The auction brought in $145,900, which went to Liane, after probate, in December 1920.

Anna's friends agreed that the real tragedy of her death was its timing: She missed seeing the end of the war by only three months. The ferocity continued right up to the Armistice, which was signed on November 11, 1918, in the forests outside Compiègne—walking distance from the chateau that Anna had bought, where she would have been with bells on, no doubt, had she been alive. After the Treaty of Versailles was signed on June 28, 1919, it was estimated that the war had cost 8,600,000 soldiers' lives (not including civilian casualties). France alone had lost 1,384,000 in battle.

It wasn't only Anna who didn't survive the Great War; neither did her brand of musical theater. The revue format lived on, with Ziegfeld's *Follies* and such worthy competition as *George White's Scandals* (1919-39), the *Greenwich Village Follies* (1919-28), and the *Music Box Revues* (1921-24). But these never pretended to have plots; they were just glorified vaudeville. George M. Cohan had started something, and with the onset of peace, his baton was taken up by Gershwin, Kern, and Wodehouse. Snappy, modern musicals like *Oh, Boy!* (1917), *Lady, Be Good!* (1924), *No, No, Nanette* (1925), *Good News* and *Funny Face* (both 1927) took over where Anna's quaintly overblown shows had left off. These new shows had actual plots, plus songs that arose from character and situation. New numbers or specialties weren't dropped in willy-nilly. They weren't star vehicles, either, so they could be revived, and produced by local theaters and high schools.

Thus, *Lady, Be Good!* and *Anything Goes* will live on, while Anna's five biggest hits—*Papa's Wife, The Little Duchess, The Parisian Model, Miss Innocence,* and *Follow Me*—died with her. Even the huge hit *Florodora* proved unrevivable.

Florenz Ziegfeld continued to careen between success and failure, fortune and bankruptcy for the fourteen years by which he survived Anna. His *Follies* ran almost continuously (missing only three years) through 1931. They got bigger and gaudier through the years, the Ziegfeld Girls getting more and more naked (somehow one can't picture an Anna Held Girl doffing her clothing onstage as Ziegfeld Girl Kay Laurell famously did). Ziegfeld gave a helping hand to many a fledgling star through the *Follies:* Over the years he helped launch the careers of Fanny Brice, W.C. Fields, Will Rogers, Eddie Cantor, Nora Bayes, Leon Errol, and Bert Williams.

But most of all, there were Ziegfeld's "Glorified American Girls," dotting the *Follies* like precious jewels. From the show's inception through the early thirties, every girl in America with a sense of glamour wanted to join the *Follies.* Being able to sing, dance, or act in sketches helped—but some of the girls did nothing more than stand there and look devastating in costumes. An amazing number of *Follies* Girls went on to impressive stage or film careers: Among them Lina Basquette, Louise Brooks, Ina Claire, Marion Davies, Billie Dove, Justine Johnstone, Martha Mansfield, Mae Murray, Mary Nolan, Ann Pennington, Barbara Stanwyck, Lilyan Tashman, and Olive Thomas. A startling number of alumni also died young and impoverished, leading to the formation in 1935 of the Ziegfeld Club. Still extant today and staffed by the few remaining *Follies* Girls, the club helped out its sisters in need.

In addition to his *Follies,* there were also Ziegfeld's popular *Midnight Frolics,* a more intimate (and naughtier) show atop the New Amsterdam roof. These shows, inaugurated in 1915, ran through 1922, by which time Prohibition put a dent in such beer-garden-type entertainments. Somehow they weren't as much fun after the champagne corks stopped popping. He also produced or coproduced another twenty-one non-*Follies* shows between 1918 and 1932. Not all of them were hits: Such ephermeral fare as *Rose Briar, Annie Dear, Betsy,* and *Smiles* quickly sank and have vanished from the public mind. But Ziegfeld did enjoy a number of smash successes in his latter-day career. *Sally* (1920) proved a great vehicle for Marilyn Miller, as *Kid Boots* (1923) and *Whoopee* (1928) did for Eddie Cantor. The operettas *Rio Rita* (1927), *Rosalie* (1928) and *Bitter Sweet* (1929) also enjoyed healthy runs and produced a number of song hits. And of course there was *Show Boat* (1927), one of the most influential musicals of its era.

Ziegfeld's marriage to Billie Burke was a stormy one, and many felt that only Burke's steel core and their daughter Patricia kept them together. He remained loyal to the increasingly self-destructive Lillian Lorraine, and his serious affairs with Olive Thomas and Marilyn Miller tested Burke's patience. His gambling never abated, and the stock market crash of 1929 wiped him out, both financially and emotionally. He carried on, dabbling in film and radio as well as theater, but he was never the same. The flashing-eyed, intense, and enthusiastic youth who had charmed Anna to America back in 1896 was a long-distant memory. Ziegfeld was a tired old man, five hundred thousand dollars in debt, when he died of a heart attack in Cedars of Lebanon Hospital in Los Angeles on July 22, 1932. He was sixty-five years old, and some feel the musical review never recovered from his loss.

Billie Burke worked for decades to pay off Ziegfeld's debts; indeed, her remarkable film career was begun out of financial necessity. Burke spent the next two decades as one of Hollywood's most beloved and talented comediennes and character actresses, playing what she referred to dismissively as "bird-witted ladies." Best known for her role as Glinda in *The Wizard of Oz*, she also turned in remarkable performances in scores of films such as *A Bill of Divorcement, Dinner at Eight, Topper, Father of the Bride* and *The Young Philadelphians*. Late in life Burke expressed a philosophical view of her career. "I should like better parts . . . but if people will laugh at my work and keep a sound roof over my head, who am I to complain?" She returned to Broadway in several shows and also pioneered in radio and television. The keeper of Ziegfeld's flame, she coauthored two autobiographies and carefully monitored any Ziegfeld-related projects. Maintaining the public attitude of a flighty, twittering matron, Burke remained a smart and very strong woman until her death at age eighty-four on May 14, 1970.

Lillian Lorraine's life went into such a sudden spiral after Anna's death that the thought of ghostly vengeance raises its head. The 1918 *Follies* was Lorraine's last edition, and her professional association with Ziegfeld ended with the 1920 *Nine O'Clock Review*. One critic of that show noted her "droning voice, which always seems a yard or so behind the musicians," adding that she was "attractive enough to make one almost forgive her for being there at all." That same year she was evicted from her apartment for throwing loud parties, and in 1921 she injured her spine in a fall outside a nightclub. Lorraine's bookings fell off through the decade: a handful of unsuccessful Broadway shows and vaudeville tours, along with embarrassing newspaper stories about her health and financial problems. In 1941 she was hauled off to Bellevue Hospital when her cheap apartment caught fire. Lorraine finally found marital happiness with accountant Jack O'Brien, but she died broke and forgotten in 1955. A handful of show business friends saved her from a pauper's grave, and she was buried in Cavalry Cemetery.

The acting career of Anna's good friend Lillian Russell had pretty much ended by the time of Anna's death. Happily married to publisher Alexander Moore, Russell became involved in politics and campaigned for women's suffrage, and in 1921 she was appointed by President Warren G. Harding to investigate immigration laws (she suggested a severe cutback in immigration from Europe). Russell died in 1922, in her sixty-first year.

Anna would still recognize much of her beloved Paris, though not the Folies-Bergère or La Scala; the buildings remain at their original sites but are so remodeled that they are unrecognizable. But the rue Faubourg Saint-Honore remains a landmark of Belle Époque Paris, crowded with chic stores. Anna's home at number 86 still stands today, across from the Élysée Palace. Its ground floor is now the home of a fashionable antiques shop. Very little, however, remains of Anna's New York. All of the theaters where she performed—the Herald Square, the Lyric, the Manhattan, the Casino, the Knickerbocker, Joe Weber's, the Broadway, the New York—are long gone, most of them torn down in the 1920s and 1930s. Anna's first New York home, the Hotel Netherland, and her last, the neighboring Savoy, are also gone, replaced by huge boxlike office buildings. Only the Ansonia remains, a beautiful but battered old dowager at Seventy-second and Broadway.

Anna's legend began to fade in the jazz-crazed 1920s, but she was never entirely forgotten. In the mid-1930s, an operetta called *The Queen of Broadway*, based on Anna's life, briefly played at Brooklyn's Hopkinson Theater. Then MGM optioned the story of Ziegfeld's life to be made into a super-production called *The Great Ziegfeld*, starring William Powell and crammed with musical numbers (the director, Robert Z. Leonard, was an ex-husband of former *Miss Innocence* performer Mae Murray). Dewy-eyed Viennese actress Luise Rainer was cast as Anna, who was written as rather more naive and languid than the real-life prototype. There was the usual Hollywood bio-pic rewriting of facts; the *Follies* were Ziegfeld's idea, with Anna opposed, for example. And the scene showing Anna listening to Gershwin's *Rhapsody in Blue* performed in the *Follies* is enough to give one historical whiplash.

Oddly, the 1913 New Year's Ball—which might have been concocted by a screenwriter—was stripped of its drama; the star-crossed Held/Ziegfeld/Burke triangle of that night is not utilized. Lillian Lorraine (renamed Audrey Dane, for legal reasons) was played by Virginia Bruce as a venal gold digger. Powell was quite good as Ziegfeld, and Rainer won an Academy Award as Anna; her comedy scenes were brilliant, but it was her teary-eyed phone call to the newly married Ziegfeld that clinched it: "Allo, Flo . . . I am so happy for you today" (in real life, of course, Anna had not even sent a telegram). MGM's Anna crawled away to die of a broken heart, leaving Ziegfeld to Billie Burke— as Burke was played by Powell's frequent costar Myrna Loy, the film pretty much turned into *The Thin Man Goes to the Follies*. But *The Great Ziegfeld* reawakened the public's interest in Anna and turned her into a figure of suffering, broken-hearted tragedy. Anna later turned up as characters in the 1978 TV-movie *Ziegfeld: The Man and His Women* (as played by Barbara Parkins) and the 1980 Broadway musical *Tintypes* ("She was the Farrah Fawcett of her day," averred actress Carolyn Mignini).

With due respect to the Misses Mignini and Fawcett, Anna was much more than this. She bridged the gap in popular culture between the floral, candy-box sweetheart of the late nineteenth century and the new woman of the twentieth. When Anna arrived in New York in 1896, she was the very image of the popular musical comedy girl, like her contemporaries Lillian Russell, Lulu Glaser, Della Fox, May Irwin, and Edna May. All flipped-up petticoats, naughty glances from behind lace fans, and double entendres; these were charming, empty-headed bon-bons, good for a laugh and a flash of a shapely ankle. Anna quickly became their queen and prize example.

But—and this is what made Anna unique—she was able to change with the times and even influence them herself. By the time of her last Broadway show in 1916, the candy-box girl was on her way out; the flapper was on the horizon. And Anna was leading the way. She was as still as modern as this morning's newspaper, leading the path into the 1920s and 1930s for starlets of the era like Charlotte Greenwood, Ina Claire, Vivienne Segal, Ruth Chatterton, Tallulah Bankhead, and Lynn Fontanne, who made their mark at the close of World War I. Amazingly, Anna kept bringing in not only her old fans but new adherents to her honest, modern, and humorous performances. It's doubtful her career could have lasted much longer. An aging Anna smoking cigarettes and making hard-edged Nöel Coward wisecracks—that simply would not have played. But above all other actresses, Anna Held managed to epitomize both the starry-eyed baby doll of 1896 and the clear-eyed woman of 1916, without ever seeming to be old-fashioned or wearing out her welcome. It wasn't until after her death that people were able to stand back and realize what an icon, a snap-shot of her era she was.

After her mother's death, Liane (billed as Anna Held Jr.) took a twenty-four-minute vaudeville act on the road. She bounced through various careers in the 1920s and 1930s—actress, typist, reporter—before opening the Anna Held Tea Shop in upstate New York. In the early 1930s she married government worker J. Dodd Martensen and had a daughter, Antoinette. "Grandma bathed in milk, but 'Anna Held 3rd' uses soap," read the caption of a newspaper photo of baby Antoinette in the bathtub.

Liane never got over being Anna's daughter, and Anna's death did not even slow down her obsession with her mother. "I'm contented and happy, and all in spite of being a famous daughter," she said in the late 1930s. But Anna preyed on her mind. She worked on an autobiography, *My Mother Was an Actress,* with newspaperman George Bye. But the manuscript went into a trunk and was forgotten. Then, in 1954, a completely rewritten version was published, called *Anna Held: Memoires.* The French-language work was written as Anna's own autobiography, as compiled by her daughter. When the book came out in English, as *Anna Held and Flo Ziegfeld* (1979), it was still purported to be in Anna's own words, though Liane was listed as the author. Both editions were put out by small presses and were pretty much ignored by critics and book buyers alike. But they were used as sources by most Ziegfeld biographers and helped to disseminate many questionable rumors.

By the 1960s the now elderly and white-haired Liane had moved to San Jacinto, a tiny California town, and opened the storefront Anna Held Museum. The few belongings she had held onto were lovingly displayed: framed photos, a tablecloth and napkins embroidered AHZ, Ziegfeld's silver brushes, curtains from Anna's Paris home, a bedspread, jeweled stockings, evening shoes, and as a grand finale, a department-store mannequin decked out in Anna's nightclothes at a dressing table. In 1981, after Anna had appeared as a character in *Tintypes,* Liane took her museum on tour to New York: "I wanted to share my heritage with people," she said. "Anna Held and the Statue of Liberty are two French contributions to the United States that have enchanted the American public. . . . She brought entertainment and joy to everybody in her day."

New York was indeed enchanted by Liane and her little exhibit, but she soon returned to San Jacinto, where her health began to fail. With Liane's death on May 22, 1988, the last thread was broken, and Anna Held once and for all retreated into the past.

Sources

First, a general note on the text and on the major sources: None of the quotes or conversations in this book has been invented; all are taken directly from published interviews, autobiographies, or private correspondence. As mentioned in the text, Anna Held was not conversant in English until about 1898, and any previous interviews were probably paraphrased or translated. If I feel an interview was not in Anna's words but simply a press release, I note this in the book.

The main source used was the Billy Rose Theater Collection at the New York Public Library at Lincoln Center. The rare books, newspaper and magazine clippings files, and extensive scrapbooks are a national treasure and without them (and the library's hardworking, helpful staff), this book would not have been possible. From these sources, I was able to trace Anna's life and career, the dates of her shows and her ocean voyages, the routes of her theatrical tours. Most of the interviews and critics' reviews quoted in this book were found in this collection.

I also used as sources Liane Carrera's two memoirs: her unpublished notes from the late 1930s and her 1979 book *Anna Held and Flo Ziegfeld*. Both of these books had to be approached with extreme caution, as Liane's stories changed from year to year and often contradicted themselves. When these books were used, I was sure to note that they consisted of Liane's personal opinions and may have only a passing relationship with reality.

Throughout the book, I mention other shows and stars who appeared onstage during Anna's career. These details were culled from *American Musical Theater* and *The Oxford Companion to American Theater* (both Bordman), *A Pictorial*

History of the American Theater (Blum and Willis), *Great Stars of the American Theater* (Blum), and *Broadway* (Bloom). I also discuss the various New York theaters in which Anna performed; details on them were available in *From the Bowery to Broadway* (Fields), *Lost New York* (Silver), *New York Then and Now* (Watson), and especially *Lost Broadway Theaters* (Van Hoogstraten).

Prologue

The quote "The ballroom was filled with fashion's throng; / It shone with a thousand lights" is taken from the opening lines of "Bird in a Gilded Cage" (1899).

1. Heaven Will Protect the Working Girl

Anna covered her tracks well, and her childhood was extremely difficult to trace. Her Warsaw birthplace was finally proved during World War I (see chapter 8), but her birthdate remains something of a mystery. When researching his book *The Ziegfeld Touch*, Richard Ziegfeld was unable to find any record of Anna's birth in either Warsaw or Paris. Though her generally acknowledged birthdate was March 18, 1873, there were other stories as well: Her tombstone says 1872; one book (*Great Jews on Stage and Screen*, Lyman) says 1865, as does a 1956 letter to the *New York Times*. Her early career and published interviews with her childhood neighbors and London coworkers led me to estimate her birthdate as 1870. It may actually have been two or three years earlier or later. Details of Anna's childhood also came from those interviews with early neighbors and coworkers, all of whom were very eager to "tell on her" after she became famous. Some stories were taken from a lengthy article, "My Beginnings," which appeared in *The Theatre* magazine in July 1907. While this article was certainly ghostwritten, it contains so many phrases and stories often repeated by Anna that it was probably based on first-hand interviews with her. But again, just because Anna told these stories does not mean they were true. Facts on nineteenth-century Poland and its Jews come from the books *The Jews in Poland* (Abramsky, Jachimczyk, and Polonsky), *The Jews in Polish Culture* (Hertz), and *Bright Star of Exile* (Rosenfeld), as well as stories from my own family, who fled Eastern Europe about the same time (and for the same reasons) as did Anna's family. The plight of Jewish refugees in nineteenth-century Paris was detailed in *The Jews in Modern France* (Malino and Wasserstein) and *Fin de Siècle Paris* (Weber); and the Victorian Jewish community in London in the books *London's East End* (Berment) and *Living London* (Sims). Anna's early career in the Yiddish theater was discussed in newspaper interviews with her coworkers and with Anna herself, and in the Jacob Adler biography *Bright Star of Exile* (Rosenfeld). The world of the Paris music halls of the 1890s was colorfully covered in the books *Folies-Bergère* (Derval), *Lautrec on Lautrec* (Huisman and Dortu), *La Belle Otero* (Lewis), *That Was Yvette* (Knapp and Chipman), *Fin de Siècle Paris* (Weber), and the biography of that singular star *Le Petomane* (Nohain and Caradec). Anna's Parisian music hall career was also extensively covered in U.S. and London newspapers (the latter obtained through London's National Museum of the Performing Arts). The marriage to Maximo Carrera and Liane's birth were both brushed over and reimagined by Anna and are difficult to pin down. Using Anna's own interviews, Liane's various reminiscences, and articles by Chicago newspaperwoman Amy Leslie, I was able to cobble together as many facts as can be ascertained at this late date. Details about Anna's neighborhood and home on the rue Faubourg Saint-Honoré were obtained through Anna's own interviews, reporters' stories, Liane's detailed memoirs (her memories of this house do ring true in her books), Stanley Loomis's book about the de Praslin murder, *A Crime of Passion*, and from modern-day Parisians Jo Lowrey and Richard Erickson. The early life and career of Florenz Ziegfeld Jr.—indeed, most biographical details about him throughout this book—come from his Lincoln Center files and from the full-length biographies by Burke, Cantor, Carter, Farnsworth, Higham, Ziegfeld (Patricia), and Ziegfeld (Richard and Paulette). As with Liane Carrera's books, these biographies do not always agree with each other, so I was careful to weigh sources, compare stories, and consider the reliability (and agendas) of authors before deciding which facts seemed the most likely. Eugen Sandow's career was well covered in the Ziegfeld books, as well as in *Sandow the Magnificent* (Chapman). Biographical details of Charles Evans, William Hoey, and "Teddy" Marks are from their *Variety* obituaries and from the invaluable book *The Oxford Companion to American Theater* (Bordman). A huge scrapbook devoted entirely to *A Parlor Match* also exists at Lincoln Center.

2. It Pays to Advertise

Social and architectural details of turn-of-the-century Manhattan come from the books *The Epic of New York City* (Ellis), *Fifth Avenue, 1911, From Start to Finish* (Gray), *Lost New York* (Silver), *New York 1900* (Stern, Gilmartin, and Massengale), *New York Then and Now* (Watson), and *On Fifth Avenue Then and Now* (Wist), as well as from my own two decades as an inquisitive New York pedestrian. Facts on Lillian Russell's life and career are from her biography, *Lillian Russell: The Era of Plush* (Morrell), as well as from her *Variety* obituary and from the books *American Musical Theater* and *The Oxford Companion to American Theater* (both Bordman), *A Pictorial History of the American Theater* (Blum and Willis), and *Great Stars of the American Theater* (Blum). Stories of theatrical publicity men come from various Ziegfeld biographies, as well as from *Behind the Curtains of Broadway's Beauty Trust* (Page), *Forty-Odd Years in the Literary Shop* (Ford), and *Winchell* (Gabler). The early years of vaudeville are best covered in the classic *American Vaudeville* (Gilbert). Oliver Morosco's opinion of pre-earthquake San Francisco is from his biography, *The Oracle of Broadway* (Morosco and Dugger). Biographical details of Charles Bigelow come from his files at Lincoln Center (he is sadly absent from all theatrical books I perused). The early history of motoring comes from Mark Sullivan's exhaustive series *Our Times*, as well as from *This Fabulous Century* (Bowen), *The Adventurous World of Paris 1900–1914* (Gosling) and *Edwardian Promenade* (Laver). Details on Harry B. Smith are from his autobiography *First Nights and First Editions* and from *The Oxford Companion to American Theater*.

3. The Belle of New York

Ladies' fashions and corsets of the turn of the (last) century are described in *Edwardian Promenade* (Laver), *Our Times* (Sullivan), and *The Light of the Home* (Green). I have also used my own hands-on experience as assistant curator of a Baltimore costume history museum for two years (I have tried on period corsets and discovered first-hand that slouching is quite impossible in them). January 1, 1900, was described in *America 1900* (Crichton). The life of the touring theater troupe was fully covered in *Trouping* (Lewis), and train travel of the period in *The Good Old Days—They Were Terrible!* (Bettmann). The world of Anna's Paris in the early twentieth century was written of in *The Adventurous World of Paris 1900–1914* (Gosling) and *Fin de Siècle Paris* (Weber). The colorful chorus girl Frankie Bailey has never had a biography, so details on her life were taken from her *Variety* obituary.

4. Poor Little Rich Girl

The frigid East Coast winter of 1903–04 was well covered in newspapers at the time and mentioned in articles in Anna's Lincoln Center scrapbooks. The disastrous Iroquois Theater fire was covered in *The Oxford Companion to American Theater* (Bordman) and in the harrowing *The Great Chicago Theater Disaster* (Everett). Its effect on the theatrical managers was noted in *The Shuberts of Broadway* (McNamara). The unsettling invitation to Louis Mott's 1904 hanging still exists in one of Anna's scrapbooks. The background on Weber and Fields comes primarily from the Fields' biography *From the Bowery to Broadway*; also from *Variety* obituaries and from *The Oxford Companion to American Theater*. The further automobiling information comes from the sources named above in chapter 2. Information on the Ansonia and its neighborhood is from *Upper West Side Story* (Salwen) and *New York Then and Now* (Watson). The decor of Anna's apartment there was mentioned at length in her interviews. The opening of New York's subway system was covered in *The Epic of New York City* (Ellis), *New York Then and Now* (Watson), and *Crossroads of the World: The Story of Times Square* (Laas). That latter book also had much information on the renaming of Times Square and the first New Year's celebration at that intersection, in 1904–05. Marie Dressler's quote about Anna is from her 1934 autobiography, *Life Story of an Ugly Duckling*. The formation of the Theater Syndicate was from various Ziegfeld biographies, and from *The Oxford Companion to American Theater* and *The Shuberts of Broadway*. The marvelous quote about Erlanger is from Wodehouse and Bolton's memoirs, *Bring On the Girls!* Details on Julian Mitchell's bizarre and admirable directing career are from his *Variety* obituary and *The Oxford Companion to American Theater*, as well as from *Bring On the Girls!* Amy Leslie's biography stems from *The Oxford Companion to American Theater*.

5. A Lucky Star

The Great Jewel Robbery of 1906 was covered ad nauseum in the press; Liane Carrera's personal opinions of the affair are from her various memoirs, published and unpublished. The "glass ass" story is from Beatrice Lillie's delightful autobiography *Every Other Inch a Lady*. The development of electric lighting in Times Square is from *Crossroads of the World: The Story of Times Square* (Laas). The birth of Ziegfeld's *Follies* was well covered in all of his biographies (see bibliography), as well as in his Lincoln Center files. Richard and Paulette Ziegfeld's book was particularly helpful as far as cast lists and opening dates. Anna's onstage quarrel with Charles Bigelow is well documented in Bigelow's Lincoln Center file. Facts on the 1907 financial panic are from *Our Times* (Sullivan). Anna's 1908 shoulder troubles were mentioned in a note from Ziegfeld to Charles Hanlon (April 27, 1908); the note appears in an original manuscript obtained from John K. King Used and Rare Books. The abortion story has been mentioned in several of Ziegfeld's biographies, but all have used Liane Carrera's 1954 (French) and 1979 (English) memoirs as the source. None of these authors had access to her unpublished 1930s memoirs, which tell a different, and often conflicting, story; this tends to cast suspicion on Liane's entire account. Anna's unspecified illness at the time is mentioned in a recently discovered letter from Ziegfeld to Hanlon of November 8, 1908 (King manuscript). Additional information comes from Richard Ziegfeld's interview with Liane's friend and estate executor Alexander Hegedus, and from my own conversations with Anna's descendants. Additional information on abortion in the early twentieth century comes from *The Light of the Home* (Green). In the end, only Anna and Ziegfeld knew what really happened; anything else can only be conjecture.

6. The Mansion of the Aching Hearts

Ziegfeld's methods for choosing show girls were mentioned in his biographies and in a filmed short subject he made, circa 1931. The world of the New York chorus girl was fleshed out in *Behind the Curtains of Broadway's Beauty Trust* (Page) and two hilarious (but hard-to-find) novels, *Show Girl* (McEvoy) and *The Sorrows of a Show Girl* (McGaffey). Early "aeroplaning" was covered in *Our Times* (Sullivan), *This Fabulous Century* (Bowen) and *Edwardian Promenade* (Laver). Lillian Lorraine's Lincoln Center files provided information on her life and career. The Ziegfeld/ Shubert fisticuffs of June 10, 1909, were covered in the biographies of both of those men. The enormous change in women's fashion in 1908 and 1909 was outlined in Anna's own interviews and in *Edwardian Promenade* and *Our Times*. Again, my own experience as a costume historian also came in handy. The adventures and fates of Nena Blake and Ursula March were mentioned in Anna's *Miss Innocence* scrapbook. The only accounts of Anna discovering Lillian Lorraine's Ansonia apartment are in Liane Carrera's various memoirs and must therefore be viewed with the appropriate caution.

7. The Unchastened Woman

Details of Anna's London engagements of 1910 were provided by the National Museum of the Performing Arts, London. The bizarre tale of Cherry de St. Maurice is contained in Anna's Lincoln Center files. Charles Hanlon's colorful obituary and his private correspondence to and from Ziegfeld and Anna were provided by John K. King Used and Rare Books. The background on ocean travel and specific ships of the early twentieth century is from *The Sway of the Grand Saloon* (Brinnen); Anna's annual comings and goings were obsessively covered in the press, so her ships and arrival/departure dates were quite easy to pin down. Michael Leavitt's *Variety* obituary provided his biographical facts; *Variety* and *The Oxford Companion to American Theater* (Bordman) provided information on John Cort's life and career. The public battle between Ziegfeld and Freddie Gersheimer was well covered in Lillian Lorraine's Lincoln Center file. The ragtime music and dance revolution was colorfully and entertainingly written of in *Our Times* (Sullivan) and the delightfully cranky *Welcome to Our City* (Street). Architectural changes in Manhattan between 1910 and World War I were written of in *The Epic of New York City* (Ellis), *Lost New York* (Silver), *New York Then and Now* (Watson), and *On Fifth Avenue Then and Now* (Wist). The Kinemacolor films of 1913 were detailed not only in Anna's Lincoln Center files but also in *From the Bowery to Broadway* (Fields). Liane Carrera's theatrical career has its own file at Lincoln Center. Biographical details on Billie Burke are from her autobiography *With a Feather on My Nose* and from *Great Stars of the American Theater* (Blum).

8. Under Two Flags

Out of the many books on World War I, the ones I chose were Martin Gilbert's superb *The First World War* (which served as the source for the Strachey and Masterman quotes), *Our Times* (Sullivan), *Edwardian Promenade* (Laver), *This Fabulous Century* (Bowen), as well as the nurses' memoirs *My Beloved Poilus* (anonymous) and *Helping France* (Gaines). H.B. Marinelli's *Variety* obituary was used for details of his career. The life and career of Oliver Morosco comes from his biography, *The Oracle of Broadway* (Morosco and Dugger), and his *Variety* obituary, as well as from *Without Lying Down: Frances Marion and the Powerful Women of Hollywood* (Beauchamp) and *The Oxford Companion to American Theater* (Bordman). Specifics about the making of *Madame la Presidente* are from Anna's files at Lincoln Center and the Academy of Motion Picture Arts and Sciences. The only known copy of *Madame la Presidente* resides at UCLA. Additional facts about the motion picture industry in 1916 were gleaned from my research into my biography of Theda Bara. The local tourism board supplied background material on the Compiègne region.

9. The Last Rose of Summer

The MacQueen-Pope quotes on chorus girls are from *Edwardian Promenade* (Laver). Anti-German actions in the United States during 1917 were documented in Ray Cunningham's Web site on World War I. Details on Anna's last tour, in *Follow Me*, are from a chorus member's scrapbook, which was donated anonymously to Lincoln Center. Facts on multiple myeloma's symptoms and treatment are from the Mayo Clinic, Rochester, and Imperial Cancer Research Fund. The date that Dr. Overton took Anna's treatment over from Dr. McCaskey is noted on her death certificate.

Epilogue

I personally visited Anna's grave, which I found through the delightful Web site www.findagrave.com. The owners of Gate of Heaven Cemetery were extremely helpful and friendly. Ziegfeld's later life was gleaned from his various biographies; Billie Burke's from the sources noted in chapter 7, above. The current-day state of Anna's Parisian haunts was ferreted out (and photographed) by Parisienne Jo Lowrey; the corresponding New York sites by myself. I got details of Liane Carrera's later life from her Lincoln Center files and from her daughter and granddaughter; Liane's friend Miles Kreuger told me of her "museum" (the handouts for this are also found at Lincoln Center).

Bibliography

Abramsky, Chimen; Maciej Jachimczyk; and Anthony Polonsky. *The Jews in Poland.* New York: Basil Blackwell, 1986.

Anonymous. *My Beloved Poilus.* St. John, N.B.: Barnes, 1917.

Bartelt, Chuck, and Barbara Bergeron, eds. *Variety Obituaries.* New York: Garland, 1989.

Beauchamp, Cari. *Without Lying Down: Frances Marion and the Powerful Women of Hollywood.* New York: Simon and Schuster, 1997.

Berenson, Edward. *The Trial of Madame Caillaux.* Berkeley and Los Angeles: Univ. of California Press, 1992.

Berment, Chaim. *London's East End.* New York: Macmillan, 1975.

Bettmann, Otto L. *The Good Old Days—They Were Terrible!* New York: Random House, 1974.

Bloom, Ken. *Broadway.* New York: Facts on File, 1991.

Blum, Daniel. *Great Stars of the American Theater.* New York: Greenberg, 1952.

Blum, Daniel, and John Willis. *A Pictorial History of the American Theater.* New York: Crown, 1977.

Bolton, Guy, and P.G. Wodehouse. *Bring On the Girls!* New York: Simon and Schuster, 1953.

Bordman, Gerald. *American Musical Theater: A Chronicle.* New York: Oxford Univ. Press, 1986.

————. *The Oxford Companion to American Theater.* New York: Oxford Univ. Press, 1992.

Bowen, Ezra, ed. *This Fabulous Century.* New York: Time, 1970.

Brinnen, John Malcolm. *The Sway of the Grand Saloon: A Social History of the North Atlantic.* New York: Delacorte, 1971.

Burke, Billie, and Cameron Shipp. *With a Feather on My Nose.* New York: Appleton-Century-Crofts, 1949.

Cantor, Eddie, and David Freeman. *Ziegfeld: The Great Glorifier.* New York: Alfred H. King, 1934.

Carrera, Liane. *Memoires: Une Étoile Français au Ciel de l'Ameriqué.* Paris: La Nef de Paris Editions, 1954.

Carrera, Liane, and George Bye. "My Mother Was an Actress." Unpublished, c. 1938.

Carrera, Liane, and Guy Daniels. *Anna Held and Flo Ziegfeld.* Hicksville, N.Y.: Exposition, 1979.

Carter, Randolph. *Ziegfeld: The Time of His Life.* London: Bernard, 1974.

Chapman, David L. *Sandow the Magnificent: Eugen Sandow and the Beginnings of Bodybuilding.* Urbana: Univ. of Illinois Press, 1994.

Crichton, Judy. *America 1900: The Turning Point.* New York: Henry Holt, 1998.

Culbertson, Judi, and Tom Randall. *Permanent New Yorkers.* Chelsea, Vt.: Chelsea Green, 1987.

Derval, Paul. *Folies-Bergère.* New York: E.P. Dutton, 1955.

Dressler, Marie. *Life Story of an Ugly Duckling.* New York: Robert M. McBride, 1924.

Ellis, Edward Robb. *The Epic of New York City.* New York: Coward-McCann, 1966.

Everett, Marshall. *The Great Chicago Theater Disaster.* N.p.: D.B. McCurdy, 1904.

Farnsworth, Marjorie. *The Ziegfeld Follies.* New York: Putnam, 1956.

Fields, Armond, and L. Marc Fields. *From the Bowery to Broadway: Lew Fields and the Roots of American Popular Theater.* New York: Oxford Univ. Press, 1993.

Ford, James L. *Forty-Odd Years in the Literary Shop.* New York: E.P. Dutton, 1921.

Gabler, Neal. *Winchell: Gossip, Power and the Culture of Celebrity.* New York: Alfred A. Knopf, 1995.

Gaines, Ruth. *Helping France: The Red Cross in the Devastated Area.* New York: E.P. Dutton, 1919.

Gilbert, Douglas. *American Vaudeville.* New York: Whittlesey House, 1940.

Gilbert, Martin. *The First World War: A Complete History.* New York: Henry Holt, 1994.

Gish, Lillian, and Ann Pinchot. *The Movies, Mr. Griffith, and Me.* Englewood Cliffs, N.J.: Prentice-Hall, 1969.

Gosling, Nigel. *The Adventurous World of Paris 1900–1914.* New York: William Morrow, 1978.

Gray, Christopher, ed. *Fifth Avenue, 1911, From Start to Finish.* Mineola, N.Y.: Dover, 1994.

Green, Harvey. *The Light of the Home.* New York: Pantheon, 1983.

Hertz, Aleksander. *The Jews in Polish Culture.* Evanston, Ill.: Northwestern Univ. Press, 1988.

Higham, Charles. *Ziegfeld.* Chicago: Henry Regnery, 1973.

Huisman, Edita P., and M.G. Dortu. *Lautrec on Lautrec.* New York: Viking, 1964.

Katz, Ephraim. *The Film Encyclopedia.* New York: HarperCollins, 1994.

Knapp, Bettina, and Myra Chipman. *That Was Yvette.* London: Frederick Muller, 1966.

Laas, William. *Crossroads of the World: The Story of Times Square.* New York: Popular Library, 1965.

Laver, James. *Edwardian Promenade.* Boston: Houghton Mifflin, 1958.

Lewis, Arthur H. *La Belle Otero.* New York: Trident, 1967.

Lewis, Philip C. *Trouping: How the Show Came to Town.* New York: Harper and Row, 1972.

Lillie, Beatrice, and James Brough. *Every Other Inch a Lady.* Garden City, N.Y.: Doubleday, 1972.

Loomis, Stanley. *A Crime of Passion.* New York: J.P. Lippincott, 1967.

Lyman, Darryl. *Great Jews on Stage and Screen.* Middle Village, N.Y.: Jonathan David, 1987.

Malino, Frances, and Bernard Wasserstein, eds. *The Jews in Modern France.* Brandeis Univ. Press, 1985.

McEvoy, J.P. *Show Girl.* New York: Simon and Schuster, 1928.

McGaffey, Kenneth. *The Sorrows of a Showgirl.* Chicago: J.I. Austen, 1908.

McNamara, Brooks. *The Shuberts of Broadway.* New York: Oxford Univ. Press, 1990.

Morosco, Helen, and Leonard Paul Dugger. *The Oracle of Broadway.* Caldwell, Idaho: Caxton Publishing, 1944.

Morrell, Parker. *Lillian Russell: The Era of Plush.* New York: Random House, 1940.

Nohain, Jean, and F. Caradec. *Le Petomane.* Los Angeles: Sherbourne, 1968.

Page, Will A. *Behind the Curtains of Broadway's Beauty Trust.* New York: Edward A. Miller, 1926.

Rosenfeld, Luli. *Bright Star of Exile: Jacob Adler and the Yiddish Theater.* New York: Thomas Y. Crowell, 1977.

Salwen, Peter. *Upper West Side Story.* New York: Abbeville, 1989.

Silver, Nathan. *Lost New York.* New York: American Legacy, 1982.

Sims, George R. *Living London.* London: Cassell, 1902.

Smith, Harry B. *First Nights and First Editions.* Boston: Little, Brown, 1931.

Stern, Robert A.M.; Gregory Gilmartin; and John Massengale. *New York 1900.* New York: Rizzoli International, 1983.

Street, Julian. *Welcome to Our City*. New York: John Lane, 1912.

Sullivan, Mark. *Our Times*, 5 vols. New York: Charles Scribner's Sons, 1926–33.

Van Hoogstraten, Nicholas. *Lost Broadway Theaters*. New York: Princeton Architectural Press, 1991.

Watson, Edward B. *New York Then and Now*. Mineola, N.Y.: Dover, 1976.

Weber, Eugen. *Fin de Siècle Paris*. Harvard Univ. Press, 1986.

West, Mae. *Goodness Had Nothing to Do with It*. Englewood Cliffs, N.J., Prentice Hall, 1959.

Wist, Ronda. *On Fifth Avenue Then and Now*. New York: Birch Lane, 1992.

Ziegfeld, Patricia. *The Ziegfelds' Girl*. Boston: Little, Brown, 1964.

Ziegfeld, Richard, and Paulette Ziegfeld. *The Ziegfeld Touch*. New York: Harry N. Abrams, 1993.

Index